MW01048399

ALASTAIR SAWDAY'S

Special

places to stay

BRITISH HOTELS, INNS AND OTHER PLACES

Edited by Stephen Tate

Typesetting, Conversion & Repro: .....   Avonset, Bath

Design: .... Caroline King
           & Springboard Design, Bristol

Mapping: .... Springboard Design, Bristol

Maps: .... Maps in Minutes ™ 1999
           © Crown Copyright, Ordnance Survey 1999

Printing: .... Stige, Italy

UK Distribution: .... Portfolio, Greenford, Middlesex

US Distribution: .... The Globe Pequot Press,
           Guilford, Connecticut

Published in November 2001.

Alastair Sawday Publishing Co. Ltd
The Home Farm Stables, Barrow Gurney, Bristol BS48 3RW
Tel: +44 (0)1275 464891 Fax: +44 (0)1275 464887
E-mail: info@specialplacestostay.com Web: www. specialplacestostay.com

The Globe Pequot Press
P. O. Box 480, Guilford, Connecticut 06437, USA
Tel: +1 203 458 4500 Fax: +1 203 458 4601
E-mail: info@globe-pequot.com Web: www.globe-pequot.com

Third edition.

Copyright © November 2001 Alastair Sawday Publishing Co. Ltd

A catalogue record for this book is available from the British Library.

Alastair Sawday has asserted his right to be identified as the author of this work.

ISBN 1-901970-20-5 in the UK

ISBN 0-7627-1246-5 in the US

Printed in Italy.

The publishers have made every effort to ensure the accuracy of the information in this book at the time of going to press. However, they cannot accept any responsibility for any loss, injury or inconvenience resulting from the use of information contained therein.

ALASTAIR SAWDAY'S

Special
places to stay

BRITISH HOTELS, INNS AND OTHER PLACES

" Because everyone's seeking the same thing:
an imaginary place, their own castle in the air,
and their very own special corner of it."

Haruki Murakami

The Globe Pequot Press

Guilford
Connecticut, USA

ASP

Alastair Sawday Publishing
Bristol, UK

Contents

Contents

Quick reference indices - places which are: wheelchair-friendly, good for people of limited mobility, restaurants with rooms; places which use mostly organic or home-grown produce; places which have: rooms for under £80, pools and tennis courts.

Hotel Soap Opera

Annual Events 2002

What is Alastair Sawday Publishing?

www.specialplacestostay.com

Alastair Sawday's Special Places to Stay series

The Little Earth Book - edition 2

Order forms

Report form

Index by property name

Index by place name

Exchange rate table

Explanation of symbols

Acknowledgements

Hotels, Inns and other Special Places to Stay in Britain have taken a bashing in 2001, especially if they have been in or near a Food and Mouth Disease outbreak. Great swathes of the countryside, diseased or not, have been avoided by travellers and tourists. On top of all that the strong pound has maintained a siren call from countries with lower prices and fewer clouds. So, pity the poor hotel-keeper. One of them, who had spent 25 years building up his business in Cumbria, told me that Foot and Mouth had been the last straw. He was selling up and emigrating.

Given the misery among many hotel-owners after such a dreadful, disease-stricken, start to the 2001 season it has been a difficult year for visiting and inspecting. Many, however, have seen this book as bringing a boost to their flagging businesses so Stephen Tate has been able to bring a little cheer to some. But it has been a long, uphill struggle for this 3rd edition and I salute Stephen for his tenacity and good humour - and for his great success. It is, again, a superb book. It is packed with 'attitude' therefore with a richly eclectic selection of brilliant hotels, inns and other places. Stephen's wry sense of humour has added immeasurably to the quality of this edition, he has bounced ably on a springboard built up in two editions by Tom Bell. There has been much background support from many people: Jonathan Goodall inspecting, Jackie King advising, Annie Shillito managing and Julia Richardson creating a book out of Stephen's long haul.

Finally I would like to thank the many hotel owners and other professionals who have inspired us; people like Richard Johnston, Sheila MacDonald, Andrea Bolwig, Belinda Rushworth-Lund, Hugo Jeune - all of them running their hotels with passion, flair and a sense of fun.

Alastair Sawday

Series Editor:................. Alastair Sawday

Editor:........................... Stephen Tate

Managing Editor:......... Annie Shillito

Production Manager:.... Julia Richardson

Administration:............. Rachel Brook, Laura Kinch, Jo Boissevain

Accounts:...................... Bridget Bishop

Inspections:.................. Jeremy Bolam, Erlend Clouston,
Jenny Colbourne, Rosie Ferguson,
Jonathan Goodall, David Griffiths,
Joanne MacInnes, Sheila and Rob Macpherson.

Special thanks, too, to those people not mentioned here who visited often at short notice - just one or two places for us.

And special thanks to Grace.

A word from Alastair Sawday

This book packs a terrific punch. Inside is a tightly selected collection of the best, the most entertaining, original, authentic and beautiful places to stay. Most are hotels, but there are pubs, inns, guest houses and those other special places which we think our readers would enjoy which don't fit a convenient category.

In fact I'd worry if you could not enjoy most of these places. We have a lighthouse, a windmill or two, castles, restaurants-with-rooms, an arts club, a Lutyens manor and other exquisite homes. Their owners are as varied and interesting a bunch as you could want to share time with: artists, musicians, landowners, historic-house restorers, fishermen, computer whizzes - humanity in much of its glittering variety is here. This is rarely the case with hotels in general; their employees come and go and are cajoled and squeezed into the company mould. Perhaps you know what I mean by the 'executive smile'? I do hope you never meet one through these pages.

There is a slow revolution going on throughout Britain as people are waking up to the delights of real food, real ale and real hotels. The organic food revolution is the most visible part of this sea-change, and we plan to encourage the change in the shift among hotels to more organic food, more locally-produced food and less pompous ways of doing their thing. The hotel business is still thickly peopled with those whose idea of a hotel is rooted in the Edwardian era when guests wanted to be treated as if they were all members of the upper classes. Our age, however, is more egalitarian and more of us want to be treated first and foremost as human beings. Most of our readers want an easy-going relationship with interesting people who'll look after them well. The days of Jeeves are almost numbered - though I confess to hoping he'll never entirely disappear.

If you wish to be anonymous then perhaps these are not ideal places. But if you want to feel welcomed and valued then Special Places will reach those parts other hotels fail to reach. Their owners are decent, authentic folk; fascinating, cultural, some even a touch eccentric - one way or another you are likely to enjoy them, and they you.

Let us know if we have not got it right.

Alastair Sawday

Introduction

This guide includes a collection of diverse places; they will appeal to the open-minded, to those who shun the banal and rigidly conventional and to all those who dream of leaving the motorway far behind for the middle of nowhere, or the centre of somewhere. It also destroys the myth that every British hotel is prohibitively expensive. It celebrates an endangered species - the indefatigably independent hotel owner, innkeeper and restaurateur. Members of this rare breed spend their days doing whatever it takes to make their places shine. It is hard work and far less glamorous than our dreams would have us believe. Hours are long, margins tight.

The government doesn't help much as business rates go up and unrealistic employment laws squeeze budgets. The year 2001 will particularly stick in the hoteliers' craw. We heard a lot about the plight of farmers in the wake of the Foot and Mouth epidemic, less about the rural leisure industry which employs many millions more. The government talked about compensation and rural aid packages as the nation went to the polls, but the resulting paperwork was mind-boggling and the issue slipped off the front pages. Meanwhile, debts mounted as the countryside remained closed and disturbing images of slaughtered livestock were beamed round the world; tourism ground to a halt, staff were laid off and debts mounted.

Somehow, most hoteliers survived to fight another day. In doing so, they keep alive a hugely worthwhile tradition - they entertain us on our travels, they welcome us with generosity and warmth, they cook with passion and imagination, they fill our glasses and they give us time and space to recharge our batteries. This book is one small but significant way of celebrating and supporting their endeavours.

How do we choose our Special Places?

We search for the best and write a book without fixed boundaries. We like to include anywhere that practises the art of hospitality with flair, good humour and commitment. We visit every property and evaluate each place on its own merits, not by comparison. The key considerations are atmosphere, value for money and style. We like people who do their own thing, though idiosyncrasy is no excuse for poor standards. Good views are more important than bellboys, and a good walk more appealing than a fitness centre. If your idea of a weekend away is to check into the Heathrow Hilton, then this book is not for you.

Introduction

What to expect

This edition sees an increase in the number of places in Scotland - where we have also included places in the Orkney Islands for the first time - Wales, and English towns and cities.

England

Lose yourself down windy lanes and happen upon unexpected treasures. Explore the old parts of market towns. In the cities, hop on a bus and see where it takes you, and one of the best ways of seeing London is on foot; take a Tube somewhere, then amble back to your hotel. The Lake District, the West Country and the Cotswolds remain firm favourites and this edition has wonderful new places to visit alongside the established favourites. But be tempted by fabulous places in less obvious parts of the country such as Northumberland, Essex and Birmingham.

Wales

The Welsh countryside is rich and varied and the range of places in this edition puts the whole country within your reach: from the impressive mountain scenery of Snowdonia National Park and the sandy beaches of the Isle of Anglesey in the north, via the beautiful undulating countryside of mid-Wales and the challenging hill-walking terrain of the Brecon Beacons, to the windswept rocky coastline of Pembrokeshire and the lushness of the Gower Peninsula in the west and south.

Scotland

The lochs, mountains and islands north of the border make up Britain's last real wilderness; this is truly somewhere to escape. The Highlands are majestic in snow or shine and the Western Isles are more than worth the adventure to get there. Less visited is the east coast with its windswept landscape of sandy beaches and towering cliffs. This edition includes new places from which to explore it all.

Hotels, Inns and Other Places

About half the places in this book are hotels and 57 are inns. The remainder we call 'other places', of which are restaurants-with-rooms, the remainder defy any obvious pigeon-hole.

Hotels range from the small and sweet to the grand and gracious. Room prices often vary according to the size of the room; but though the huge Queen Anne four-poster may have sea views, the small twin is kept to the same standard and you can enjoy the same view from the reception rooms.

Introduction

Inns come in three types: the smart inn - part-hotel - which aims to provide a high level of luxury and service; the dining pub, which generally has both a bar and a more formal restaurant; and the traditional inn where all mix under the same roof and bedrooms vary from simple to extremely stylish. Bars may stay open late, so ask about noise levels, especially if you are a light sleeper.

Restaurants with rooms are starting to blossom all over the country, offering excellent service and good value for money. Owners are knowledgeable and passionate about food. It is often more a way of life than a job and their efforts have done much to raise the standard of restaurant food in Britain.

Other places are ones that do not fit easily into any of the above categories but are nonetheless too good to miss. They include an organic farm, Pullman railway carriages, a couple of arts clubs, a cliff-topping castle... the term gives us latitude to include the unconventional.

How to use this book

Map

Each property is flagged with its entry number on maps at the front of the book. Our maps are only rough guides. You will get lost if you try navigating with them. We recommend the WH Smith/AA road map of Britain, which is clear and easy to use.

Bedrooms and Bathrooms

A 'double' means one double bed, a 'twin' means two single beds, a 'double/twin' means two single beds that can be made up into a large double. A 'triple' or 'family' room may have any mix of beds (sometimes sofa-beds) for 3, 4 or more people. A 'suite' may be one large room with a sitting area or it may have two or more interconnecting rooms and one or more bathrooms. Extra beds and cots for children can often be provided; ask about extra costs when booking.

Assume all bedrooms have en suite bathrooms unless it is stated otherwise in the text; we let you know when a room has either a shared bathroom, or a private one. However, things do change so check when you book. If you are staying more than one night, consider using your towels more than once and be kinder to the environment.

Introduction

Prices

The basic room price is for two people sharing, with breakfast included unless it is specified otherwise. The lowest price is usually for the least expensive room in low season; the highest price for the most expensive room in high season. Check when booking if there are offers available.

Singles

Room prices for single people are given separately; if a place does not have a single room, the price refers to single occupancy of a double or a twin. Most owners charge a supplement for single occupancy - understandable as it requires the same amount of work to clean. Some do not, which is generous. The price and standard of single rooms remains a thorny issue. In the main, owners do not actively encourage single people, though there are notable exceptions and these are mentioned in the text.

The more remote places and some restaurants-with-rooms prefer to offer dinner, bed and breakfast rates only. The price is listed per person and includes a three-course evening meal. Where both room-only and dinner, B&B rates are listed, the latter usually saves you a few pounds but check whether there are certain conditions attached when booking. Special Dinner B&B deals are often available at much-reduced prices. These are for two nights or more and usually get cheaper the longer you stay. Keep an eye on our web site at www.specialplacestostay.com as we plan to introduce an online noticeboard, which will enable owners to post up last-minute offers.

Practical Matters

Booking

Most hotels require a deposit to secure a room. You are likely to lose part or all of it if you cancel, or if you have given your credit card details, a sum may be deducted. Check the exact terms when you book and have the hotel confirm the agreement in writing. Many hotels only accept a minimum two-night stay at weekends, while a handful insist on a minimum of three nights over a Bank Holiday weekend.

Meals

The standard of cooking coming out of the kitchens in this book is exceptional. The best ingredients are not cheap but the resulting food can be truly memorable. Check our symbols for those places that actively source their meat, fish and other produce locally wherever possible, or grow their own vegetables and herbs, or rear their own meat for the table. And those places that only use organic produce and have been certified by the Soil Association.

Introduction

Breakfast

A full cooked breakfast or a Continental breakfast is included in the room price unless stated otherwise. Continental breakfasts are substantial, never just bread and jam. Breakfast times are either given, or flexible.

Lunch and dinner

About 95% of our places either offer lunch, or evening meals, or both. If you have special dietary needs, let them know when booking; our symbol shows which places cater for vegetarians. Restaurants may close one or two evenings a week and we try to report this but double-check to be sure.

Problems, problems...

You are paying to be looked after, so if the hot water isn't hot or your chicken isn't chicken, you are entitled to complain. If you have a problem, speak to a member of staff there and then, or ask to speak to the owner or manager who should be keen to deal with it swiftly and efficiently. If you get nowhere, please let us know.

Tipping

Tipping, if you are satisfied with the level of service or the kindness of those looking after you, will be appreciated. However, it is not obligatory.

Hotel telephones

Ask for the price per minute before making a call as charges vary enormously. The country code for the US from the UK is **011**.

Credit and debit cards

MasterCard and Visa are generally welcome; American Express is sometimes accepted, Diners Card hardly ever. Debit cards, such as Switch, are widely accepted. A few places take cash and cheques only.

Smoking

Most bedrooms and nearly all dining rooms and restaurants are non-smoking. Some places are entirely non-smoking and this is mentioned in the text. Inns are less likely to have smoking restrictions, but their restaurants usually do.

Children

Our symbol shows you which places welcome children of all ages - although it doesn't necessarily mean there are 'facilities' for them We mention in italics at the end of the description those that only accept children over a certain age. In many places, baby-sitting can be arranged with advance

notice, while some may also provide children's suppers. Many hotels prefer
not to allow children in the restaurant after a certain time in the evening.

Pets

Obviously, where pets are welcome, owners expect you to control them
at all times. Please be extremely considerate. Our symbol means pets are
allowed in some bedrooms. That does not mean they are also allowed in
the sitting room, dining room or swimming pool. There may be a pet
supplement to pay and always let the hotel know beforehand, or Fido
may have to sleep in the car.

Leisure

The relevant symbol says where there is a swimming pool or tennis
court. Many places have croquet lawns, while others may provide free
or discounted membership to local leisure centres. Sauna and massage
treatment may also be available in-house. There are often lots of activities,
such as fishing and horse-riding, that can be arranged for you locally.
We don't always mention these so it's worth checking.

Arrival and departure times

These vary, but on the whole your room should be ready by mid-afternoon,
while you will be expected to vacate it on the morning you leave, by around
11am. Many hotels are happy for you to linger... but not in your room.

Subscription

All owners pay a fee to be included in this book. It is an expensive book
to produce, but it is not a directory. Hotels cannot buy their way in – the
payment is a fee, not a bribe. We keep editorial control over what we write.
The words are ours and ours alone.

Black holes

We never include places that fall short of our standards just to offer
coverage in a particular area. This book is about staying in special places,
not just any old place.

Quick reference indices

At the back of the book is a quick reference guide to help direct you to the
type of places that suit you, be they restaurants with rooms, places that do
organic or home-grown food, or places with rooms under £40 per person
per night.

Introduction

www.specialplacestostay.com

Our web site has online entries for many of the places featured here as well as many from our other books. Each entry has up-to-date prices, hot links to owners' web sites and their email addresses. More information about the web site can be found at the back of the book.

Environment

We try to reduce our impact on the environment where possible by:

- planting trees to compensate for our carbon emissions as calculated by Edinburgh University. We are officially a Carbon Neutral® publishing company and the emissions directly related with the paper production, printing and distribution of this book have been made Carbon Neutral® through the planting of indigenous woodlands with Future Forests.

- re-using paper, recycling stationery, tins, bottles, etc.

- encouraging staff use of bicycles - they're loaned free - and encouraging car sharing.

- celebrating the use of organic, home - and locally-produced food.

- publishing books that support, in however small a way, the rural economy and small-scale businesses.

- encouraging our owners to follow recommendations made to them by the Energy Efficiency Centre.

Disclaimer

We make no claims to pure objectivity in judging our special places to stay. They are here because we like them. Our opinions and tastes are ours alone; we hope you share them.

And Finally

Your feedback is important because it helps us keep the series up to date. We want to hear whether your stay was absolutely wonderful or whether there were any problems - passing on praise is as important to us as clearing up a complaint. Please fill out the report form at the back of the book, or email us at britishhotels@sawdays.co.uk. Finally, please tell us of any treasured find for this or any other edition in the series. We will send you a free book if your recommendation leads to its inclusion.

Happy travels.

Stephen Tate

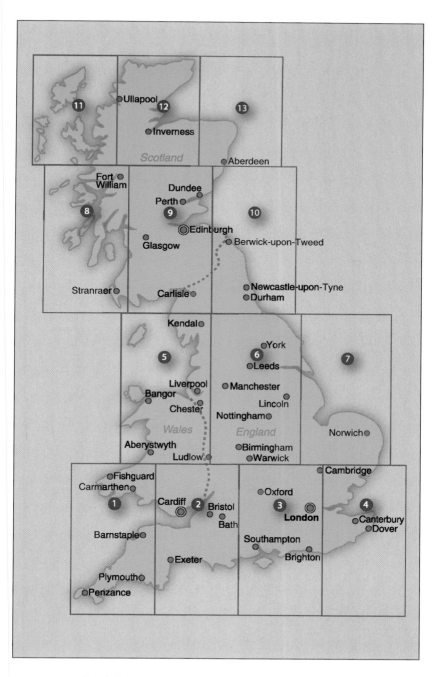

Guide to our map page numbers

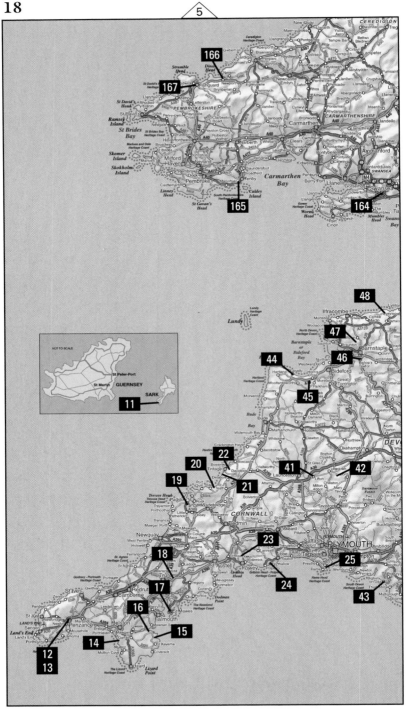

Map 1

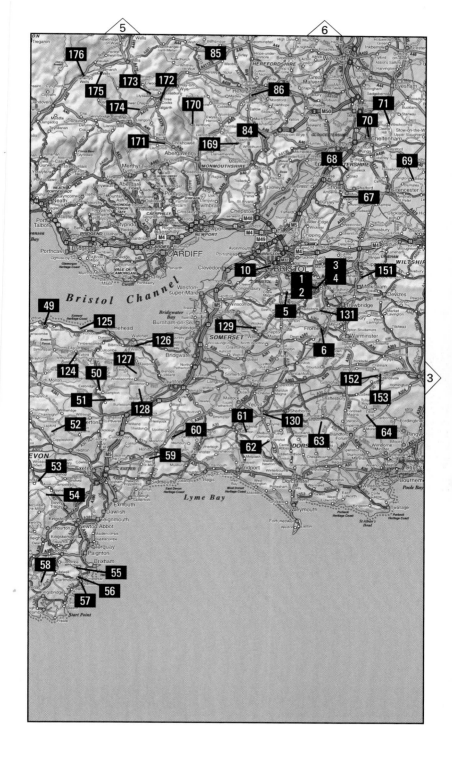

Map 2

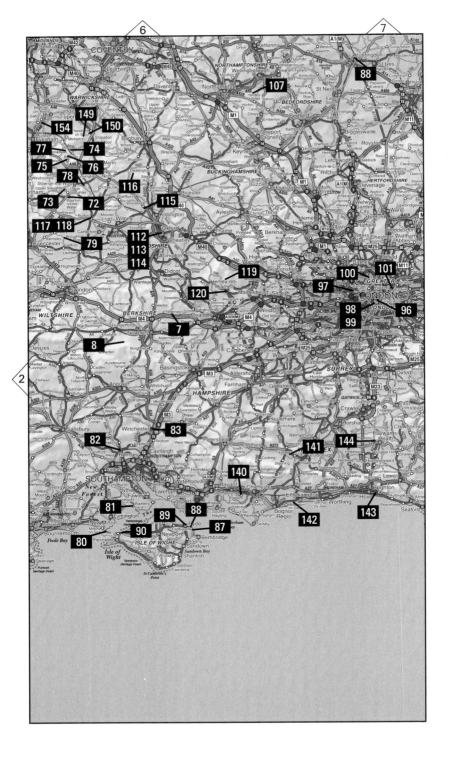

Map 3

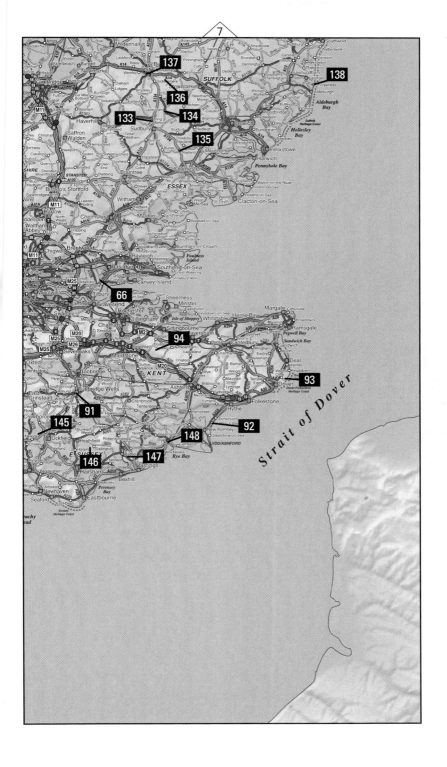

Map 4

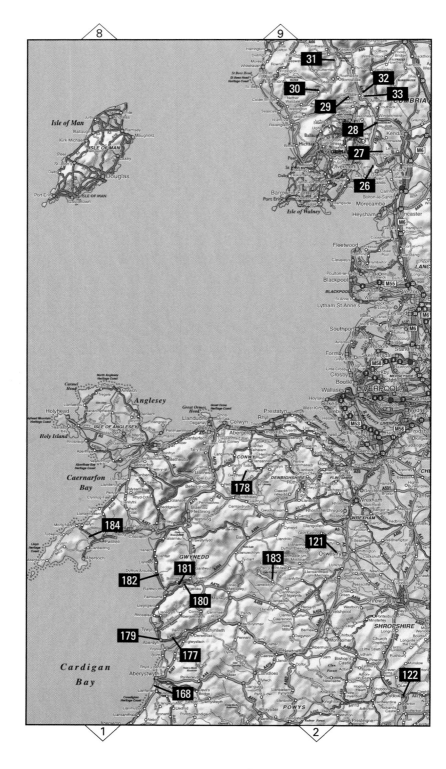

Map 5

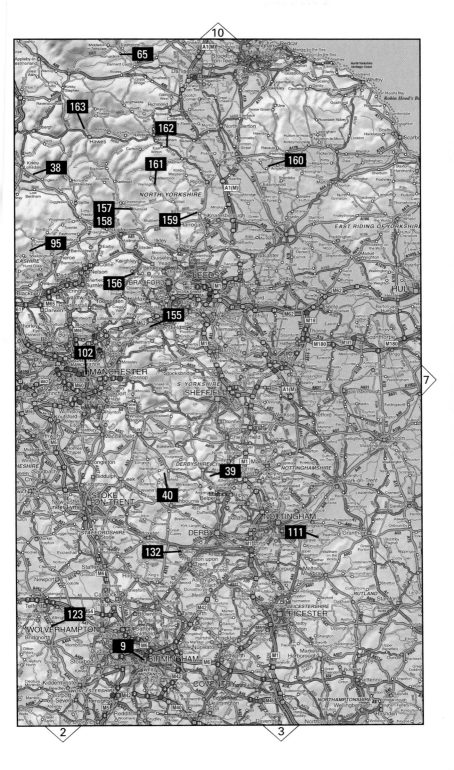

Map 6

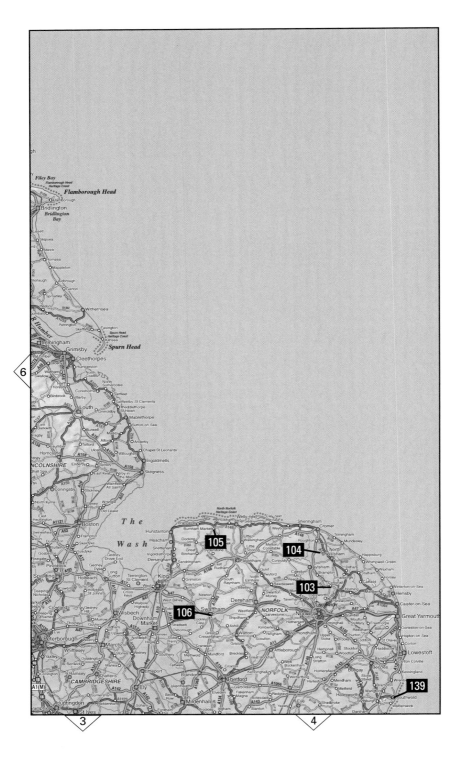

Map 7

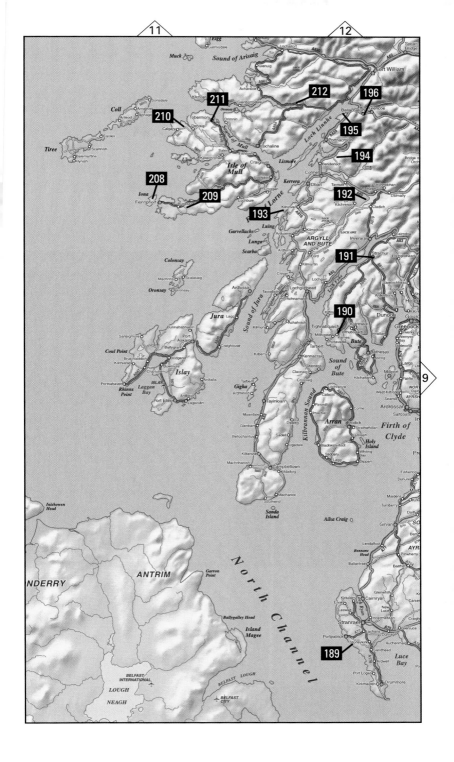

Map 8

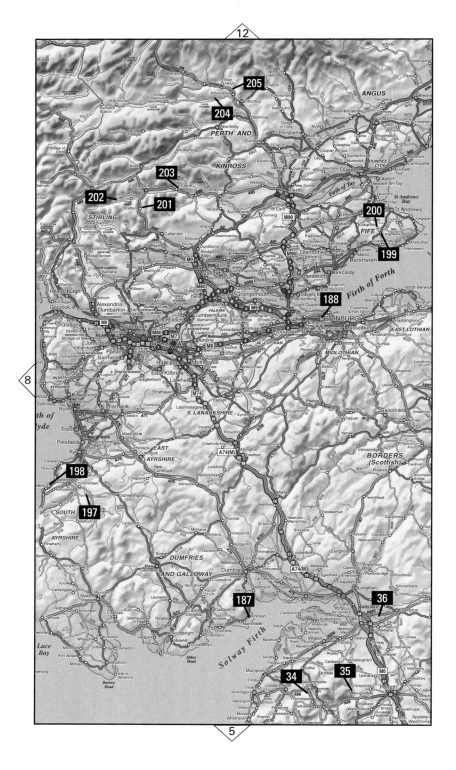

Map 9

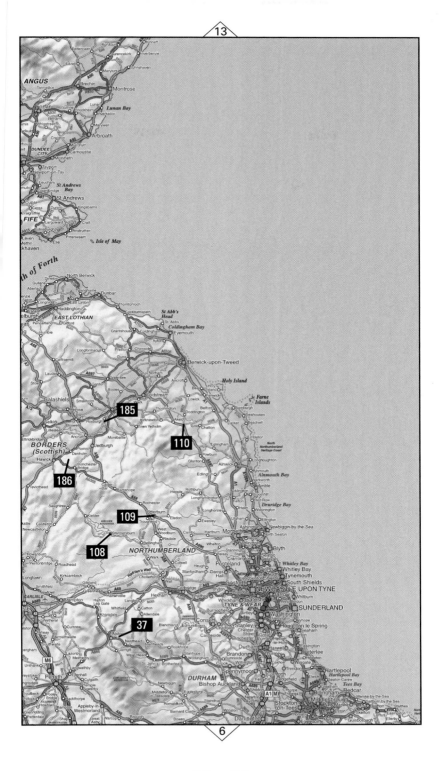

Map 10

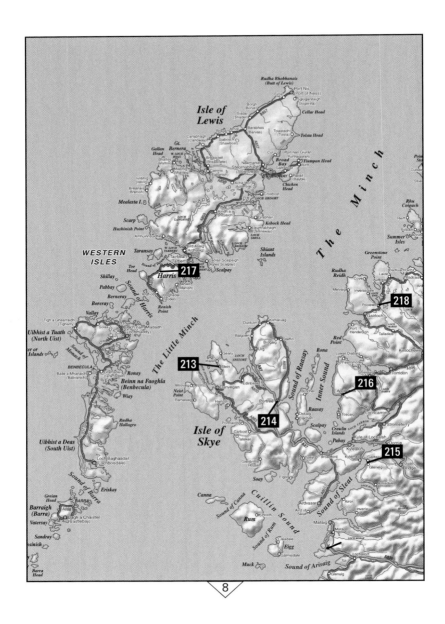

Map 11

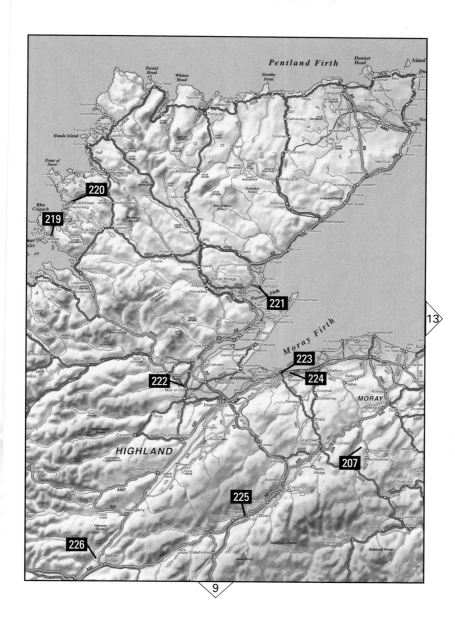

Map 12

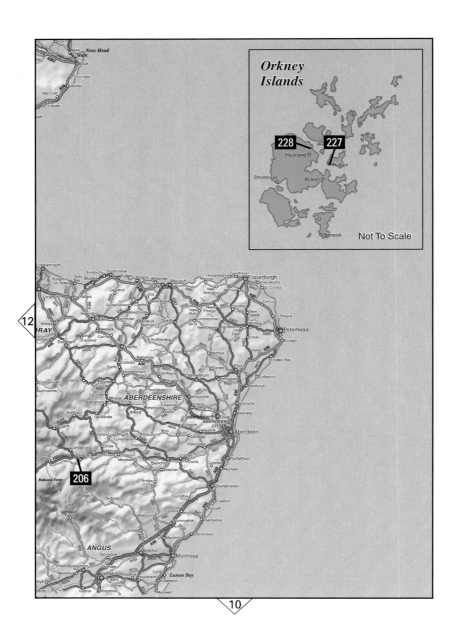

Map 13

England

The way to ensure summer in England
is to have it framed on the wall.

Horace Walpole

The Queensberry Hotel and Olive Tree Restaurant
Russel Street
Bath
Bath and N. E. Somerset
BA1 2QF

Tel: 01225 447928
Fax: 01225 446065
E-mail: enquiries@bathqueensberry.com
Web: www.bathqueensberry.com

Stephen and Penny Ross

The Queensberry is an old favourite, grand but totally unpretentious and immensely enjoyable. It is rare to find a hotel of this size and elegance still in private hands, rarer still to find the owners so actively deployed. Stephen is 'everywhere' and even though he no longer cooks in the famous basement restaurant, his Dauphinoise potatoes remain, rightly, legendary. The bedrooms are magnificent - contemporary and dramatic, with bold, inspirational colours and fabrics. If you feel like spoiling yourself, have breakfast brought up to you – croissants, orange juice, fresh coffee, warm milk and a newspaper. Then, pad around in wonderful white bathrobes feeling a million dollars. The bath runs in seconds, the shower imitates a monsoon. At night, pop down to supper and when you get back your bed will have been turned down, your towels refreshed. As for the home-made fudge after supper... just wonderful. All this in a John Wood house in the centre of Bath, a minute's walk from the Assembly Rooms.

Rooms: 15 doubles, 13 doubles/twins, 1 four-poster.
Price: £120-£210; singles from £90.
Meals: Breakfast 7.30-9.30am, 8-10am Sundays; Continental included, Full English £9.50. Lunch from £13. Dinner from £24.
Closed: Christmas & New Year.

Take London Road (A4) towards Bath centre until it becomes Paragon. 1st right into Lansdown, second left into Bennett St, then first right into Russel St.

Map No: 2

Paradise House

Holloway
Bath
Bath and N. E. Somerset
BA2 4PX

Tel: 01225 317723
Fax: 01225 482005
E-mail: info@paradise-house.co.uk
Web: www.paradise-house.co.uk

David and Annie Lanz

The magical 180-degree panoramic view from the garden at Paradise House, with the Royal Crescent and the Abbey floodlit at night, is a dazzling advertisement for Bath. It draws you out as soon as you enter the house. In summer, hot air balloons float across low enough for you to hear the roar of the burners. Wonderful. Most of the rooms make full use of the view; the best have bay windows. In the past year, two more garden rooms have been added in an extension built from Bath stone - it's a remarkable achievement in keeping with the original house (planners took six years to approve the plans) and David is justly proud. All the rooms have a soft, luxurious country feel, with drapes, wicker chairs and good bathrooms. Downstairs, the sitting room has lovely stone-arched French windows - the house seems to use glass in all the right places. Two doors up on Holloway - the old Roman Road into Bath - the old Monastery is owned by a music teacher; afternoon tea in the garden can sometimes be very special as the sound of piano music drifts gently across. Bells may peal, too. *Seven minutes' walk from the centre.*

Rooms: 2 four-poster, 1 family,
4 twins, 4 doubles.
Price: £75-£130; singles £55-£85.
Meals: Breakfast until 9.30am. Lunch &
dinner available in Bath.
Closed: Christmas.

From Bath train station follow one-way system to Churchill Bridge. Take A367 exit from r'bout up hill. After 0.75 miles left at Andrews estate agents. Left down hill into cul-de-sac. On left.

Map No: 2

2

Apsley House

141 Newbridge Hill
Bath
Bath and N. E. Somerset
BA1 3PT

David and Annie Lanz

Tel: 01225 336966
Fax: 01225 425462
E-mail: info@apsley-house.co.uk
Web: www.apsley-house.co.uk

Apsley House takes its name from the Duke of Wellington's main London residence which had the mighty address 'No.1 London'. The Iron Duke is thought to have lived here, though if he did, the tempo was probably a little stiffer than it is now with David and Annie at the helm. Take a drink from the bar, then collapse into one of the sofas in the drawing room. It's full of great furniture and fabrics, tallboy porter chairs, gilt mirrors and rich Colefax and Fowler curtains. There's also a huge, arched window, overlooking the garden. The dining room is separated by an arch and antique screens and shares the same warm elegance, with fresh flowers on all the tables and nice touches like jugs of iced water at breakfast. Upstairs, most of the pretty bedrooms are huge and have good bathrooms. Morning papers are dropped off at your door, your clothes can be laundered, and there's a car park, which in this city is precious indeed. *Children over five welcome.*

Rooms: 1 four-poster, 5 twin/doubles, 3 doubles.
Price: £75-£120; singles £55-£85.
Meals: Breakfast until 9am weekdays, 9.30am weekends. Lunch & dinner available locally.
Closed: Christmas.

A4 west into Bath. Keep right at 1st mini-r'bout. Continue for about 2 miles, then follow 'Bristol A4' signs. Pass Total garage on right. At next lights, branch right. Hotel on left after 1 mile.

Dorian House

One Upper Oldfield Park
Bath
Bath and N. E. Somerset
BA2 3JX

Kathryn and Tim Hugh

Tel: 01225 426336
Fax: 01225 444699
E-mail: dorian.house@which.net
Web: www.dorianhouse.co.uk

A cellist with a love of interior design is rare enough, but to find one running a hotel amid the beautiful surroundings of Bath is exceptional. Tim is the London Symphony Orchestra's principal cellist and was once taught by the late and great Jacqueline du Pré: "She played with abandon - she was herself", he says of his tutor. Be yourself in the cosy, spoiling luxury of this converted Victorian house; it feels more home than hotel. Tim and Kathryn have restored everything inside - the original tiled hallway is lovely. Sit with afternoon tea in deep sofas in the lounge, or enjoy one of six types of champagne in comfortable bedrooms all named after cellists; no surprise that the most exquisite - and the most secluded - is du Pré; a huge four-poster bed is reached up a flight of stairs. Every room is decorated with beautiful fabrics and Egyptian linen; those on the first floor are more traditional, those on the second more contemporary, with Scandanavian pine and sloping ceilings. Tim's artwork is everywhere; he plays regularly at one gallery in Portugal that pays him in paintings. Relaxation assured, maybe some music, too.

Rooms: 3 four-posters, 3 doubles, 2 twin/doubles, 2 family, 1 single.
Price: £65-£140; singles £47-£59.
Meals: Breakfast 8-9am weekdays, 8.30-9.30am weekends; other times by arrangement. Good restaurants nearby.
Closed: Christmas.

From Bath centre, follow signs to Shepton Mallet to sausage-shaped r'bout, A37 up hill, then 1st right. House 3rd on left, signed.

Map No: 2

Hunstrete House

Pensford
Nr. Bath
Bath and N. E. Somerset
BS39 4NS

Tel: 01761 490490
Fax: 01761 490732
E-mail: user@hunstretehouse.co.uk
Web: www.hunstretehouse.co.uk

House manager: David Hennigan

At last, a grand country house hotel where you're encouraged to leave your Wellington boots at the back door and curl up, shoeless, in front of the fire for tea. There's been a house here for over 1,000 years – the Lewin of Bristol once paid a rent of 10 salmon a year; what stands today goes back to the 1650s when it was built as a hunting lodge. It's impossible to pick out just one feature for praise; elegant long curtains, oils everywhere, gilt-framed mirrors, chandeliers, columns, high ceilings, striking fabrics... just room after room full of exquisite antiques, all with large windows giving long views out past plinths and urns to deer park beyond. There's a courtyard, with weeping pear trees and terracotta pots where you can eat in summer, croquet, a tennis court and bedrooms full of antiques and all the trimmings – bathrobes, bowls of fruit, old radios. Stroll through the magnificent six-acre Victorian walled garden on your way to the outdoor pool and see the gardeners picking carrots for the pot - they ask the chef what he wants every day. All this within easy striking distance of Bath and Bristol.

Rooms: 18 twins/doubles,
1 four-poster, 3 suites.
Price: £125-£195; suites from £240.
Dinner, B&B £100-£170 p.p.
Meals: Breakfast 7.30-10am. Lunch
from £15.95. Dinner, 3 courses,
from £40.
Closed: Never.

*From Bristol, south on A37, then left at
Chelwood r'bout onto A368.
After 4 miles, left and hotel 1st left again.*

Map No: 2

Number Four

Catherine Street
Frome
Bath and N. E. Somerset
BA11 1DA

Tel: 01373 455690
Fax: 01373 455992
Web: www.indialinktravel.co.uk

Pie Chambers and Sunil Sethi

Amid the narrow, meandering streets of Frome beats the heart of authentic India; warm, exotic and beguiling. Number Four is part restaurant and part oasis. Sunil is Punjabi and Pie has been travelling to Asia for years, cultivating native methods of dyeing and weaving to create designs that adorn the whole of this lovely house; she has a shop nearby as well. The restaurant captures the sense of rural India with hand-made curtains, tablecloths and cushions of terracotta and mustard, mixed with wooden tables, a stone floor and an open-plan kitchen lined with shelves of spices. Elsewhere, ethnic meets modern in the bedrooms; Pie is partial to designer taps, especially the beautiful plumbing accessories of architect Arne Jacobsen and designer Philippe Starck. My favourite bedroom looked onto a tiny courtyard of lush, shade-loving ferns and plants; just the place to try a garam masala omelette for breakfast on sunnier mornings. Sunil and Pie both cook by instinct, rather than to a menu, and the results are superb. As Sunil put it: "This is where your trip to India starts." *Not licensed. BYO.*

Rooms: 1 double; 2 twins, 1 single, sharing bathroom (shower).
Price: £35-£55; singles £25-£40.
Meals: Breakfast until 10am. Dinner £12.50-£17.50.
Closed: November & February-March. Restaurant open to non-residents Fridays or Saturdays. Groups by arrangement.

From Frome centre, follow signs to Shepton Mallet up Bath St. Right at mini-r'bout into Christchurch St West, then 4th right after Ship Inn down Catherine St. Restaurant on right. Free parking available.

Map No: 2

The Royal Oak Hotel

The Square
Yattendon
Berkshire
RG18 0UG

Tel: 01635 201325
Fax: 01635 201926
E-mail: theroyaloakhotel@hotmail.com

Corinne and Robbie Macrae

Corinne, who is French, would never forgive me if I didn't mention her garden; she loves it, and rightly so. It is English through and through, walled by ancient red bricks, bordered on one side by gently-sloping tiled roofs, with lots of colour and shade. There's also a French twist - vines under which you can eat, or fall asleep. Yattendon has a deep country feel; unspoiled, quiet and pretty, with a village store, old red-brick cottages and the handsome Royal Oak - a 300-year-old inn. Inside, Robbie, who cooks, and Corrine have mixed the traditional and the contemporary to great effect; cool yellows and greens in the stunning restaurant – you'll eat well here; a warm and elegant sitting room with rugs and open fire; and a smart but traditional bar, with a terracotta-tiled floor, old red-brick walls and timber frames. The bedrooms are excellent, too; fresh, uncluttered, with a hint of French chic – lace and good linen, antiques and big white towels, and spotless bathrooms. Nothing nasty in sight. A good place to escape to and only an hour from London.

Rooms: 4 doubles, 1 twin/double.
Price: £115-£125; singles £105.
Meals: Breakfast 7-9.30am;
Continental £8, full English £11.
Brasserie lunch & dinner £12-£25.
Restaurant dinner, 3 courses, £35.
Closed: Never.

*M4, junc.13, A34 south for under
1 mile. Take 1st left past petrol station,
then 1st left again onto B4009.
Continue through Hermitage, then
branch right to Yattendon.*

Map No: 3

Crown & Garter

Inkpen Common
Hungerford
Berkshire
RG17 9QR

Tel: 01488 668325
Fax: 01488 669072
E-mail: peter@crowngarter.freeserve.co.uk
Web: www.crownandgarter.com

Candida Leaver and Peter Starling

The Crown & Garter lies in a lush paradise just south of the M4 motorway. Quiet lanes dip through fields and woodland, past cottages draped in honeysuckle - England rarely feels this dreamy. Candida and Peter left catering careers in London to resuscitate this unspoilt 16th-century inn. The charming bedrooms in a new-build around a pretty garden are the best surprise of all. Candida has resourcefully blended voile and Bennison fabrics with painted floorboards, recycled furniture and handmade cushions to create colourful, eclectic rooms - none are the same. The bar is full of odd curios, testament to Candida's maxim that "if your partner's short on chat, there should be lots to look at"; the wonderful throne-like chair by the front door is actually part wine box, part trapdoor but is often mistaken for an antique. Bistro-style food includes homemade pasta and paté, and the ales are all local. Peter loves cycling and will suggest routes. There are also plenty of super walks across Inkpen Common and a pretty beer garden under an old oak tree. Hard to imagine London's so close. *No smoking in bedrooms.*

Rooms: 7 doubles, 3 twins.
Price: £65; singles £45.
Meals: Breakfast 7.30-8.30am weekdays, 8.30-9.30am weekends. Bar lunch from £6. Dinner, 2 courses, from £10. Inn closed Mondays & Tuesday lunchtimes.
Closed: Never.

From M4, junc. 13, A34 Basingstoke, then left on A4 towards Hungerford. After 2 miles, left, signed Kintbury/Inkpen. In Kintbury, left opp. corner shop, marked Inkpen Rd. Inn on left after 2 miles.

Map No: 3

Birmingham

Hotel du Vin & Bistro

Church Road
Birmingham
B3 2NR

Tel: 0121 2360559
Fax: 0121 2360889
E-mail: info@birmingham.hotelduvin.com
Web: www.hotelduvin.com

Manager: Michael Warren

Oh la la, the Hotel du Vin 'micro-chain' has done it again. Their latest and fourth venture has converted the disused Birmingham & West Midlands eye hospital into a palace of art, style and fun on five floors, set around a Parisian-style courtyard full of bronze statues and palm trees. They've kept the sweeping double staircase, the granite pillars and an oddly-shaped Victorian lift designed to take stretchers, but the rest bears their unmistakable signature. The restaurant is emphatically French; the waiters' uniforms, the Lautrec posters, and small tables, set comfortably apart, transport you to Paris. There's a cosy cellar bar, with squidgy sofas and funky lobster art, and the 'Bubble Lounge', done in the style of Venice's Café Florin, stocks 60 kinds of champagne. Minimalist bedrooms please the eye, with Henderson & Redfearn furniture, natural fabrics, huge beds - the biggest measures eight-feet square - and bathrooms with roll-top Edwardian baths and "monsoon-like" showers. Pamper yourself silly in the health and fitness suite, then relax with a long cocktail, before discovering a city on the up.

Rooms: 55 twin/doubles, 1 principle suite, 10 suites
Price: £110-£135; suites £175-£395.
Meals: Breakfast until 9.30am weekdays, until 10am weekends; Continental £8.50, Full English £11.50. Lunch & dinner, à la carte, 2 courses £16-£20.
Closed: Never.

From M6, junc. 6, A38(M) Aston Expressway into city centre. Over flyover, then left up slip road, signed Snowhill Station. Take 2nd exit at r'bout, then 1st left, 3rd right and 1st right into Church St.

9

Hotel du Vin & Bistro
The Sugar House
Narrow Lewins Mead
Bristol
BS1 2NU

Tel: 0117 925 5577
Fax: 0117 925 1199
E-mail:
info@bristol.hotelduvin.com
Web: www.hotelduvin.com

Manager: Stuart Kennedy

Robin Hutson and his team get better and better as they cover the country with their reinvention of the grand townhouse hotel, turning 'grand' to 'casual' in the process, to the joy of all. This, their third venture and first in a big city, will win awards, as have the other two, but it's the inherent good value that's most notable - if they can do such luxury for these prices, then others must look to their laurels. There's lots of space, stone walls, floorboards, rugs, squishy sofas and sandblasted beams. A sprinkle of tables and chairs around a fountain in the courtyard adds further style, as does the fire that shoots up a 100-foot chimney in the glass-fronted lobby, a remnant of the building's warehouse past. Up the steel staircase, spectacular bedrooms have a minimalist Manhattan-loft feel - low-slung furniture, handmade beds, off-white walls, hessian and big bathrooms, with walk-through showers, and baths. But always at the heart of a Hotel du Vin beats the bistro, French to the core, full of life and a great place to be. You can also play billiards or walk into the *humidor* and buy a Havana.

Rooms: 25 doubles, 5 twins, 10 suites.
Price: £109-£130; suites £160-£225.
Meals: Breakfast 7-9.30am weekdays, 8-10am weekends; Continental £8.50, Full English £11.50. Lunch & dinner in bistro, 3 courses with bottle of house wine, about £35.
Closed: Never.

M4, junc. 19, M32 into Bristol, then right at lights, following signs to city centre (past House of Fraser). Left at big r'bout onto two-lane inner ring road. After about 500 yards, double back at traffic lights. Hotel on left down small side road after 100 yards.

Map No: 2

La Sablonnerie

Little Sark
Sark, Via Guernsey
Channel Islands
GY9 0SD

Tel: 01481 832061
Fax: 01481 832408

Elizabeth Perrée

If you tell Elizabeth which ferry you're arriving on, she'll send down her horse and carriage to meet you. "Small, sweet world of wave-encompassed wonder", wrote Swinburne of Sark. The tiny community of 500 people lives under a spell, governed feudally and sharing this magic island with horses, sheep, cattle, carpets of wild flowers and birds. There are wild cliff walks, thick woodland, sandy coves, wonderful deep rock pools, aquamarine seas. No cars, only bikes, horse and carriage and the odd tractor. In the hotel - a 400-year-old farmhouse - there is no TV, no radio, no trouser press... just a dreamy peace, kindness, starched cotton sheets, woollen blankets and food to die for. The Perrées still farm and, as a result, the hotel is almost self-sufficient; you also get home-baked bread and lobsters straight from the sea. Elizabeth is Sercquaise - her mother's family were part of the 1565 colonisation - and she knows her land well enough to lead you to the island's secrets.

Rooms: 6 twins, 5 doubles, 6 family, 1 suite; 2 twins, 2 doubles sharing 2 bathrooms.
Price: £95-£155. Dinner, B&B £59.50-£75.50 p.p.
Meals: Breakfast times flexible. Dinner, 5 courses, £30.
Closed: Second Monday in October until Wednesday before Easter.

Take ferry to Sark and ask!

Map No: 1

Penzance Arts Club

Chapel House
Chapel Street, Penzance
Cornwall
TR18 4AQ

Tel: 01736 363761
Fax: 01736 363761
E-mail: reception@penzanceartsclub.co.uk
Web: www.chycor.co.uk/arts-club

Belinda Rushworth-Lund

Amusing, quirky and original... the Arts Club has brought a little fun to old Penzance. Belinda has created an easy-going but vital cultural centre where you can fall into bed after a night of poetry and jazz in the bar, or an evening of fish in the gaily-coloured restaurant. The bar is a feast of ideas and art, with paintings all over the walls and a mix of comfortable and attractive furniture, marble open fireplaces, driftwood, wooden floors and a handsome wooden table. The little garden and balcony off the bar have fine views over the harbour. The bedrooms are attractive, colourful and surprisingly comfortable, and are as charmingly flamboyant as the bar is raffish. There is elegance too, for the house was once the Portuguese embassy in more prosperous Penzance days. Not luxurious - the touches of scruffiness don't matter at all - but terrific value and one of the most engagingly individual places in this book. Rather than 'exclusive' – how we lament the word – this is 'inclusive'; a must for the open-minded.

Rooms: 1 double, 3 family, all en suite shower and sharing wc.
Price: £50-£70; singles £30-£45. Children under 14 sharing with parents half price.
Meals: Breakfast 8.30-9.30am; early breakfast on request. Tapas from £3. Lunch & dinner, 3 courses, £15-£20.
Closed: Never. Restaurant closed Sundays (& Mondays in winter).

In Penzance, drive along harbourside with sea on your left. Opposite the docks, turn right into Quay St (by the Dolphin pub). Up hill and house on right opp. St. Mary's Church.

Map No: 1

The Summer House Restaurant with Rooms

Cornwall Terrace
Penzance
Cornwall
TR18 4HL
Linda and Ciro Zaino

Tel: 01736 363744
Fax: 01736 360959
E-mail: summerhouse@dial.pipex.com
Web: www.summerhouse-cornwall.com

Don't rush through; stay awhile - this is fun, and you'll get so well fed. After trawling through the hotels of Britain to find ones to include in this book, the Summer House was a glittering catch. It is stylish, imaginative, bustling, informal, colourful... a happy marriage of sunshine yellows, strong Tuscan shades and wooden floors. Squashy sofas rub shoulders with pieces of pure Gothic carving, a glass wall floods the house with light, and walls show local artists. The restaurant continues the Mediterranean theme, its elegant room spilling out into a walled garden alive with terracotta pots and palm trees. Food is a vital part of the hotel - *le patron mange ici*. Ciro loves simple food and fresh ingredients; the fish is wonderfully fresh and lovingly displayed. The bedrooms have an eclectic mix of family pieces and beautiful 'collectables', and are as lively and colourful as the hotel itself. Linda and Ciro run it with huge energy and enthusiasm. A place where guests can unwind and talk to each other. *Children over 12 welcome.*

Rooms: 2 doubles and 3 twin/doubles.
Price: £60-£80; singles from £55.
Meals: Breakfast until 9.30am. Packed lunch from £6. Dinner, 3 courses, £21.50.
Closed: Occasionally in January & February. Restaurant closed Sundays & Mondays.

With sea on left, drive along harbourside, past Jubilee open-air pool, then immediate right after Queens Hotel. House 30m up on left.

Halzephron

Gunwalloe
Helston
Cornwall
TR12 7QB

Angela Davy Thomas

Tel: 01326 240406
Fax: 01326 241442
E-mail: halzephroninn@bandbcornwall.net
Web: www.halzephron.co.uk

An opera singer running an old smuggler's inn on the remote Lizard Peninsula - incomparable. Angela is carrying on a tradition started by her late husband, Harry - the bottom-worn armchair in the bar is a fond memento. Funny, charming, she runs the whole show with cheery ebullience. The inn has been taking in guests (and smugglers, judging by the shaft behind the bar that connects to an underground passage) for 500 years. It reopened in 1958 as the Halzephron; old Cornish for 'cliffs of hell' and testament to the numerous ships dashed onto this beautiful but treacherous coastline. The inn has two cosy rooms, with deep-sprung beds, patchwork quilts, the odd heirloom, fresh fruit and cafetière coffee. Downstairs, Angela has created some marvellous eating areas - the mock sea cove in wood-panelled marine-blue, lit overhead by a necklace of tiny lights, is delightful. Food is taken seriously here - freshly cooked, carefully presented, with a supporting cast of 10 local cheeses. Just the job after a visit to Gunwalloe's 13th-century church or the unspoilt fishing villages of Cadgwith, Coverack and Mullion.

Rooms: 2 doubles.
Price: £70; singles £40.
Meals: Breakfast 8-9am. Lunch £10-£15. Packed lunch £12. Dinner, 3 courses, £22.
Closed: Christmas Day.

From Helston, A3083, signed The Lizard, past Culdrose air base, then right, signed Gunwalloe, for 2 miles. Inn on left after houses.

Trengilly Wartha Inn

Nancenoy, Constantine
Falmouth
Cornwall
TR11 5RP

Tel: 01326 340332
Fax: 01326 340332
E-mail: trengilly@compuserve.com

Michael and Helen Maguire & Nigel and Isabel Logan

It's hard to believe the Helford river is navigable up to this point, simply because it's quite hard to navigate a car up the narrow, steep lanes of this deeply rural hideaway. It's worth the effort. Trengilly has won all the awards a pub can win: 'Best Free House of the Year', 'Pub of the Year', 'Best Dining Pub in Cornwall', and it really is everything you'd want from a country inn. The ales are honourable, the wooden settles comfy and the bar meals good. In summer, the garden fills – the locals *all* come here; and there's a jazzy restaurant - pastel blues and pale yellows - and a no-smoking conservatory, too. The hotel sitting room is as cosy as you could wish for with lots of books, cricket and political biographies, and an open fire. All bar one of the bedrooms have valley views; some have simple old pine beds, some Laura Ashley, others whitewashed. There's a small lake at the bottom of the six-acre garden, breakfast is a feast – scrambled duck eggs with smoked trout, maybe – and you can even arrive by horse – there are posts to tie up to. Locals do.

Rooms: 4 doubles, 1 twin, 2 family; 1 twin with private bathroom.
Price: £60-£88; singles £48.
Meals: Breakfast until 9.30am. Bar meals £4-£15. Dinner, 2 courses, £20; 3 courses, £25.
Closed: Never.

Approaching Falmouth on A39, follow Constantine signs. After about 7 miles, as you approach village, inn is clearly signed left, then right.

Map No: 1

Tregildry Hotel

Gillan
Manaccan
Cornwall
TR12 6HG

Tel: 01326 231378
Fax: 01326 231561
E-mail: trgildry@globalnet.co.uk
Web: www.tregildryhotel.co.uk

Huw and Lynne Phillips

Take your pick - Gillan Creek, the Helford River, Falmouth Bay and the Roseland Peninsula - the sea views here are absolutely stunning. At the bottom of the hill, the road ends and there are great views across the creek to St. Anthony's Church. At low tide hidden stepping stones will take you there, but be warned; they are slippery. Back up the hill, Tregildry makes the most of the view. Lynne and Huw rescued the place from neglect and gave the big downstairs rooms lots of windows. They are now smart, light and airy, full of squishy sofas and rattan armchairs, with piles of magazines, bursting bookshelves and Mediterranean colours. Wonderful food in the restaurant (Cornish crab cakes, spicy tiger prawns, rack of lamb) and a different table each evening so you don't miss the view, though pre-dinner drinks under parasols on the terrace insure against this (there are sun loungers, too). Bedrooms have a soft, clean country feel: fresh flowers, more rattan furniture, pinks, yellows and greens; all but two have seaward views. A track leads down to the coastal path and the cove below.

Rooms: 7 doubles, 3 twins.
Price: Dinner, B&B £70-£75 p.p.; singles £70-£85.
Meals: Breakfast 8.30-9.30am. Dinner, 4 courses, included. Light lunch by arrangement.
Closed: 1 November-1 March.

South from Helston on A3083, past naval base on left, then left on B3293 for St. Keverne. After 3 miles, left to Manaccan, then follow signs for Gillan. Signed down hill and right in village.

Map No: 1

The St. Mawes Hotel

The Sea Front
St. Mawes
Cornwall
TR2 5DW

Tel: 01326 270266
Fax: 01326 270170
E-mail: stmaweshotel@compuserve.com
Web: www.stmaweshotel.co.uk

Emma Burrows and Henry Hare

Unstinting determination and a passion for fun marks out The St. Mawes. Emma took the hotel over from her parents, who ran it for nigh-on 30 years. With partner Henry, she gave the place a complete overhaul. But as the last drops of paint were drying, fate intervened and 3,500 gallons of water flooded the entire place. They had to start all over again. More recently, three balcony rooms have been transformed into a busy brasserie. From a balcony table, the view over St. Mawes Bay is gorgeous; gleaming yachts bob gently in a calm swell that shimmers like liquid gold in the sun; at night, lights on the quayside cast swirling, soupy patterns into the shallows. The hotel is a lazy amble from the sea; take a dip before breakfast, served outside in the French style - the road goes nowhere, so you won't be disturbed. The hub of the hotel is a lively ground-floor bar that opens onto the street in summer. Mediterranean colours, wooden floors and sofas keep things informal - expect to meet some lively locals. Bedrooms are simple and stylish, with good beds, wicker chairs, flowers and white walls that absorb the light. Come and join the party.

Rooms: 3 doubles, 2 twins.
Price: £50-£110; singles £25-£80.
Meals: Breakfast 9-9.30am weekdays, 9-10.30am weekends. Lunch and dinner in bar or new brasserie. Light lunch from £3.95; dinner, 3 courses, from £20. Cream teas also available.
Closed: Never.

The hotel is on the seafront in the town. Parking available opposite in public car park (£6 a day in high season, free in low season).

Map No: 1

Manor Cottage

Tresillian
Truro
Cornwall
TR2 4BN

Tel: 01872 520212
E-mail: man.cott@cwcom.net
Web: www.manorcottage.com

Carlton Moyle and Gillian Jackson

Don't let the slightly shabby exterior of this engagingly unpretentious restaurant with rooms put you off - locals break out in nostalgic smiles at the mere mention of the place, their memory jogged about some sublime dish that Carlton once whisked up for them. This is a small, very relaxed operation and everything you come across is the work of either Carlton or Gillian; they painted the yellow walls, polished the wooden floors, hung the big mirror, arranged the flowers. They even planted the plumbago and passionflower that wander on the stone walls in the conservatory where you eat. Carlton cooks from Thursday to Saturday - the restaurant is closed for the rest of the week, presumably to let him get on with his other chores; he put in the bathrooms. They're excellent, some with hand-painted tiles. Bedrooms are small, but, for their price, superb and full of pretty things. You might have a Heal's of London bed, a hint of Art Deco or scented candles. Wonderful old farm quilts hang on the banister, so grab one and roast away till morning. A little noise from the road, but it's worth it.

Rooms: 2 doubles; 1 double with private shower; 1 twin, 1 single sharing shower.
Price: £48-£60; singles £25-£40.
Meals: Breakfast 7.30-9.30am. Dinner, 3 courses, £26.
Closed: Occasionally. Restaurant open Thursday-Saturday.

From Truro, east A390, for about 3 miles. House on left when entering village, signed.

Map No: 1

18

Number 6

6 Middle Street
Padstow
Cornwall
PL28 8AP

Tel: 01841 532093
Fax: 01841 532093

Karen Scott

If you dream of the Mediterranean, pack your bags and head to Padstow. Number 6 is the sort of place you hope to stumble upon in the back street of an unspoilt fishing village in the south of France. Karen came here to cook, to live by the sea, to fulfil the dream. Her place is perfect: small, informal and brilliantly decorated. It's not a place to come looking for spa baths and room service, but if you crave style without pretension, attentive but easy-going service and superb fish straight from the sea, then pick up the phone. Checkerboard floors, ferns in urns, wooden blinds and Fired Earth paints in the restaurant and a tiny courtyard garden full of pots and passionflower - book early if you want to eat here. Bedrooms are small, but perfectly formed: coir matting, the best linen, piles of pillows on wooden beds and wonderful bathrooms that bring the beach to you. The house is bang next door to Rick Stein's deli. They can book you a table at his restaurant, but make sure you eat here, too. Perfect. *Children over 12 welcome.*

Rooms: 2 doubles.
Price: £60-£65; singles £56.
Meals: Breakfast 8.45-9.30am. Dinner, 2 courses, £19.50; 3 courses, £23.50.
Closed: Occasionally in winter - please check.

From Wadebridge, A389 west into Padstow. Parking not available in centre, but you can drop off bags. Parking is a five-minute walk away.

Map No: 1

The Port Gaverne Hotel

Port Gaverne
Nr. Port Isaac
Cornwall
PL29 3SQ

Tel: 01208 880244
Fax: 01208 880151

Graham & Annabelle Sylvester

This is a new venture for the Sylvesters. Having successfully created the relaxed country house splendour of Polsue Manor, Graham and Annabelle are breathing new life into a seaside hotel. Their natural bonhomie and eye for detail is set to turn Port Gaverne into a stylish enclave on the north Cornish coast. This 17th-century inn lies in a rocky funnel-shaped cove near the pretty fishing village of Port Isaac – it's safe to swim. Bedrooms in the oldest part of the building have beamed-ceiling character, while those in the modern wing have received the Sylvester treatment - clean, elegant and comfortable, with access to a small balcony. Downstairs, hunker down in a warren-like bar of snug cubby-holes; ideal recuperation after a hike along the coast, or a stroll up a sweet inland valley - both walks start outside the inn. A wonderful stained glass sailing rigger leads to a formal restaurant, serving freshly cooked food in a modern English style. Come for the sea, come for quiet relaxation. *Opening Easter 2002.*

Rooms: 16: 9 doubles, 2 twins, 1 triple, 4 family.
Price: £70-£90; singles £45-£55.
Meals: Breakfast 8.30-9.30am. Bar lunch from £4.50. Dinner, 4 courses, £20.
Closed: January-mid-February.

From Wadebridge, B3314, then B3267, following signs to Port Isaac. In village, follow road right to Port Gaverne. Inn up lane from cove on left.

Map No: 1

20

The Mill House Inn

Trebarwith
Nr. Tintagel
Cornwall
PL34 0HD

Tel: 01840 770200
Fax: 01840 770647
E-mail: management@themillhouseinn.co.uk
Web: www.themillhouseinn.co.uk

Nigel Peters, John Beach and John Bamford

It's no surprise the folk behind the Mill House Inn work in the movie business. Imagine the initial pitch - put the atmosphere of a stylish London bistro in an old mill house next to the rolling surf of the north Cornish coast, then provide chic, affordable rooms. Such a cracking idea, it's a wonder no-one thought of it before. Arrive down a steep winding lane to a pretty woodland setting, ambling along at its own contented pace. All you need is within walking distance – a glorious sandy beach to suit sunbather or body surfer and coastal trails that lead to Tintagel, official home of the Arthurian legends. Inside, a dark and cosy bar has easy-going panache, with old floorboards, gnarled wooden tables and blissed-out tunes. The dining room over the old mill stream is light and elegant; sea blues, crisp, white linen and chapel chairs create a tongue-in-cheek formality - chef Phil Griffin trained under Marco Pierre White. There's a snug living room for guests, with lots of old movies and CDs, and state-of-the-art equipment to play them on. A funky oasis for the chintz-weary generation.

Rooms: 8 doubles, 1 family, 1 single.
Price: £60-£80; singles £40-£50.
Meals: Breakfast 8.30-10.30am. Bar lunch from £3.95-£7.95. Dinner, à la carte, 3 courses approx. £20.
Closed: Never.

From Tintagel, B3263 south, following signs to Trebarwith Strand. Inn at bottom of steep hill.

Map No: 1

Trebrea Lodge

Trenale
Tintagel
Cornwall
PL34 0HR

Tel: 01840 770410
Fax: 01840 770092

John Charlick and Sean Devlin

We'd wager a pound or two that people who 'discover' Trebrea either tell everyone or no-one about it, and guess mostly it's the latter. It has perfect combinations: formal but cosy, small but grand, warm and intimate, yet never oppressive or remotely pretentious. You start in the bright red-carpeted hall where wooden stairs flanked by fine large oils lead up to the drawing room. The view from here is uplifting, stretching across fields to cliff-topping Tintagel church, the Atlantic beyond. Up still further to the bedrooms that manage the clever trick of being crisp and elegant, yet cosy and homely as well. Beautiful furniture, bright colours, crisp linen; one has an enormous oak four-poster. Downstairs, there's a very snug smoking room and honesty bar piled high with magazines, where, in winter, lulled by a crackling fire, you fall asleep easily. Across the hall is a panelled dining room, candlelit in the evenings, where Sean serves up great things. Outside, there are five acres of grounds and woodland, and the North Cornish coast is only one mile away. *Children over 12 welcome.*

Rooms: 3 twins, 4 doubles.
Price: £78-£98; singles £63.50-£69.
Meals: Breakfast 8.30-9.30am. Dinner, 4 courses, £24.50. Packed lunch by arrangement.
Closed: January.

On B3263 leaving Tintagel to the north, turn right into Trenale Lane beside R.C. church. In Trenale, turn right towards Trewarmett.
Hotel is 0.25 miles on left.

Map No: 1

Cormorant on the River

Golant
Nr. Fowey
Cornwall
PL23 1LL

Tel: 01726 833426
Fax: 01726 833574
E-mail: relax@cormoranthotels.co.uk
Web: www.cormoranthotels.co.uk

Carrie and Colin King

Golant is well-hidden from Cornwall's tourist trail and the Cormorant is well-hidden from Golant. You drive along the quay, then climb a short, steep hill. The reward is a breathtaking view of the Fowey estuary (pronounced 'Foy'), flowing through a wooded landscape. Boats tug on their moorings and birds glide lazily over the water - this is a very English paradise. The view is so good the architect made sure it leapt into every room; 10 of the 11 bedrooms have French windows. They're fabulous to wake up in, and not bad to sleep in either, with comfy beds, pastel colours and spotless bathrooms. From the entrance, steps lead to a huge light-filled sitting room with log fire, colourful pictures and a big map of the estuary to help plan adventures - walks start from the door. There's a small bar with a good smattering of whiskies and a pretty dining room themed on the legend of Tristam, Yseult and jilted King Mark (the love story was made into an opera by Wagner; a nearby 13th-century church once belonged in the king's domain). In summer, have tea under parasols on the terraced lawn and watch the boats zip by. A marvellous spot.

Rooms: 11 twin/doubles.
Price: £80-£130; singles from £55 (winter only).
Meals: Breakfast until 9.30am. Dinner, 4 courses, from £20.
Closed: Never.

A390 west towards St. Austell, then B3269 to Fowey. After 6 miles, left to Golant. Continue into village, along quay, hotel signed right, up very steep hill.

Map No: 1

Talland Bay Hotel

Talland
Nr. Looe
Cornwall
PL13 2JB

Tel: 01503 272667
Fax: 01503 272940
E-mail: tallandbay@aol.com
Web: www.tallandbayhotel.co.uk

Annie and Barrington Rosier

Decidedly old-fashioned, with decidedly old-fashioned ideas about looking after people. If you want to be by yourself you may curl up with a book at the end of the garden, or just lie by the pool and listen to the seagulls. A peaceful place, with two acres of subtropical gardens and a beautifully mown lawn ending in a ha-ha and a 150-foot drop down to the bay, with long views out to sea. The air is clear and fresh, and the sea view through pine trees has a Mediterranean feel, reflected in the style and flavour of the hotel's food. The house is surprisingly ancient, mentioned in the Domesday book and once owned by the famous Trelawney family. French windows open from the sitting room, dining room (both part-panelled), bar and library onto a paved terrace and a heated swimming pool. There's a little upstairs sitting area, too. The bedrooms are traditional-luxurious, Laura Ashley in parts, impeccable and bathed in light. The traditions go as far as croquet and a Cornish clotted cream tea, as well as lots of fresh fish and seafood from Looe, including lobster, crab and scallops.

Rooms: 20 twin/doubles, 2 singles.
Price: £86-£160; singles £43-£80.
Meals: Breakfast until 9.30am. Light lunch £4-£12. Packed lunch from £5. Dinner, 3 courses, £23.
Closed: 10 January-mid-February.

From Looe, A387 towards Polperro. Ignore 1st sign to Talland. After 2 miles, left at crossroads and follow signs.

Map No: 1

24

Halfway House Inn
Fore Street
Kingsand, Cawsand Bay
Cornwall
PL10 1NA

Tel: 01752 822279
Fax: 01752 823146
E-mail: david.riggs@virgin.net
Web: www.connexions.co.uk/halfway

Sarah and David Riggs
Manager: Justine Tidmarsh

Kingsand is a dream, a shaded warren of narrow, car-free lanes and brightly-painted cottages, with the sea stretching out on one side and hills rising behind. At its heart is the Halfway House, a snug, traditional inn, where the local fishermen drop off their catch at the kitchen door before coming in for a pint. Inside, back-to-back woodburners warm both sides of the room, pictures of ships hang on stone walls and, somewhere, there's a barometer. Look carefully and you'll find a photo of the clock tower being drenched by a wave, then take 30 paces outside and you'll be standing 80ft below the clock. There's masses of fresh fish to tempt you - the fish soup is a meal in itself - but the philosophy here is 'eat whatever you want, wherever you want' so they'll do you ham, egg and chips if that's what you feel like. Sunday lunches are huge and very popular. Bedrooms are simple and spotless with a dash of colour, a sprinkling of books and fresh flowers - nothing nasty, just excellent value. Sandy beaches, coastal walks, surfing, sailing, historic houses, gardens... something for everyone. Bring your bucket and spade.

Rooms: 3 doubles, 1 twin, 1 family, 1 single.
Price: £55; family £70; single £27.50.
Meals: Breakfast 8.30-9.30am. Lunch & dinner £5-£25; book in advance.
Closed: Never.

6 miles west of Saltash, leave A38 for Torpoint on A374. Follow signs, first, for Mount Edgcumbe Country Park (B3247), then, for Kingsand. Inn opposite Post Office. Public car park next door £1.50.

Map No: 1

Aynsome Manor Hotel

Cartmel
Nr. Grange-over-Sands
Cumbria
LA11 6HH

Tel: 015395 36653
Fax: 015395 36016
E-mail: info@aynsomemanorhotel.co.uk
Web: www.aynsomemanorhotel.co.uk

Christopher and Andrea Varley

Stand at the front door and look away from the house. Three-quarters of a mile across ancient meadows Cartmel Priory stands, magnificent after 800 years, still the heart of a small, thriving community. The view is almost medieval. You can strike out across fields to the village and discover its gentle secrets. The house, too, echoes with history - it was the home of the descendants of the Earl of Pembroke and, in 1930, it gave up a long-held secret when a suit of chain armour dating back to 1335 was found behind a wall in an attic bedroom. There's a *tongue-and-ball* ceiling in the panelled dining room and, in the hall, a melodious grandfather clock, a wood and coal fire and carved-oak panels, the gift of an 1839 storm. A cantilevered spiral staircase with cupola-domed window leads up to the first-floor sitting room where newspapers hang from poles and there's an Adams-style marble fireplace. The bedrooms vary in size and are simple and comfortable, some with gently sloping floors. Racegoers will love the National Hunt racecourse. *No under fives in the restaurant.*

Rooms: 4 twins, 5 doubles, 1 four-poster, 2 family.
Price: £69-£80; singles from £39. Dinner, B&B £48-£62 p.p.
Meals: Breakfast 8.30-9.30am. Dinner, 4 courses, £22.
Closed: January.

Leave A590 (M6 - Barrow road) at top of Lindale Hill. Follow signs left to Cartmel. Hotel on right 3 miles from A590.

Map No: 5

The Old Vicarage

Church Road
Witherslack
Cumbria
LA11 6RS

Tel: 015395 52381
Fax: 015395 52373
E-mail: hotel@oldvicarage.com
Web: www.oldvicarage.com

Jill and Roger Brown, Irene and Stanley Reeve

Thank goodness for the Browns and the Reeves. The potted history of these four effervescent souls is that about 20 years ago they escaped the rat race 'down south', swapped suits, first for overalls (the house needed a major make-over), then aprons. They have been indulging their passions ever since, number one on the list being food. Everyone I spoke to in the area had eaten here and thoroughly recommended it; the TV cameras have, of course, paid a visit. The baton has been passed to the next generation with James, Jill and Roger's son, now in the kitchen. Add to this, rooms of simple, stylish luxury and you have guests as happy as the owners. Rooms in the main house look out over the garden and are closer to the fun; those in Orchard House are bigger, better and utterly secluded – stroll through the damson trees and past the tennis court on your way up. Maps and routes for walkers, high teas and chairs for children, and Yewbarrow Fell ('The Noddle') is just behind. A ten-minute walk to the top brings spectacular views. Quite simply, heaven-sent and down-to-earth.

Rooms: 1 family, 6 doubles, 4 twins, 1 four-poster.
Price: £98-£138; four-poster £158; singles from £65. Dinner, B&B £65-£100 p.p.
Meals: Breakfast 8-9.30am. Dinner, 3 courses from £25. Sunday lunch £15.50. Packed lunch also available.
Closed: Never.

*M6, junc. 36, then A590 towards Barrow.
After 6 miles, right signed Witherslack.
In village, left after phone box. House
on left just before church.*

Map No: 5

Miller Howe Hotel & Restaurant

Rayrigg Road
Bowness-on-Windermere
Cumbria
LA23 1EY

Tel: 015394 42536
Fax: 015394 45664
E-mail: lakeview@millerhowe.com
Web: www.millerhowe.com

Charles Garside

Many places claim to have the best view in England but this must rank as one of the strongest contenders. Looking over Lake Windermere to hills, fells and mountains, it's absolutely breathtaking, whatever the season. Celebrated chef John Tovey established Miller Howe's reputation in the Seventies, maintaining that the secret was to attract the right staff to this wonderful location. Many of the original team remain, under the present stewardship of Charles Garside, a former national newspaper editor who left Fleet Street to take up the challenge of running a hotel in 1997. Charles likes to welcome guests with a friendly arm round the shoulder and is a stickler for good service. Comfortable reception rooms are in a lavish country house style, while a dining room of honey limestone tiles, wrought-iron verdigris and gilded ceilings draws the view to your table; menus helpfully identify the landscape. Handsome bedrooms exude traditional elegance, while three new suites in a converted cottage provide luxurious privacy. Perfect anytime. *Children eight and over welcome. Free use of nearby leisure complex.*

Rooms: Main house: 7 twin/doubles, 5 doubles. Cottage: 3 suites.
Price: Dinner B&B £75-£135 p.p. (house); £135-£175 p.p. (cottage).
Meals: Breakfast 8.30-9.30am. Light lunch from £7. Picnics £14. Afternoon teas £4.50-£9.99. Dinner, 5 courses, included; non-residents £39.50.
Closed: 6-18 January.

From Kendal, A591 to Windermere, then left at mini-r'bout onto A592 towards Bowness. Hotel 0.25 miles on right.

Old Dungeon Ghyll

Great Langdale
Ambleside
Cumbria
LA22 9JY

Tel: 015394 37272
Fax: 015394 37272
E-mail: neil.odg@lineone.net
Web: www.odg.co.uk

Neil and Jane Walmsley

This is an old favourite of those hardy mountaineers and it comes as no surprise to learn that Tenzing and Hillary stayed here. The hotel is at the head of the valley, surrounded by spectacular peaks, heaven for hikers and climbers, a place to escape to. The scenery is breathtaking, and this is a solid and genuine base... as unpretentious as can be. The bedrooms are eclectically decorated with the odd brass bed, patchwork quilts, maybe floral wallpaper and patterned carpets. They are also blissfully free of phones and TVs - you wouldn't want them here, not when you can go downstairs. In winter, the fire crackles comfortably in the sitting room, the food is all home-cooked (fresh bread, teacakes and flapjacks every day) and there's a small snug residents' bar. Best of all is the famous hikers' bar – hotel wedding parties always seem to end up here. Guitars and fiddles appear (do they carry them over the mountain?), *ceilidhs* break out, laughter is the main language and it's all overseen by Neil, Jane and great staff. Come to walk and to leave the city far behind.

Rooms: 4 twin/doubles; 1 twin, 2 family, 3 singles, 4 doubles, all sharing 4 baths and 1 shower.
Price: £64-£75.
Meals: Breakfast 8.30-9.30am. Bar snacks from £6. Packed lunch £3.95. Dinner, 3 courses, £18.50.
Closed: 24-26 December.

On A593, from Ambleside towards Coniston, turn right onto B5343. Hotel signed on right after 5 miles, past Great Langdale campsite.

The Wasdale Head Inn
Wasdale Head
Gosforth
Cumbria
CA20 1EX

Tel: 019467 26229
Fax: 019467 26334
E-mail: wasdaleheadinn@msn.com
Web: www.wasdale.com

Howard Christie

Wasdale Head is incomparable, perfect and unique. The vastness of the scenery is awesome and its remoteness second-to-none. No great surprise then to discover this is the recognised birth place of world mountain climbing. The residents' bar is its 'holy of holies', with original photos taken by the Abrahams brothers, the pioneers of climbing photography, hanging reverently on the walls. Wasdale remains blissfully free of the outside world; you'll not find even the faintest whiff of commercialism here. The inn is warm and intimate, lively and fun. In the hikers' bar, blackboards give regular weather updates alongside the daily specials, while the restaurant is full of old climbing memorabilia. Outside, the beer garden has spectacular views of Kirk Fell, Great Gable and Scafell, England's highest peak. Bedrooms are split between chalet-style rooms in the main house and more luxurious rooms in nearby cottages. Howard is part of the mountain rescue team, so expect the best advice. Expect tall tales, too, as he stars in the annual 'Biggest Liar in the World' competition held nearby. The drive from Windermere, weather permitting, is arguably the best in England.

Rooms: 3 suites, 5 doubles, 1 twin, 1 triple, 2 singles.
Price: £70-£90; singles £35-£45.
Meals: Breakfast 7.30-9am. Bar meals from £3. Dinner, 4 courses, £22.
Closed: Never.

From Gosforth, A595 east, via Wellington, following signs to Wasdale Head; from Windermere, cross Wrynose & Hardknott passes to Great Langdale, then literally 'first right' every time to inn.

Map No: 5

Swinside Lodge

Grange Road
Newlands, Keswick
Cumbria
CA12 5UE

Kevin and Susan Kniveton

Tel: 017687 72948
Fax: 017687 72948
E-mail: info@swinsidelodge-hotel.co.uk
Web: www.swinsidelodge-hotel.co.uk

A short stroll takes you to the edge of Derwentwater – the Queen of the Lakes. Immediately behind, fells rise and spirits soar. At Swinside – a small-scale model of English country house elegance – reception rooms are crisp and fresh, with fine period furniture offset by pastel blues and yellows. In the bold dining room, deep reds combine with candle-lamps burning oil... formal, yet very relaxed. There are lots of books in the sitting rooms, maps for walkers, bowls of fruit, fresh flowers and no clutter. Every tiny detail has been well thought out, not least in the bedrooms where flair and forethought have pulled off a maestro's touch – the rooms have been furnished with cream furniture to make them feel bigger than they are, and it works a treat. The bedrooms are all good and two are huge. You'll find drapes, more crisp materials and uplifting views – you can watch the weather change. Food is honest and delicious; perhaps try asparagus and herb risotto, celery and apple soup, lamb, or warm chocolate mousse. *Children over 10 welcome.*

Rooms: 2 twins, 5 doubles.
Price: Dinner, B&B, £65-£87 p.p.
Meals: Breakfast 8.30-9.30am. Dinner, 4 courses, included; non-residents £28. Booking essential.
Closed: Never.

M6, junc. 40, then A66 west past Keswick. Over r'bout, then 2nd left, signed Portiscale and Grange. Follow signs to Grange for 2 miles. House signed on right.

Map No: 6

Michaels Nook

Grasmere
Ambleside
Cumbria
LA22 9RP

Tel: 015394 35496
Fax: 015394 35645
E-mail: m-nook@wordsworth-grasmere.co.uk
Web: www.grasmere-hotels.co.uk

Reg and Elizabeth Gifford

The immense luxury of Michaels Nook is offered in the most understated way, making it easy to understand why it is one of Britain's finest country house hotels. Expect the best of everything: a Michelin-starred restaurant, a treasure trove of antique furniture, Honduran mahogany staircase and panelling, sumptuously rich fabrics and bold décor. Bedrooms are superb: high four-posters, drapes, armoires, maybe an aubergine-coloured *chaise longue,* or a big old cast-iron bath with the equivalent of a Victorian power shower – marvellous. The suite has some lovely Chinese lacquer furniture and a big window to frame the lakeland view. Reg has been here for 30 odd years and presides over it all with gentle good humour and an unpretentious Cumbrian warmth. You'll meet his Great Danes, too – they're as friendly as they are big. He won best of breed at Crufts in 1997 and 2000, yet still has a soft spot for Scruffs. There are three acres of landscaped gardens, 10 acres of hillside and you can walk into the fells from the front door.

Rooms: 2 suites, 1 four-poster,
11 twin/doubles.
Price: Dinner, B&B £85-£137.50 p.p.;
suites £160 p.p.; singles from £148 p.p.
Meals: Breakfast 8.30-9.30am. Dinner,
4 courses, included.
Closed: Never.

From Windermere, A591 north to Grasmere, then right on A591 at the Swan pub between the pub and its car park. Hotel signed right.

Map No: 5

32

White Moss House

Rydal Water
Grasmere
Cumbria
LA22 9SE

Tel: 015394 35295
Fax: 015394 35516
E-mail: sue@whitemoss.com
Web: www.whitemoss.com

Susan and Peter Dixon

This is the epicentre of Wordsworth country; walk north a mile to his home at Dove Cottage or west to his somewhat more salubrious house at Rydal Mount. The paths are old and you can follow his footsteps up fell and through wood. He knew White Moss, too - he bought it for his son and came here to escape. The Dixons have lived here for 21 years - they took over from Susan's parents - and they have kept the feel of a home: flowers everywhere, a woodburning stove, pretty floral fabrics and lots of comfy sofas and chairs. There's a small bar in an old linen cupboard, and after-dinner coffee in the sitting room brings out the house-party feel. Upstairs, bedrooms range in size, but not comfort. All are different, with maybe a glazed pine-panelled bay window, old wooden beds and a sprinkling of books and magazines. All have good views, and bathrooms have Radox to soothe fell-fallen feet. There's also the small matter of the food, all cooked by Peter. Five courses of famed indulgence await - expect to have taste buds tickled.

Rooms: 2 doubles, 3 twin/doubles; 1 cottage, sleeps 4.
Price: Dinner, B&B £65-£90 p.p.
Meals: Breakfast 8.30-9.30am. Packed lunch £5. Dinner, 5 courses, included; non-residents £30.
Closed: 1 December-mid-February. Restaurant closed Sunday nights.

North from Ambleside on A591. House signed on right at north end of Rydal Water.

Map No: 5

The Pheasant

Bassenthwaite Lake
Nr. Cockermouth
Cumbria
CA13 9YE

Matthew Wylie

Tel: 017687 76234
Fax: 017687 76002
E-mail: pheasant@easynet.co.uk
Web: www.the-pheasant.co.uk

The snug bar at The Pheasant, a treasured relic of its days as a coaching inn, is tremendous, the walls a shiny combination of 300 years of nicotine and polish. It's wonderful. There's also a low-slung wooden bar where the barman guards his 28 malts. The inn has since turned into a hotel, and drinks are usually served in one of the sitting rooms, where elegance is piled upon elegance in an utterly understated way: gilt mirrors, sprays of garden flowers, trim carpets, rugs and fresh yellow walls, fine furniture and a beam or two - everything is just right, immaculate yet immediately relaxing. The bedrooms have been beautifully refurbished this year; the odd hidden beam has been revealed, mellow lighting added, warm colours put on the walls and a rug or two thrown in for good measure. All are elegant and you still come across Housekeeping armed with feather dusters - perfect. There's a kennel for visiting dogs, Skiddaw to be scaled and Bassenthwaite Lake to be paddled. *Children over eight welcome.*

Rooms: Main house: 2 suites, 1 single, 10 twin/doubles; Garden Lodge: 2 doubles, 1 single.
Price: £110-£160; singles £65-£80. Dinner, B&B £71-£98 p.p. (minimum 2 nights).
Meals: Breakfast 7.30-9.30am. Light lunch from £5. Dinner, 3 courses, £21.95-£30.
Closed: Christmas Day.

The hotel is signed left on the A66, 7 miles north-west of Keswick.

The Mill Hotel

Mungrisdale
Nr. Penrith
Cumbria
CA11 0XR

Tel: 017687 79659
Fax: 017687 79155
E-mail: quinlan.themill@evesham.net
Web: www.themillhotel.com

Richard and Eleanor Quinlan

A small, eclectic bolt hole, this 1651 mill house on the northern border of the lakes has a stream racing past that is fed by fells that rise behind. Richard and Eleanor belong to that band of innkeepers who do their own thing instinctively and immaculately - this is the antithesis of a big, impersonal hotel. Richard comes out to greet you at the car, to help with the bags, to show you up to your room, and finally, invites you down for drinks "whenever you're ready". Downstairs you'll find a tiny library and a homely sitting room with rocking chair, ancient stone fireplace, wood carvings and piles of reference books on every subject under the sun. All the while, Eleanor has been cooking up five courses of heaven for your supper, all home-made (and organic where possible), from the olive bread to the watercress soup; breakfasts, too, are first class. Bedrooms range in size, but not style. The old mill, wrapped in *clematis montana*, has its own sitting room where you can fall asleep to the sound of the river. In the main house, beams, bowls of fruit, African art, fresh flowers and good linen induce perfect slumber.

Rooms: 4 doubles, 3 twins; 1 double,
1 twin with shared bath.
Price: Dinner, B&B £59-£79 p.p.
Meals: Breakfast 8.30-9.15am. Dinner,
5 courses, included.
Closed: 1 November-1 March.

*Mungrisdale is signed north from A66,
7 miles west of Penrith. The hotel is next
door to the Mill Inn.*

Map No: 9

Crosby Lodge

High Crosby
Crosby-on-Eden, nr. Carlisle
Cumbria
CA6 4QZ

Tel: 01228 573618
Fax: 01228 573428
E-mail: crosbylodge@crosby-eden.demon.co.uk
Web: www.crosbylodge.co.uk

Michael and Patricia Sedgwick

Come to elope - Gretna is close - or just to escape. Patricia never seems to stop, though she wasn't in a hurry. Walking round outside, we came across the blacksmith, the donkey and a Shetland pony - and there could be grandchildren out there. Not that you'd mind. Crosby Lodge is relaxed and unpretentious enough to thrive on its 'take-us-as-you-find-us' approach. It's very much a family affair. Michael and Patricia came here 30-odd years ago and now their children, James and Pippa, have both joined the firm. Inside is warm and cosy with the odd *chaise longue*, fenders round open fires, lots of rugs and oak furniture. Bedrooms are fun. Pat won't have "square corners", so you get arches and alcoves instead. They're big and bright with good fabrics and colours, and you might get arrow slits or a lovely gnarled half-tester as well. The food is all home-made - soups, breads and ice-creams - and you can eat out on the terrace in summer. Wild flowers grow in the garden, the fabulous Eden Valley starts over the fence and Hadrian's Wall is less than 10 miles away.

Rooms: 2 half-testers, 3 family,
5 twin/doubles, 1 single.
Price: £115-£150; singles £82-£85.
Meals: Breakfast 7.30-9.30am. Lunch from £5.
Dinner, 4 courses, £29; à la carte, £13-£30.
Closed: 24 December-21 January.

M6, Junc.44, then A689 east for 3.5 miles. Turn right to Low Crosby, through village and house signed right less than 1 mile.

Lovelady Shield

Nenthead Road
Nr. Alston
Cumbria
CA9 3LF
Peter and Marie Haynes

Tel: 01434 381203
Fax: 01434 381515
E-mail: enquiries@lovelady.co.uk
Web: www.lovelady.co.uk

This area of the High Pennines is remote and utterly unspoilt. You can walk straight out from Lovelady; the river Nent runs through the garden and at the bridge, four footpaths meet. The house, hidden away down a long and suitably bumpy drive, was rebuilt in 1832. The cellars date from 1690, the foundations from the 14th century when a convent stood here. No noise, but antiphonic sheep bleat in the fields and if you sleep with your window open, you can hear the river. Peter and Marie have been here four years and run the place with a hint of eccentricity and a lot of good-natured charm. A small rag-rolled bar and pretty sitting rooms give a low key, country house feel. Long windows in all rooms bring the views inside and French windows open up in summer for Pimms on the lawn. The food is wonderful; you eat in the very pretty dining room surrounded by gilt mirrors, sash windows and fresh flowers. Upstairs, dark hallways lead through old pine doors to bright bedrooms with window seats, maybe a sofa, good furniture and Scrabble; most have gorgeous views.

Rooms: 1 four-poster, 7 doubles, 2 twins.
Price: Dinner, B&B £60-£110 p.p.
Meals: Breakfast 8-9am. Dinner, 4 courses, included. Non-residents £32. Lunch by arrangement.
Closed: Never.

From Alston, A689 west for 2 miles. House signed left at junction of B6294.

Map No: 10

Hipping Hall

Cowan Bridge
Kirkby Lonsdale
Cumbria
LA6 2JJ

Tel: 015242 71187
Fax: 015242 72452
E-mail: hippinghal@aol.com
Web: www.dedicate.co.uk/hipping-hall

Richard, Jean and Tamara Skelton

One of Lancashire's best kept secrets, Hipping Hall is the surviving remnant of a 15th-century hamlet; the only other clues are an old stone wash-house, a stream and a spring-fed pond, while the ancient well is now part of a flagstoned conservatory. The Skeltons have kept the feel much as it always was - informal, stylish and relaxed – adding a treasure trove of antiques, paintings, prints and numerous teddy bears and dolls as well. Jean's father used to deal in antiques but she prefers to call her love of old things a hobby - there's a tiny curio shop in one of the cellars. Groups can dine in true house-party style in the Great Hall (once the hamlet's town hall), surrounded by old oak floors, rugs, candles and beams, but guests usually eat in an old morning room now converted into an intimate dining room. Jean cooks like an angel and Richard grows vegetables for the table organically. Bedrooms are warm and homely, full of bookshelves, and bathrooms are spotless. Wander in three acres of garden, or majestic countryside - a footpath leads over Leck Fell to Barbondale. Ingleton waterfalls are also close by. *Pets welcome in the cottage suites.*

Rooms: 2 twins, 3 doubles, 2 cottage suites.
Price: From £96; singles from £75.
Meals: Breakfast 8.30-9.30am. Dinner, à la carte, 3 courses, from £18. Morning coffee, lunch and afternoon tea daily.
Closed: 27 December-February; private parties by arrangement.

M6, junc. 36, then A65 east.
House on left, 2.5 miles after Kirkby Lonsdale.

Map No: 6

Riber Hall

Matlock
Derbyshire
DE4 5JU

Tel: 01629 582795
Fax: 01629 580475
E-mail: info@riber-hall.co.uk
Web: www.riber-hall.co.uk

Alex Biggin

Alex is wonderfully 'old school', very much his own man, and has run this 14th-century Elizabethan manor house for 30 years with one foot in the past. The sitting room and dining room fires smoulder all year round making the house feel grand, warm and intimate. Bedrooms are great fun, the majority having antique four-posters, timber-framed walls, mullioned windows, rich thick fabrics, beams and good furniture. There are lots of spoiling touches - beds are turned down discreetly, and you can luxuriate with Royal Spa toiletries in super bathrooms; each room has umbrellas, fresh fruit and home-made shortbread. There's a secret conservatory full of colour and scent all year, and a walled orchard garden with long views for those seeking pure tranquillity. The award-winning food is excellent and Alex is a gentle host, easy to talk to and speaks with passion about Spain, New World wines and local wildlife. Chatsworth House is close by. *Children over 10 welcome.*

Rooms: 9 four-posters, 2 twins,
3 doubles.
Price: £127-£170; singles £97-£112.
Meals: Breakfast 7-9.30am;
Continental included, Full English £8.
Lunch from £13. Dinner from £28.50.
Closed: Never.

From Matlock, A615 to Tansley, then right by Royal Oak (Alders Lane). Wind up hill for 1 mile to hotel.

Map No: 6

Biggin Hall

Biggin-by-Hartington
Buxton
Derbyshire
SK17 0DH

Tel: 01298 84451
Fax: 01298 84681
E-mail: bigginhall@compuserve.com
Web: www.bigginhall.co.uk

James Moffett

Biggin Hall, a 17th-century Grade II*-listed farmhouse, lies knee-deep in lovely countryside. A path from the house leads out past the geese hut and stables to fields, hills, woods, rivers and waterfalls. Not far away is the 1831 Cromford and High Peak Railway - one of the first in the world - now the preserve of cyclists and walkers. James, gently-spoken and humorous, knows his patch of England well and will guide you to its many secrets. He came here 26 years ago and started his labour of love, the restoration of Biggin Hall, keeping its fine old character - stone-flagged floors, old beams, the original fireplace, mullioned windows and leaded lights - while adding contemporary comforts. The bedrooms in the old house have bags of character and there's also a pretty dining room for good, wholesome home-cooked English food. The view through its big window is a seamless transition from garden to paddock, then country beyond. Not surprising that guests go away gleamingly happy. *Children over 11 welcome and pets by arrangement.*

Rooms: Main house: 6 doubles/twins, 1 suite (two singles), 1 four-poster suite. Outbuildings: 5 one-bedroom studio apartments, 2 doubles/twins and 1 suite.
Price: £84-£104; suite £104-£124; singles £55. Apartments £35-£45 p.p.
Meals: Breakfast until 8-9am; Continental included, Full English £3.80. Dinner, 4 courses, £15.50. Teas and packed lunch also available.
Closed: Never.

From A515 take turning to Biggin between Ashbourne and Buxton. Turn right just after Waterloo pub up drive to Biggin Hall.

Map No: 6

The Arundell Arms

Lifton
Devon
PL16 0AA

Tel: 01566 784666
Fax: 01566 784494
E-mail: reservations@arundellarms.com
Web: www.arundellarms.com

Anne Voss-Bark

Just a tiny pretence about liking fish, and fishing, would not be amiss - though Anne and her staff are so kind they'd welcome anyone. She was once Woman Hotelier of the Year, an award richly deserved. Her husband was a contributor to *The Times* on fly-fishing, and most guests come with a strong sense of piscatorial purpose, perhaps for a fishing course. The hotel has 20 miles of its own water on the Tamar and five tributaries. You can be alone here all day, eyes peeled for an otter or kingfisher, fishing for wild trout and salmon, or sea-trout at night. Then back to country house warmth, log fires and perhaps to an "exceptional" (*Daily Telegraph*) meal, where no doubt the piscivorous will be in raptures. But this is a haven for anyone, with a games room and skittle alley, and a good bar with a dartboard. We heard a guest whisper: "I'm in heaven".

Rooms: 9 doubles, 11 twins, 7 singles.
Price: £93-£120; singles £46.50-£79. Dinner, B&B £73-£96 p.p.
Meals: Breakfast until 10am. Bar meals from £5. Dinner, à la carte, 3 courses approx £37; Menu of the Day, 4 courses, £31.
Closed: 24-26 December.

A30 south-west from Exeter, past Okehampton. The village of Lifton is 0.5 miles off the A30, 3 miles east of Launceston and signed. Hotel in centre of village.

Map No: 1

Devon

Lewtrenchard Manor

Lewdown
Nr. Okehampton
Devon
EX20 4PN

Tel: 01566 783256
Fax: 01566 783332
E-mail: s&j@lewtrenchard.co.uk
Web: www.lewtrenchard.co.uk

Sue and James Murray

A thrilling, historical mansion, outstanding in every way – I entered the hall almost expecting to be set upon by hounds. Your senses just explode with the magnificence of it all; the roaring fire in the huge stone fireplace, the acres of panelling, the stained-glass crests, the mullioned windows... only Victorian radiators belie the fact you're not in 16th-century England. Sue and James arrive moments later to provide the perfect counterbalance to the formality of their home. Our tour took in every corner - far too much to mention. Highlights include hand-painted muses on wooden panelling, Queen Henrietta Maria's four-poster, and Anthony and Cleopatra – two African leopard skins that were once the pets of James's father. Incredibly, all this fades to insignificance upon entering the 1602 gallery, with its honeycombed, plaster-moulded ceiling, its grand piano, its 1725 Bible – one of the most beautiful rooms I have ever seen. Bedrooms are exemplary as well and tremendous value for money. Need I say, the gardens are outstanding, too. Unmissable.

Rooms: 4 twin/king doubles, 2 doubles, 2 four-posters, 1 suite.
Price: £120-£175; singles from £90.
Meals: Breakfast 8-9.30am. Lunch, bistro restaurant, from £2.95 (Monday-Saturday), main restaurant, 3 courses, £32 (booking essential), Sunday lunch £19.50. Dinner, 3 courses, £32.
Closed: Never.

From Exeter, leave A30 on slip road for A386. At T-junction, right, then 1st left, signed Lewdown. After 6 miles, left for Lewtrenchard. House signed left after 0.75 miles.

Map No: 1

42

The Henley

Folly Hill
Bigbury-on-Sea
Devon
TQ7 4AR

Tel: 01548 810240
Fax: 01548 810240
E-mail: enquiries@thehenleyhotel.co.uk

Martyn Scarterfield and Petra Lampe

The view from this Edwardian summer house is truly uplifting, a head-clearing vision of sand, sea and lush headland. The garden falls away gently, disappearing over a shallow cliff to an inviting expanse of golden sand and white surf – nothing jars the eye and a footpath leads the way down. Inside, the hotel entrance, with its bold red walls, creates a lovely first impression, and leads to two sitting areas and a conservatory, all decorated with homely elegance. A dining room of Lloyd Loom chairs, pot plants and sea grass sucks in the view to maximum effect; every table has its own special portion and in the evening provides a lovely candlelit setting for Martyn's fresh and unpretentious style of cooking; one reviewer said the view and food combined made them feel content with the world. Bedrooms are small and adequate; all have the view. Reach the island by a narrow causeway at low tide, or by sea tractor at high tide, while the beach is popular with surfers. A friendly, informal retreat.

Rooms: 6 doubles.
Price: £74-£84; singles £47-£52.
Meals: Breakfast: Until 9am. Dinner, 3 courses, £20.
Closed: November-March.

From A38, A3121 to Modbury, then B3392 to Bigbury-on-Sea. Hotel on left as road slopes down towards sea.

The Red Lion Hotel

The Pier
Clovelly
Devon
EX39 5TF

John Rous

Tel: 01237 431237
Fax: 01237 431044
Web: www.clovelly.co.uk
E-mail: redlion@clovelly.co.uk

Manager: Michael Corbett

Clovelly has been spared time's march, partly because of its position - it is completely car-free - and partly because it is a tenanted estate. The houses perch like seagulls' nests on ledges cut into the cliff; many still have original cob walls of red earth and straw. A steep cobbled path snakes down to a small harbour. The Red Lion is right on the quayside, looking out across the Atlantic – you'll hear the sound of the sea from every room. It's an eccentric place, but pleasantly so, with laid-back staff and a friendly manager - Michael cuts a striking figure in this seafaring enclave, dressed impeccably in a suit whatever the weather. Smart bedrooms are up to date, thanks to a recent makeover; all have sea or harbour views. Wonderful seafood is literally delivered from the fishing boat to the kitchen. Travel out to Lundy Island wildlife sanctuary, or walk along Hobby Drive, a beautiful coastal walk laid out in the early 1800s. The late Christine Hamlyn, anointed 'Queen of Clovelly', restored many of the cottages and is still loved by villagers. There's nowhere quite like it. *The New Inn, in the village, has eight en suite rooms.*

Rooms: 7 doubles, 2 twins, 2 family.
Price: £85-£104; singles £42.50-£67.25. Dinner B&B £110-£144.50 p.p. (min. 2 nights).
Meals: Breakfast 8.30-9.30am. Bar lunch from £3.25. Dinner, set menu, £25.
Closed: Never.

From Bideford, A39 towards Bude for 12 miles, then right at r'bout, signed Clovelly. Left fork before Visitor Centre, then left at white rails down steep hill to hotel.

Map No: 1

44

The Hoops Country Inn & Hotel

Horns Cross
Nr. Clovelly, Bideford
Devon
EX39 5DL

Gay Marriott

Tel: 01237 451222
Fax: 01237 451247
E-mail: sales@hoopsinn.co.uk
Web: www.hoopsinn.co.uk

Arriving at The Hoops Inn is like stepping into a timewarp blissfully out of kilter with the outside world. It's changed little in 800 years; there are just fewer smugglers rubbing shoulders with the local gentry at the bar these days. This feeling of splendid disorientation is increased by the lack of road signs to say you've actually arrived in the tiny hamlet of Hoops (from Hoopspink, the Devon word for bullfinch). The signs were taken down during the Second World War to confuse the enemy in the event of an invasion and never put back. The bar has a mellow tick-tock atmosphere, with lots of irregular beams, uneven floors, snug corners, low-hung doorways and five blazing fires in winter - just the place to savour a newspaper (they're provided free) with a local ale. Above the bar, lavish baroque-style rooms are magnificent; the four-poster beds were made from one massive oak bed that originally slept up to 20 people (sic.). The coachhouse rooms are along a corridor, past a pretty courtyard - a lovely spot for afternoon tea. Though smaller, they have the same luxurious period feel. Ample proof, along with the fresh fish and vegetarian menu, that this is special throughout.

Rooms: 4 doubles, 2 twin/doubles, 1 family, 1 twin, 3 four-posters, 1 suite.
Price: £80-£140; singles £53-£85.
Meals: Breakfast 7.30-10am weekdays, 8-10.30am weekends; later by arrangement. Bar lunch from £8.50. Dinner, 2 courses, £12-£18.
Closed: Christmas Day.

From Bideford, A39 towards Bude (North Devon Coastal Road) for 6 miles. Just past Horns Cross, road dips. Inn on right.

Map No: 1

Halmpstone Manor

Bishop's Tawton
Barnstaple
Devon
EX32 0EA

Tel: 01271 830321
Fax: 01271 830826
E-mail: charles@halmpstonemanor.co.uk
Web: www.halmpstonemanor.co.uk

Jane and Charles Stanbury

'Halmpstone' means 'Holy Boundary Stone'. The house, a 1701 Queen Anne manor that had 22 bedrooms before a fire in 1633, faces south across to Dartmoor. The proportions remain delightful. Charles was born here and has run the farm for much of his life. The dining room is panelled, fresh flowers adorn every room, pink walls cheer, family photos beam from silver frames, china figures stand on parade... all very traditional. The bedrooms are immaculate, with a decanter of free sherry, fresh fruit and more flowers, while afternoon tea is included, as are the newspapers; colours are pink and peach. Pink drapes decorate an Edwardian four-poster in one. Here décor is formal, the food excellent (monkfish in a mustard sauce, fillet of beef...) and the service impeccable, while Jane and Charles are very much 'hands-on'.

Rooms: 2 four-posters, 3 twin/doubles.
Price: £100-£140; singles £70.
Meals: Breakfast until 10am. Dinner, 5 courses, £25.
Closed: Christmas & New Year.

From Barnstaple, south on A377. Turn left, opposite petrol station, after Bishop's Tawton, signed Cobbaton and Chittlehampton. After 2 miles, turn right. House on left after 200 yards.

Map No: 1

Broomhill Art Hotel and Sculpture Gardens

Muddiford
Devon
EX31 4EX

Tel: 01271 850262
Fax: 01271 850575
E-mail: info@broomhillart.co.uk
Web: www.broomhillart.co.uk

Rinus and Aniet Van de Sande

This is real devotion to art in a raw, relaxed, and unpretentious setting. Rinus bought his first piece at the age of 17 and hasn't been able to stop since - he's now a young-looking 40-something. He and Aniet had a gallery in Holland, but after falling in love with Devon, decided to ship the contents over here. Now you'll find 250 pieces of contemporary sculpture in their wild garden, 11 international exhibitions a year in the hotel, a ceramics shop and a programme that includes jazz, bebop, lectures and poetry... if it comes along, they put it on. Every piece is original, including some in the bedrooms, and the range is wide - classical, abstract, conceptual... and as you'd expect, there are no airs and graces (leave your pearls at home), the atmosphere is completely informal, the food generous, and the wine flows. Bedrooms are simple, warm and comfortable; you might find the odd wobbly shower head, but in the midst of all this inspirational art, it pales into insignificance. A unique experience.

Rooms: 1 four-poster, 4 twin/doubles.
Price: £55-£65; singles £35-£45.
Meals: Breakfast 8-10am. Lunch from £5. Dinner, 2 courses, £16. Restaurant closed Sunday evenings.
Closed: 20 December-mid-January.

From Barnstable, north for Lynton on A39, then left onto B3230. From here, follow brown signs to the Sculpture Gardens and hotel.

Map No: 1

The Old Rectory Hotel

Martinhoe
Parracombe, Barnstaple
Devon
EX31 4QT

Tel: 01598 763368
Fax: 01598 763567
E-mail: reception@oldrectoryhotel.co.uk
Web: www.oldrectoryhotel.co.uk

Christopher and Enid Richmond

The Exmoor plateau meets the sea abruptly at Martinhoe ('hoe' is Saxon for high ground), creating a breathtaking view on the approach to the village. Yet as you quietly succumb to the genuine sense of spiritual calm, it's hard to conceive that one field away, the land skids to a halt and spectacular cliffs drop 800 feet. Built in 1800 with later additions, this former rectory stands next to an 11th-century church in a lovely three-acre garden, full of birdsong, waterfalls, a triangular maze, and mature plants, from scented azaleas to the bizarre yet majestic gunnera. This is a gentle retreat, dedicated to food, and peace and quiet. Enid has been cooking with a passion since she was a child. She makes most things, sourcing the rest locally - their water comes from a local bore hole and is truly delicious. Traditional country house-style bedrooms have Laura Ashley wallpaper and the odd Waring and Gillow antique; one has a balcony. Relax in the conservatory under a 200-year-old vine that produces juicy black grapes, or curl up in front of an open fire. Blissful. *A no-smoking hotel. Two self-catering cottages, sleep 4-8.*

Rooms: 4 doubles, 2 twin/doubles, 2 twins.
Price: £98; singles £60. Dinner B&B (includes afternoon tea) £75 p.p. Reductions for longer stays.
Meals: Breakfast 8.30-9.30am. Dinner, 5 courses, £27.
Closed: December-February.

M5, junc. 27, A361 past Tiverton, right after South Molton on A399 to Blackmoor Gate, right on A39 towards Lynton, then left after about 4 miles, signed Martinhoe. Across common, then left into village. Hotel 1st on right by church.

The Rising Sun Hotel

Harbourside
Lynmouth
Devon
EX35 6EQ
Hugo Jeune

Tel: 01598 753223
Fax: 01598 753480
E-mail: risingsunlynmouth@easynet.co.uk
Web: www.risingsunlynmouth.co.uk

A head-ducking, boat-bobbing place with an entirely unexpected level of luxury. As the tide rises, so do the boats in the tiny harbour just across the road, creating a sensation of mobility as you idle in bed under Jane Churchill fabric. The Rising Sun strides modestly through much of the village, absorbing a string of ancient houses, with low beams, twisting spaces and probably the narrowest staircase in the world. Hugo has used reclaimed timber for beams and thoughtfully padded low doorways for taller folk. A local shipwright tenderly carved the panels in the snug dining room, where the atmosphere is as delicious as the food. Design and fabric freaks can drop names to each other: Gaston y Daniela, Monkwell, Colefax and Fowler, Farrow and Ball, Telenzo - all applied with verve and superb effect. It's not pretentious, just honest good taste in small but perfect rooms. Throw open the doors of a balconied lounge and enjoy afternoon tea, with the sun streaming in and a gentle sea breeze on your face. Make time to explore this interesting little village. Walkers can head straight up the valley into good hill country.

Rooms: 1 twin, 12 doubles, 2 singles, 1 cottage suite.
Price: £94-£146; singles £63. Dinner, B&B £74.50-£102.50 p.p.
Meals: Breakfast 8.30-9.30am. Dinner, 3 courses, about £27.50.
Closed: Never.

From A39, turn into town centre and follow sign to harbour. Hotel overlooks harbour at the end on the left.

Bark House Hotel

Oakfordbridge   **Tel:** 01398 351236
Nr. Bampton
Devon
EX16 9HZ

Alastair Kameen and Justine Hill

Alastair left the family business to become a hotelier, trained at all the best places and then searched high and low for the right place to call his own. He found it a field away from the river Exe in a wooded valley, settled in and taught himself to cook, winning plaudits almost immediately. The day I visited, he was orchestrating a clean-up in the garden; nothing, it seems, is beyond his grasp. The house is quietly stylish, not grand, but soothing - you look in vain for signs of bad taste; cosily low ceilings, a basket of logs by the fire, newspapers and magazines on tables, the rooms swimming in morning light. Fresh flowers, candles and fine linen in the restaurant suit Alastair's excellent cooking. Upstairs, bedrooms are simple, spotless and perfectly cosy, with flowers from the garden and a bit of oak furniture. One has a beautiful, curved, bay window. The service is superb; morning tea is brought to your room and breakfast is a feast - flaked almonds with your yogurt, fresh juice, fruit and porridge. There's Mike, too, handy man, porter and waiter - it's that sort of place.

Rooms: 2 doubles, 2 twin/doubles; 1 double with private bath.
Price: £79-£103; singles from £39.50. Dinner, B&B from £60.75 p.p.
Meals: Breakfast 8.30-9.30am. Dinner, 3 courses, £25.
Closed: Most Mondays & Tuesdays.

From Tiverton, A396 north towards Minehead. Hotel on right, 1 mile north of junction with B3227.

Huntsham Court

Huntsham
Nr. Bampton
Devon
EX16 7NA

Tel: 01398 361365
Fax: 01398 361456
E-mail: bolwigs@huntsham.freeserve.co.uk
Web: www.huntshamcourt.co.uk

Mogens and Andrea Bolwig

Two pianos in your bedroom and a fireplace primed for combustion - such may be your lot if you draw the short straw. The whole place has a rare aura of originality. As you enter you may wonder at the lack of staff to greet you, but they are there somewhere - solicitous, informal and competent. You are likely to find music filling the great hall, a fire roaring in the hearth, perhaps the clicking of billiard balls in the distance. Or if you are late the dinner party will be in full swing around the long table; later still and there may be games in the drawing room. But I don't want to give the impression of formality; far from it. This is one of the most easy-going and unpretentious hotels in the country, one that combines good taste, irony (viz. the '50s furniture and odds and ends), all in a surprisingly grandiose setting. It may be a touch faded in places, definitely not deluxe in others, but the mood is priceless. A great place for a private party.

Rooms: 11 twin/doubles, 3 family.
Price: £130-£150.
Meals: Breakfast times flexible.
Dinner £38.
Closed: Never.

From M5, junc. 27, follow signs to Sampford Peverell, then sharp right on bridge. Continue 2 miles to Uplowman, then straight ahead for 4 miles to Huntsham.

Wigham

Morchard Bishop
Nr. Crediton
Devon
EX17 6RJ

Tel: 01363 877350
Fax: 01363 877350
E-mail: info@wigham.co.uk
Web: www.wigham.co.uk

Stephen and Dawn Chilcott

This ivy-clad house is a trimly-thatched Devon dream, hidden away on the side of a hill, half a mile from the lane. You get exactly what the picture suggests: roaring fires, baskets of logs, stone floors, low, beamed ceilings, tapestries on the walls, a curved settle here, an original 1590s oak screen wall there. Much of the wood furniture is locally made, the dining room table a great slab of polished elm around which you all sit for communal dinners. Upstairs, bedrooms are suitably cosy, with long views, timber-framed walls and generous bathrooms. But that is only half the story. Wigham is also a 30-acre, fully organic farm and - from the sausage at breakfast to the lamb at supper - the meat is all home-reared. Stephen, remarkably, farms it single-handedly while Dawn manages the kitchen, making the breads, the soups, the ice creams. They even make their own butter and if you are lucky, you'll arrive as Stephen is washing the milk churns. If you want, help on the farm for a day; if not take home a box of organic meats, some organic wool or honey. There's a heated pool with a view, too.

Rooms: 1 four-poster, 2 doubles, 2 triples.
Price: Dinner, B&B £62-£79 p.p.
Meals: Breakfast 8.30-10am. Dinner, 3 courses, included.
Closed: Occasionally in winter.

A377 west from Crediton, then right to Morchard Bishop, signed. Leave village on Eastington road and fork right by postbox in wall. House signed right at bottom of hill.

Map No: 2

Easton Court

Easton Cross
Chagford
Devon
TQ13 8JL

Tel: 01647 433469
Fax: 01647 433654
E-mail: stay@easton.co.uk
Web: www.easton.co.uk

Debra and Paul Witting

"I often try and always fail to define the peculiar charm of Easton Court," wrote the author Evelyn Waugh of this old manor house. He completed *Brideshead Revisited* and *A Handful of Dust* here in the 1930s, sitting at a table near the window in what is now a small bar. The literary associations don't stop there - Patrick Leigh Fermor and Alec Waugh both found the muse in plentiful supply during long stays. Debra and Paul obviously love the house, too. They're a young, friendly couple who left behind the world of corporate accounting to realise a long-held dream – much to the approval of the hotel's resident ghost, according to a medium who stayed. There have been sightings of the Grey Lady, but don't imagine this to be a spooky house. Far from it. Built in 1450, it has lots of old world charm, with uneven floors, beams and big stone fireplaces. Bedrooms have been nicely refurbished in a simple cottage style; most have framed views of the pretty garden. There's also a snug library room, with leather armchairs, while a light, zesty dining room is good for breakfast, or dinner; chef George Davies is ex-Gidleigh Park.

Rooms: 1 four-poster, 4 doubles, 2 twin/doubles, 1 twin.
Price: £80-£110. Dinner B&B £65-£80 p.p.
Meals: Breakfast 8.30-9.30am. Dinner, 3 courses, £23. Cream teas available.
Closed: January.

From Exeter, A30 towards Okehampton to Whiddon Down (15 miles), then A382 south towards Moretonhampstead for 3 miles. Hotel 2on left at x-roads, signed Chagford right.

Map No: 2

Blackaller

North Bovey
Moretonhampstead
Devon
TQ13 8QY

Hazel Phillips and Peter Hunt

Tel: 01647 440322
Fax: 01647 441131
E-mail: peter@blackaller.fsbusiness.co.uk
Web: www.blackaller.co.uk

Small and perfectly formed, this is the sort of place you dream of. Have absolutely *no* reservations about coming here unless you are after a city-slick hotel. Sparkling, polished pine floors, walking sticks for hikers, whitewashed walls to soak up Dartmoor's magical light, wood carvings, stone fireplaces and candles in the dining room. Peter and Hazel couldn't be nicer and keep themselves busy spinning wool, collecting honey, rearing sheep, making soups - the normal things in life. Don't think of eating elsewhere - the food here is gorgeous, much of it organic. Bedrooms are perfect - cosy and comfy with more of those white walls - but it's the relaxed mood of this superb little place that is priceless. Outside, stone walls and old water troughs full of flowers, then across the lawn the river tumbles past. In summer, sit out for a sundowner or come in November and watch the salmon run up. You are in the middle of nowhere; walks from the front door are reason enough to come, but we would come for the simple humanity of the place.

Rooms: 4 doubles; 1 single with private bathroom.
Price: £64-£80; singles £31-£48.
Meals: Breakfast 8.30-9am. Dinner (Wednesday-Saturday only) £24.
Closed: January & February.

From M5, A30 to Okehampton, then B3212 to Moretonhampstead. Take Princetown road, left at newsagent into Pound Street to North Bovey. Entering village, right at top of hill, signed.

Map No: 2

Fingals
Dittisham
Dartmouth
Devon
TQ6 0JA

Richard Johnston

Tel: 01803 722398
Fax: 01803 722401
E-mail: richard@fingals.co.uk
Web: www.fingals.co.uk

Where else can one find this magic? Richard miraculously combines a rare *laissez-faire* management style with a passionate commitment to doing things well. He is ever-present without intruding, fun without challenging, spontaneous without being demanding. This is his place, his style, his gesture of defiance to the rest of the hotel world. He does things his way, and most people love it. And he is backed by Sheila, whose kindness and perennial good nature are a constant source of wonder. The food is good, the meals around the big table memorable, the comfort indisputable. You may find children and dogs wandering freely, happy adults - certainly - and Sheila's ducks being marshalled home in the evening. The indoor pool beckons, sauna and jacuzzi, ping-pong and croquet for all, perhaps tennis on the lawn and cosy conversation in the bar. But don't be misled, you can do peace and quiet here, too. Perfect for the open-hearted.

Rooms: 8 doubles, 1 twin, 1 family.
Self-catering barn with 1 double,
1 twin sharing bathroom.
Price: £70-£110. Variable single supp.
Meals: Breakfast any time after 9am.
Dinner £27.50.
Closed: 2 January-26 March.

A381 south from Totnes, up hill, left towards Cornworthy/Ashprington. Turn right at ruined gatehouse near Cornworthy to Dittisham. Descend steep hill. Hotel signed on right after the bridge and up hill.

Map No: 2

Barrington House

Mount Boone
Dartmouth
Devon
TQ6 9HZ
Lizzie Baldwin

Tel: 01803 835545
Fax: 01803 835545
E-mail: enquiries@barrington-house.com
Web: www.barrington-house.com

General Eisenhower billeted here prior to the Normandy landings and one can only assume he left this lovely spot feeling rested and ready for the arduous task ahead. The south-facing garden overlooks the Dart estuary and has magnificent views across to Kingswear and out to sea past the castle. The house was originally built for a member of the Peake-Frean family, whose biscuit empire brought us the famous 'Nice' biscuit. More recently, Simon and Lizzie have created a fabulous place to stay in the colonial style. Smart, uncluttered rooms are a delightful mix of kilim rugs, wall hangings, grey slate, polished pine floors, huge modern sofas and a welcoming open fire; the dining room opens out onto the garden for afternoon tea, or lazy contemplation after breakfast. Big bedrooms have radiant, yellow walls that absorb the light and swish bathrooms, full of luxurious extras; all have sea views. The Baldwins are a relaxed young couple full of good advice; the gentle river trip to Totnes sounds divine. *3% surcharge when paying by credit card. Self-catering penthouse sleeps six.*

Rooms: 2 doubles, 1 twin.
Price: £70-£90; singles from £50 (low season only). Self-catering £350-£825 p.w.
Meals: Breakfast until 9.15am. Packed lunch £5.50. Dinner, 3 courses, from £21.
Closed: Never.

Entering Dartmouth on A3122, turn right opp. top gate to Royal Naval College into Townstal Rd, then 1st left into Mount Boone. Barrington House 3rd on left, signed.

Map No: 2

The Gunfield Hotel

Castle Road
Dartmouth
Devon
TQ6 0JN

Mike and Lucy Swash

Tel: 01803 834571
Fax: 01803 834772
E-mail: enquiry@gunfield.co.uk
Web: www.gunfield.co.uk

The Gunfield will soon be an institution in Dartmouth. At the heart of it are youthful, enthusiastic owners and staff, so it's lively and fun. Then there's the position right on the water's edge and the Devon coastal path, the waterside deck for breakfasts and barbecues in fine weather, the garden for sun-worshippers, the pontoon for boat taxis to the town quays and motor boat trips out to beaches. You can moor your own boat, too. The view follows you around wherever you go. The bistro, the restaurant and the lovely carved wooden bar all have river views, as do the great bedrooms. Colours are fun - terracotta, reds and oranges - the four-poster room has its own balcony and the octagonal turret rooms are exceptional. Back outside, there's also 'one-gun point', a grassy outcrop with a canon that hasn't moved since 1550, a good place to watch the traffic of the high seas: sailing dinghies, fishing boats, yachts and ocean cruisers all glide by. There are bicycles and water sports, you can go on wildlife cruises, even golf can be arranged. *Pets by arrangement.*

Rooms: 1 four-poster, 4 twin/doubles, 2 doubles; 1 four-poster with private bath; 2 turret rooms (let to same party) sharing bath.
Price: £70-£145; singles from £45.
Meals: Breakfast until 10am weekdays, 10.30am weekends. Dinner, 3 courses, from £22.50. Lunch available; BBQs in summer.
Closed: Never.

Into Dartmouth and follow signs to the Castle. Hotel 200m before Castle on left.

Map No: 2

Hazelwood House

Loddiswell
Nr. Kingsbridge
Devon
TQ7 4EB

Tel: 01548 821232
Fax: 01548 821318

Janie Bowman, Gillian Kean and Anabel Watson

Set amid 67 acres of woodland, meadows and orchards in an untamed river valley, Hazelwood House is no ordinary hotel. It is a place of exceptional peace and natural beauty, created more as a relaxed, unpretentious country house. It might not be for everyone, but those who like it will love it. Come through the front door, pass rows of Wellington boots and you enter a world to revive the spirit. Lectures and courses and evenings of music – classical or jazz – all play a part, all carried off with a relaxed and friendly approach. Anabel and Gillian came here 12 years ago and the place has evolved ever since. They are involved with 'Through the Heart to Peace', a peace initiative started in 1993. The atmosphere outweighs any decorative shortfalls, the food is delicious and fully organic and they produce their own spring water. Cream tea on the veranda is wonderful, or roam past ancient rhododendrons and huge camellias to fields of wild flowers or grazing sheep. *Self-catering cottages also available.*

Rooms: 15: 1 twin/double with child's bed, 1 twin, both en suite; 8 twin/doubles, 3 family, 2 singles, sharing 4 bathrooms.
Price: £50-£95; singles £35.25.
Meals: Breakfast until 10.30am. Lunch from £8. Packed lunch £5-£8. Dinner, 2 courses, from £15; 3 courses, from £18.
Closed: Never.

From Exeter, A38 south then A3121 south. Left onto B3196 south. At California Cross 1st left after petrol station. After 0.75 miles, left for Hazelwood. Gates on right.

Map No: 2

Combe House at Gittisham

Honiton
Nr. Exeter
Devon
EX14 3AD
Ruth and Ken Hunt

Tel: 01404 540400
Fax: 01404 46004
E-mail: stay@thishotel.com
Web: www.thishotel.com

Combe House claims a Saxon, Elizabethan and Caroline heritage. You meet history at every turn, with stone-mullioned windows, oak panelling, huge rooms, high ceilings and beautiful murals. The house is set in 3,500 acres of beech woods and parkland that run down to the village of Gittisham; Prince Charles once described it as "the ideal English village" - it's full of thatched cob cottages, a village green and a stunning Norman church where some of Combe's previous owners are buried in lavish tombs. All this is only two miles from Honiton. Yet amid the splendour, it's Ruth and Ken who dazzle. The welcome is genuine, the feel more country house than hotel and an atmosphere that's both refined and friendly. Enjoy wonderful fresh flower arrangements, superb food, fine furniture, luxurious bathrooms - some have murals - and as you'd expect, views over a lush valley. You can walk your socks off without leaving the estate, or else potter around the walled flower garden. Wonderful.

Rooms: 1 four-poster, 12 twin/doubles, 2 suites.
Price: £130-£186; suites £245; singles from £85.
Dinner, B&B from £88 p.p.
Meals: Breakfast 7.30-10am. Lunch, 2 courses, £12; 3 courses £16.50. Dinner, 3 courses, £28.50.
Closed: Never.

A30 south from Honiton for 2 miles, then A375 towards Sidmouth and Branscombe. House signed through beech woods.

Map No: 2

Kings Arms

Stockland
Nr. Honiton
Devon
EX14 9BS

Tel: 01404 881361
Fax: 01404 881732
E-mail: reserve@kingsarms.net
Web: www.kingsarms.net

Paul Diviani, John O'Leary and Heinz Kiefer

Stay for a week and you'll be a nearly-fledged local, a member of the skittles team, an expert in line dancing and probably a tambourine-player for the folk club. You'll also be a stone or two heavier – this is the Devon dining pub of the year 1999, the menus seemingly endless, with masses of fish, locally-reared game, even ostrich. Ramble at will and you'll find crackling fires, beams, gilt-framed mirrors, stone walls, cosy low ceilings and, eventually, the stone-flagged Farmer's Bar. It is here you meet the "fair-minded, fun-loving locals who have the fortune to dwell in such a place" – one comes down from Birmingham – they'll have you playing darts in minutes. Bedrooms are just what you'd hope for, not grand, but perfectly traditional with, maybe, a walnut bed or cushioned window seat – if you like inns, you'll be delighted. Outside – get lost in the Blackdown Hills or simply laze around inside with Princess Ida, the cat. As for Paul, "he's a tyrant to work for," said one of his staff, an enormous smile on his face.

Rooms: 2 doubles, 1 twin.
Price: £50; singles £30.
Meals: Breakfast 9-10am. Lunch from £4. Dinner, 3 courses, £14-£21.50.
Closed: Christmas Day.

From the centre of Honiton, head for north-eastern junction of A30. Just before you join, Stockland is signed right. Straight ahead for 6 miles to village.

The Fox Inn

Corscombe
Nr. Dorchester
Dorset
DT2 0NS
Susie and Martyn Lee

Tel: 01935 891330
Fax: 01935 891330
E-mail: dine@fox-inn.co.uk
Web: www.fox-inn.co.uk

Martyn was master of a nearby hunt before he became landlord of the Fox. It's a nice little irony not lost on the ex-Army man, who's turned this 17th-century thatched inn into one of the most sought after places to stay and eat in the South of England. Hospitality is first rate, food excellent and the setting is Hardy's Wessex at its most peaceful and beautiful. In days of yore, drovers on the way to market would wash their sheep in the stream opposite and stop for a pint of cider; the inn only received a full licence 40 years ago. Martyn and Susie are a delightful, stylish and amusing couple. They've kept the old feel of the inn, with clever additions like a slate-topped bar, a flower-filled conservatory with benches and a long table made from a single oak blown down during the storms of 1987. You're surrounded by eye-pleasing detail; stuffed owls in glass cases, blue gingham tableclothes, paintings, flowers, antlers, flagstones and fires in winter. Bedrooms have simple country charm with floral and mahogany touches; one in a converted loft is reached by stone steps. Special, indeed, and the sea isn't far, either.

Rooms: 2 doubles, 1 twin/double;
1 double.
Price: £80-£100; singles £55-£65.
Meals: Breakfast until 10am. Dinner, à la carte, 3 courses from £15.95.
Closed: Christmas.

From Yeovil, A37 towards Dorchester for 1 mile, then right, signed Corscombe, for 5.5 miles. Inn on left on outskirts of village. Use kitchen door to left of main entrance if arriving before 7pm.

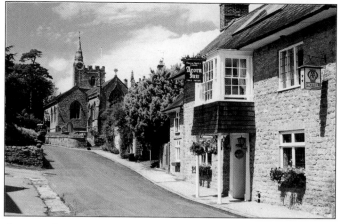

The Acorn Inn

Evershot
Dorchester
Dorset
DT2 0JW

Tel: 01935 83228
Fax: 01935 83707
E-mail: lee@acorn-inn.co.uk
Web: www.acorn-inn.co.uk

Susie and Martyn Lee

An inn for nearly 400 years, The Acorn has a tale or two to tell; Thomas Hardy called it The Sow and Acorn and let Tess rest a night here. Martyn and Susie are as local as Hardy's literature and took over determined to preserve all the traditions of an old inn, while giving the creature comforts a 21st-century zap. The result is bedrooms that creak with age *and* style; canopied four-posters rest on uneven floors. In *Tess* (all the rooms have a Hardy connection), the pub sign hangs outside the window and there's a seven-foot Edwardian mahogany bed. Downstairs, panelled and beamed bars echo to the merry chink of glass and cutlery; the food has won several awards. There's much local mirth as well; this being, above all, a locals' pub, the heart of village life. There are also open fires, a skittle alley, a small beer garden and, if you keep going, deer parks and ancient woods for revitalising Sunday strolls.

Rooms: 2 four-posters, 4 doubles, 3 twins.
Price: £80-£120; singles £55.
Meals: Breakfast times flexible. Meals in restaurant or bar, à la carte, £3.25-£15.95.
Closed: Never.

From A37 Yeovil-Dorchester, follow signs to Evershot. Inn in centre of village.

Plumber Manor

Sturminster Newton
Dorset
DT10 2AF

Tel: 01258 472507
Fax: 01258 473370
E-mail: book@plumbermanor.com
Web: www.plumbermanor.com

Richard, Alison and Brian Prideaux-Brune

The *enormous* old sofa on the landing is surely the most uncomfortable thing I have ever sat on, but it is irresistibly vast and the only discomfort Plumber has to offer. While the sofa might be old, the family is positively ancient. They go back to William the Conqueror and have lived "in the area" ever since, the last 300 years right here at Plumber. Outside, there's a large, sloping lawn, a white bridge over the river and deck chairs scattered about the well-manicured garden. Inside, the house remains more home than hotel with huge family portraits crammed on the walls; everything in this house seems to be *big*. The atmosphere is relaxed and informal without a trace of pomposity. Bedrooms in the main house are more homely; those in the converted stables are bigger with fresher colours and fabrics. Best of all at Plumber is the family triumvirate of Brian in the kitchen, Richard behind the bar, guaranteed to provide laughter, and Alison, who is simply everywhere. They know exactly how to make you feel at home. *Pets by arrangement.*

Rooms: In house: 2 doubles,
3 twin/doubles; 1 twin/double with
private bath. In Courtyard: 10
twin/doubles.
Price: £100–£155; singles from £85.
Meals: Breakfast until 9.30am. Dinner,
2 courses, from £21.50; 3 courses,
from £24.50.
Closed: February.

*From Sturminster Newton south to
Hazlebury Bryan for 2 miles. House on left.*

The Museum Inn

Farnham
Nr. Blandford Forum
Dorset
DT11 8DE

Tel: 01725 516261
Fax: 01725 516988
E-mail: themuseuminn@supernet.co.uk
Web: www.museuminn.co.uk

Vicky Elliot and Mark Stephenson

This delightful part-thatched 17th-century inn owes its name to General Augustus Lane Fox Pitt Rivers, the 'father of archaeology'; it fed and bed folk who came to see his museum, one of three he opened in the 1800s to house his fabulous collection - only the Pitt Rivers Museum in Oxford survives today. No sign either of the yaks and zebu that the General once released into a nearby pleasure park. What you will discover, though, is one of the best inns in the south of England, set in a picture postcard village of thatched cottages in the heart of Cranborne Chase. Vicky and Mark work well together - she does bubbly, he does laid-back and they've created a wonderfully warm and friendly place to stay. The smart refit has a lovely period feel, with flagstones, an inglenook fireplace, fresh flowers and a pleasing mismatch of wooden tables and chairs. Upstairs, there's a gorgeous drawing room, with lots of books, and bright, comfortable bedrooms, with antique beds and lots of prints - all impeccably done. Chef Mark Treasure is sure to win more accolades as he did elsewhere. A real find. *Only children over five in pub.*

Rooms: 8 doubles.
Price: £65-£120.
Meals: Breakfast until 10am. Light lunch from £3.95. Dinner, à la carte, 3 courses approx. £24.
Closed: Christmas Day & New Year's Eve.

From Blandford A354 towards Salisbury for 6.5 miles, then left, signed Farnham. Inn on left in village.

Rose and Crown

Romaldkirk
Barnard Castle
Durham
DL12 9EB

Tel: 01833 650213
Fax: 01833 650828
E-mail: hotel@rose-and-crown.co.uk
Web: www.rose-and-crown.co.uk

Christopher and Alison Davy

In the small locals' bar, you can sit at settles in front of the fire and read the *Stockton Times* or the *Teesdale Mercury*, while a few trophies peer down. This inn is dreamy, superbly comfortable and traditional, and built in the 1750s when Romaldkirk's famous son, Captain Bligh, was still a young sprite. The mood is softly elegant, gently informal, utterly unpretentious, warmed by smart red carpets, stone walls, beams, and a bright, panelled dining room. Alison and Christopher are easy-going perfectionists; their hard work has made the Rose and Crown the place to stay, the place to eat. You can expect vibrant rooms, with slanting eaves and window seats as well as fun contemporary colours and fabrics. The food, too, is excellent - another example of the fantastic value-for-money this place represents. Outside, the village green is surrounded by a church and untouched stone cottages; further afield, countryside, as good as any in Britain, and Barnard Castle (Barney to the locals) wait to be explored.

Rooms: 5 doubles, 7 twins.
Price: £86-£100; singles £62.
Meals: Breakfast 7.30-9.30am. Bar meals £5-£11. Dinner, 4 courses, £25.
Closed: 24-26 December.

From Barnard Castle, B6277 north for 6 miles. In village, turn right towards green and hotel on left.

The Bell Inn and Hill House

High Rd
Horndon-on-the-Hill
Essex
SS17 8LD

Tel: 01375 642463
Fax: 01375 361611
E-mail: info@bell-inn.co.uk
Web: www.bell-inn.co.uk

Christine and John Vereker

Christine is an original fixture in this Great Inn of England - her parents ran The Bell for years and she was born in one of the upstairs rooms. Full of spirit, she laughs easily and is quick to welcome the weary traveller. John is also a key figure, much admired in the trade for the pride he takes in his work. Five quirky and beautifully decorated suites in the main inn are by far the best places to stay; they're all named after famous mistresses, including Lady Hamilton, Madame du Barry and Anne Boleyn, said to be buried in the local church. Downstairs, public rooms suit the mood of the day. The breakfast room is light and airy, with attractive white table and chair coverings, while the flagstoned bar has wonderful oak panelled walls and curious French wood carvings - part of a huge collection built up by Christine's father. The bar bustles with working folk at lunchtime, then mellows in the evening. Enjoy an intimate meal in the smart, unpretentious restaurant, served by waiters in white aprons and black ties; John sends them all on wine courses. Delicious food is well presented; no surprise it picks up awards. Great value.

Rooms: The Bell: 5 suites;
Hill House: 7 doubles, 3 twins.
Price: £50-£85.
Meals: Breakfast 7-9am weekdays,
8.30-10am Saturdays, 9-10.30 Sundays;
full cooked £7.50, continental £9.50.
Bar lunch from £5.50. Set lunch menu
from £13.95. Dinner, à la carte, 3
courses about £23. No lunch/dinner
on Bank Holidays.
Closed: Christmas Day & Boxing Day.

*M25, junc. 30, A13 towards Southend for
3 miles, then B1007 to Horndon-on-the-Hill.
Inn on left in village.*

Map No: 4

Heavens Above at The Mad Hatters Restaurant
3 Cossack Square
Nailsworth
Gloucestershire
GL6 0DB

Tel: 01453 832615

Carolyn and Mike Findlay

Mike and Carolyn are inspiring. They were smallholders once, lived at the top of the hill, worked the land, kept livestock, made bellows - and earned £2,500 a year. Nine years ago they rolled down hill into town and opened a fully-organic restaurant. The locals flocked in and still do - the food here is quite delicious, some still grown back up the hill. You might get fabulous fish soup, lamb with garlic and rosemary and a mouth-puckering lemon tart. It's a place with real heart, not designed to impress, which is probably why it does. Cookery books are squashed into a pretty pine dresser and there are mellow stone walls, big bay windows, stripped wooden floors, simple pine tables. Exceptional art hangs on the walls and the place is airy with a warm rustic feel to it. Please don't worry that the bedrooms are not en suite and that you have to walk round the back to get to them. They are delightful - huge, like an artist's studio, with shiny wood floors, whitewashed walls and rag-rolled beams. A fabulous little place run with great passion and humanity. It may not be the Dorchester, but we'd prefer to stay here instead.

Rooms: 1 double, 1 twin, 1 family, sharing bathroom.
Price: £50-£60; singles £28-£35.
Meals: Breakfast times flexible. Lunch from £6.50. Dinner, 3 courses, £20-£25 (restaurant closed Sunday evenings & Mondays).
Closed: Never.

M5, junc. 13, A419 east to Stroud, then A46 south into Nailsworth. Right at r'bout, immediately left and restaurant on right, opposite the Britannia pub.

Map No: 2

Painswick Hotel

Kemps Lane
Painswick
Gloucestershire
GL6 6YB

Tel: 01452 812160
Fax: 01452 814059
E-mail: reservations@painswickhotel.com
Web: www.painswickhotel.com

Helen and Gareth Pugh

The Painswick is an absolute gem, immaculate inside and out. It was once home to a wealthy rector. He married a Catholic, unwise at the time, so he built her a small private chapel that's now a cocktail bar with a black and white tiled floor and a gold-leaf, plaster-moulded ceiling – just wonderful. To single out one room for praise is unfair - they are all superb, all treated with stunning simplicity. There's a semicircular pine-panelled dining room, with tables set to perfection, a pale yellow, clutter-free country house morning room and a big, bright and elegant sitting room that opens onto a small porticoed balcony with valley views. The bedrooms are no less magnificent; sparkling antiques, Balinese thrones, a mahogany four-poster, maybe a porter chair – even the simpler rooms feel luxurious. Amid all this grandeur, Helen and Gareth have kept the mood splendidly relaxed. Outside, the Slad Valley where writer Laurie Lee drank his cider with Rosie.

Rooms: 2 four-posters, 11 doubles, 2 twins, 2 family, 2 singles.
Price: £115-£180; singles from £75.
Meals: Breakfast until 10am. Dinner, 3 courses, £27.50; 6 course (*dégustation*) menu, £60.
Closed: Never.

From Stroud, A46 north to Painswick. Right at St Mary's church. Follow road left, then 1st right. Hotel signed on right.

Map No: 2

The Swan Hotel at Bibury

Bibury
Gloucestershire
GL7 5NW

Tel: 01285 740695
Fax: 01285 740473
E-mail: swanhot1@swanhotel-cotswolds.co.uk
Web: www.swanhotel.co.uk

Elizabeth Rose   Manager: John Stevens

The Swan must be the most photographed hotel in Britain - the setting is pure Cotswold bliss. The inside is no less enchanting, the sky-blue panelling in the entrance hall so impressive it's been listed. Everywhere there is something wonderful: Macintosh chairs sprinkled about, a baby grand piano in the lobby. The dining room is spectacular - a monument to 1920s opulence with high ceilings, claret wallpaper, oils and chandeliers - and a great place to eat. Bedrooms are equally indulgent, with a mix of old and contemporary furniture, maybe an Art Deco mirror or a ceramic bedside light the size of a barrel; every room we saw had something delightfully extravagant. There are Italian-tiled bathrooms, bathrobes and old Roberts radios; the hotel even has its own spring water. Retire at night and you'll find the bed turned down; wake in the morning and your newspaper is waiting outside your room. Go for rooms with a view at the front - the trout farm across the road is an artistic triumph. Fish nearby in the hotel's beat.

Rooms: Hotel: 3 four-posters, 1 family, 5 twins, 9 doubles; Cottage: 2 kingsize twin/doubles, with en suite jacuzzi.
Price: £165-£235; singles from £99; cottage from £240.
Meals: Breakfast 7.30-10am. Lunch from £5. Set dinner, 3 courses, £28.50; à la carte also available.
Closed: Never.

From Oxford, A40 west, past Burford, then left on B4425 to Bibury. Hotel by bridge in village.

Map No: 2

Hotel on the Park

Evesham Road
Cheltenham
Gloucestershire
GL52 2AH

Tel: 01242 518898
Fax: 01242 511526
E-mail: stay@hotelonthepark.co.uk
Web: www.hotelonthepark.co.uk

Darryl Gregory

Symmetry and style to please the eye in the heart of the spa town of Cheltenham. The attention to detail is staggering - everything has a place and is just where it should be. The style is crisp and dramatic, a homage to the Regency period in which the house was built, but there's plenty of good humour floating around, not least in Darryl himself, who's brilliant at making you feel at home. He's the first to encourage people to dive in and enjoy it all. There are lovely touches too: piles of fresh hand towels in the gents' cloakroom, where there's a sink with no plug hole - you'll work it out; newspapers hang on poles, so grab one and head into the drawing room where drapes swirl across big windows. In the restaurant you'll come across Doric columns, Greek and Roman busts, lots and lots of fun too. Upstairs, bedrooms are fabulous, crisp and artistic, all furnished to fit the period. The whole house is a treat, classically dramatic, and it's great fun.

Rooms: 4 twins, 6 doubles, 2 suites.
Price: £102.50-£162.50; singles £79.50.
Meals: Breakfast until 9.30am weekdays, 10am weekends; Continental £6.50, Full English £8.75. Dinner, 3 courses, from £22.50.
Closed: Never.

From town centre, join one-way system and exit at signpost to Evesham. Continue down Evesham Road. Hotel signed on left opposite park.

Wesley House
High Street
Winchcombe
Gloucestershire
GL54 5LJ

Tel: 01242 602366
Fax: 01242 609046
E-mail:
reservations@wesleyhouse.co.uk
Web: www.wesleyhouse.co.uk

Matthew Brown

Winchcombe was the sixth-century capital of Mercia. Wesley House, a 14th-century half-timbered town house, entices you straight off the High Street and seduces you once inside. Old timber-framed white walls, a terracotta-tiled floor and a large, crackling fire - all are perfect for lazy afternoons spent flicking through the papers. Downstairs is open-plan, the dining area stretches back in search of countryside - and finds it. French windows lead out to a small terrace where breakfast and lunch, or evening drinks, are enjoyed against the backdrop of the gentle Cotswold hills. Bedrooms have more of those ancient whitewashed, timber-framed walls that need little decoration; warm, smart, well-lit and compact, with good wooden beds, crisp sheets, new carpets and the occasional head-cracking bathroom door. One room has a lovely balcony. Find fresh milk and coffee in every room, and breakfast in bed, with home-baked bread, croissants and *pain au chocolat*, even kumquat, orange and whisky marmalade. *Children over seven and babies welcome.*

Rooms: 5 doubles.
Price: £75-£85; singles £48.
Meals: Breakfast until 10am. Lunch from £6.95. Dinner, 3 courses, £21.50-£31.
Closed: Never.

From Cheltenham, B4632 to Winchcombe. Wesley House on High Street.

Dial House

The Chestnuts
Bourton-on-the-Water
Gloucestershire
GL54 2AN

Tel: 01451 822244
Fax: 01451 810126
E-mail: info@dialhousehotel.com
Web: www.dialhousehotel.com

Jane and Adrian Campbell-Howard

The 'Venice of the Cotswolds' and such a peaceful setting, with distinctive sandstone Georgian houses and the slow, meandering River Windrush idly drifting by. Bourton is popular with the Cotswolds' traveller, drawn to the genteel buzz of village life. There's lots going on, and right in its midst stands the Dial House, built in 1698 by architect Andrew Paxford - his and his wife's initials are carved on the front. Originally the Vinehouse, it was renamed after the large sundial above the front door. Inside, Jane and Adrian have created an oasis of old world charm, with Jacobean-style furniture, wonderful four-posters, old portrait paintings and impressive stone fireplaces lit in winter. Elegant, relaxed, and friendly, it epitomises the traditional country house hotel. The best bedrooms are in the main house, with lovely antiques, a little chintz to create the country feel, and views of the village and river through leaded window panes. Rooms in an extension look out onto the walled garden, a lovely spot to keep the world at arm's length for a while, while the classic English menu takes a lot of beating.

Rooms: 1 suite, 3 four-posters, 9 doubles, 1 single.
Price: £114. Dinner B&B £75 p.p., minimum 2 nights.
Meals: Breakfast until 9.30am. Dinner, set menu, 3 courses, £14.95; à la carte also available. Packed lunch by arrangement.
Closed: Never.

From Oxford, A40 to Northleach, then right on A429 to Bourton-on-the-Water. Hotel set back from High St opp. main bridge in village.

Map No: 3

Gloucestershire

Lords of the Manor

Upper Slaughter
Nr. Bourton-on-the-Water
Gloucestershire
GL54 2JD

Tel: 01451 820243
Fax: 01451 820696
E-mail: lordsofthemanor@btinternet.com
Web: www.lordsofthemanor.com

General Manager: Iain Shelton

What a name - a form of linguistic time travel. The bar, more gentleman's club than hotel, is deeply rich with old wooden floors, low lighting and the smell of smouldering logs. Sit at a large bay window in leather sofas, staring out across rolling parkland: the perfect English landscape. A sense of tradition swirls around you, but progress is evident, too. The restaurant is nicely contemporary, looking out onto walled orchard, where pears grow in bottles; they're made into *Poire William*, then imbibed. Bedrooms are split between the main house and the converted granary; they're what you'd expect, some beamed in the eaves, others with stately four-posters. There are fruit and sherry and a feeling of deep calm. You sleep easy; the name 'slaughter' has no sinister history – it comes from *scolostre* meaning 'muddy place' and the walk over to Lower Slaughter is a good way to find out.

Rooms: 3 suites, 3 four-posters,
2 singles, 19 twin/doubles.
Price: £149-£299; singles from £99.
Meals: Breakfast 8-10am. Lunch,
2 courses, £16.95. Dinner, 3 courses,
£40. Picnic hampers available.
Closed: Never.

From Cirencester, A429 north about 16 miles, then left signed The Slaughters. In Lower Slaughter, left over bridge. Continue to Upper Slaughter and hotel signed right in village.

The Churchill Inn

Paxford
Chipping Campden
Gloucestershire
GL55 6XH

Tel: 01386 594000
Fax: 01386 594005
E-mail: the_churchill_arms@hotmail.com

Leo Brooke-Little and Sonia Kidney   Manager: Richard Barnes

Above all, The Churchill is fun. The bar is vital, full of life and warm, with stone floors and wooden tables. The feel is fresh, an engaging mixture of old and new, the atmosphere relaxed and informal and bubbling over with happy chatter. Staff are friendly and natural, and no one seems to stand on ceremony; it's 'user friendly'. The locals seem to like it that way. They were reluctantly starting to leave after lunch, when our inspector arrived at two o'clock. The bedrooms, right above the bar, are equally fun and stylish. "Frills and drapes are not us," says Sonia. Beams, old radiators and uneven floors obviously are. There are good fabrics and pastel colours with country views from the heart of the village. Although two rooms are small, good use of space keeps you from feeling closed in. The food here is good and the sticky toffee pudding perfect, according to one usually cantankerous Sunday critic. Such perfection might explain the prayer stool in one corner.

Rooms: 4 doubles.
Price: £70; singles £40.
Meals: Breakfast until 10am. Lunch £15.
Dinner £20.
Closed: Never.

*From Moreton-in-Marsh, take A44
towards Worcester/Evesham. Through
Bourton-on-the-Hill, take right at end to
Paxford. Straight through Blockley, over
railway track and tiny bridge into
Paxford. Inn is in village on right.*

Lower Brook House

Lower Street
Blockley, Moreton-in-Marsh
Gloucestershire
GL56 9DS

Tel: 01386 700286
Fax: 01386 700286
E-mail: lowerbrookhouse@cs.com
Web: www.lowerbrookhouse.co.uk

Marie Mosedale-Cooper

Marie is full of life - not the sort of person to stand in the way of progress. Lower Brook House started life as a B&B and evolved into an award-winning restaurant with rooms, but it's still more than that. Ancient stone floors, timber-framed walls, fresh flowers everywhere... and stacks of beautiful things. Settle into coral sofas next to the huge inglenook fire, toss on a log and start *War and Peace.* Next door in the restaurant, a gallery of family rogues hang on crimson walls, surrounding tables decorated with cut-glass crystal, hand-painted crockery, the best starched linen. In summer, eat breakfast and dinner in the garden, the latter by scented candle. Bedrooms are compact but with all the paraphernalia to pamper you - bathrobes, bowls of fruit, garden flowers, as well as fresh colours, stone mullioned windows, the odd exposed timber roof. The food is delicious; maybe steamed fillet of sea bass or roast loin of venison, supported by the working kitchen garden. Watch brown trout commuting up the brook to pass the time.

Rooms: 2 four-posters, 3 doubles, 2 twin/doubles.
Price: £80-£145; singles from £75.
Meals: Breakfast 8-10am. Dinner, 3 courses, £21 approx. Lunch by arrangement.
Closed: Never.

From Moreton-in-Marsh, A44 west, then right on B4479 into Blockley. House on right at bottom of hill, signed.

The Cotswold House Hotel & Restaurant

The Square
Chipping Campden
Gloucestershire
GL55 6AN

Tel: 01386 840330
Fax: 01386 840310
E-mail:
reception@cotswoldhouse.com
Web: www.cotswoldhouse.com

Christa and Ian Taylor

Few brochures quite capture the spirit of a place, often losing their way in long, wordy clichés. Cotswold House is an exception. Its CD-sized package concertinas out into a dreamy sequence of portraits that give a tantalising flavour of what to expect. We liked it so much we've used a photograph of the hotel's magnificent spiral staircase to introduce this book. The Taylors have created a beautiful place to stay out of this 19th-century wool-merchant's house in a quiet corner of the Cotswolds; the village is full of bijou shops - and free parking. "Elegant without being intimidating or pretentious," was how our inspector described the hotel. Reds, terracottas and browns draw guests into two clutter-free lounges either side of the hallway, full of antiques, flowers and paintings. Gorgeous bedrooms are done in deep National Trust colours while bathrooms are full of French colognes, balms and lotions; rooms at the front have village views. The hotel runs events through the year; expect talks on organic food to candlelit classical concerts in the pretty walled gardens. Go on, spoil yourself.

Rooms: 1 four-poster, 13 doubles, 1 single.
Price: £140-£180, singles £90.
Meals: Breakfast until 10am in restaurant; until 12am in brasserie. Brasserie meals from £7. Picnics £12-£15. Dinner, 3 courses, £35.
Closed: Never.

From Oxford, A44 north towards Evesham. 5 miles after Moreton-in-Marsh, right on B4081 to Chipping Campden. Hotel in village square by town hall.

Map No: 3

The Malt House

Broad Campden   **Tel:** 01386 840295
Nr. Chipping Campden   **Fax:** 01386 841334
Gloucestershire
GL55 6UU

Nick, Jean and Julian Brown

The very epitome of Englishness, a substantial house in the heart of an untouched village, with climbing roses, magnolia trees and deckchairs in the garden. A place that echoes to the past; you almost expect the vicar to call for tea or for a post boy to bring a telegram explaining that the London train is running late. The mellow Cotswold walls of this 1530 house hold a soft and unexpected grandeur: bright wood floors, ancient panelling, a Renaissance oil painting hanging on a wall of shimmering gold and an original fireplace throwing out the crackle of smouldering logs beneath a 17th-century mantelpiece that rises to within a foot of the ceiling. Nick is easy-going and never tires of seeing guests' faces light up as they walk in. Standards don't drop in the bedrooms either, where mullioned windows, sloping floors, gilt mirrors, a beam or two, and muralled bathrooms all wait. Contemporary splashes of colour in the fine garden suite, pretty views of the orchard paddock and hearty food keep you smiling for days.

Rooms: 6 twin/doubles, 1 four-poster, 1 garden suite.
Price: £89.50-£134.50; singles from £59.50. Dinner, B&B from £74 p.p.
Meals: Breakfast 8-9.30am weekdays, 8.30-10am weekends. Dinner, 3 courses, £29.50.
Closed: Christmas.

A44, then B4081 north into Chipping Campden. 1st right, signed Broad Campden. House on left after 1 mile.

         Map No: 3

The Fox Inn

Lower Oddington
Nr. Moreton-in-Marsh
Gloucestershire
GL56 0UR

Tel: 01451 870555
Fax: 01451 870669
E-mail: info@foxinn.net
Web: www.foxinn.net

Kirk and Sally Ritchie

Amid the grandeur of beautiful, old Cotswold country houses, The Fox evokes a wonderful sense of times past, gently at odds with the juggernaut of modern life. Low ceilings, worn flagstones, a roaring fire in winter, good food and exemplary hosts induce quiet relaxation. Kirk and Sally instinctively know how to look after their guests - the information pack found in each delightful room is carefully researched, providing the complete loafer's guide to what to do and see. Bedrooms in the 'charming inn' category sometimes leave a lot to be desired, but here they need no disclaimer; all are lovely in their own right, with antique beds, warm colours and prints of country scenes - the largest has views of the village and a lawned garden. The mellow bar is full of wooden furniture, with walls of yellow ochre that date back years, while breakfast is served in an elegant room painted a deep rose. Sit on a garden terrace from spring to autumn, thanks to awnings and outside heaters, and discover the magnificent frescoes in a nearby 11th-century church. For those who crave good old-fashioned romance.

Rooms: 3 doubles.
Price: £58-£85.
Meals: Breakfast 9am, other times by arrangement. Light lunch from £4. Dinner, à la carte, 3 courses approx. £17.50.
Closed: Christmas & New Year.

From Stow-on-the-Wold, A436 towards Chipping Norton for 3 miles, then 2nd right after VW garage, signed Lower Oddington. Inn 500 yards on right.

Map No: 3

The New Inn At Coln

Coln St-Aldwyns
Nr. Cirencester
Gloucestershire
GL7 5AN
Brian and Sandra-Anne Evans

Tel: 01285 750651
Fax: 01285 750657
E-mail: stay@new-inn.co.uk
Web: www.new-inn.co.uk

Built by decree of Elizabeth I, this lovely coaching inn in a sleepy Cotswold village provides old-fashioned hospitality at its best, with roaring fires and low beamed ceilings; a place for locals, too. The New Inn At Coln is Brian and Sandra-Anne's life - you sense this in their relaxed, personal welcome. They, and their staff, take the time to talk you through a local walk, the ales on tap, the wonderful menu; chef Alastair Ward's food is "divine". Sandra-Anne's sumptuously designed bedrooms have everything - a four-poster here, a half-tester there, a romantic floral theme brilliantly developed. Those in the converted dovecote have views out to open country where the river meanders serenely. In summer, sip drinks lazily outside under the generous shade of parasols. Golf, biking and horse riding can all be arranged; or walk into countryside from the front door, past grazing cattle and gliding swans.

Rooms: 10 doubles, 3 twin/doubles, 1 single.
Price: £99-£125; singles £85.
Meals: Breakfast 8-9.30am. Dinner, 2 courses, £23.50; 3 courses, £27.50.
Closed: Never.

From London/Oxford leave A40 soon after Burford, taking B4425 towards Bibury. After Aldsworth, left to Coln St-Aldwyns.

Map No: 3

Westover Hall

Park Lane
Milford-on-Sea, Lymington
Hampshire
SO41 0PT

Tel: 01590 643044
Fax: 01590 644490
E-mail:
westoverhallhotel@barclays.net
Web: www.westoverhallhotel.com

Nicola and Stewart Mechem

A hotel, but family-run and without the slightest hint of stuffiness. It was built for Siemens in 1897 to be the most luxurious house on the south coast; a fortune was lavished on wood alone. It is still vibrant with gleaming oak and exquisite stained glass and it's hard to stifle a gasp when you enter the hall - it's a controlled explosion of wood. The Mechems are generous and open-minded, keen that people should come to unwind and treat the place as home. Private parties can take over completely and throw the rule book towards the window. Bedrooms are exemplary; some have sea views, all are furnished with a mix of the old and the contemporary, and have spotless bathrooms. The whole place indulges you. Romantics can take to the bar or restaurant and gaze out to sea. The more active can dive outside and walk up the beach to Hurst Castle. Alternatively, sink into steamer chairs on the sun-deck at the back for great views of the Needles, or visit their nearby Mediterranean beach hut.

Rooms: 3 twins, 8 doubles, 1 family, 1 single.
Price: £120-£160. Dinner, B&B £87.50-£102.50 p.p.
Meals: Breakfast times flexible. Light lunch £5-£10. Dinner, 3 courses, £29.50.
Closed: Never.

From Lymington B3058 to Milford-on-Sea. Continue through village. House on left up hill.

Map No: 3

Master Builder's House Hotel
Bucklers Hard
Beaulieu
Hampshire
SO42 7XB

Tel: 01590 616253
Fax: 01590 616297
E-mail:
res@themasterbuilders.co.uk
Web: www.themasterbuilders.co.uk

Christine Bayley

The first thing you need to know is that the Master Builder's House is utterly comfortable. In the bedrooms there are good fabrics and king-size beds; downstairs, there's fine, comfortable furniture in rooms with great views down to the River Beaulieu. But this is an end-of-the-road idyll - you can only go further by boat - and if, during its recent renovation, they had made it grander, the house would have lost some of the warmth that makes it so special. There's a traditional terracotta-floored pub, full of sailors in summer, a hall that seems to tumble down to the water, a river view restaurant (turn left by the flying buttress), and a terrace for *al fresco* meals. Yachts and sailing boats glide down to the Solent (you can take river trips), the marshland is full of birdlife. It's a one-hour walk upstream to Beaulieu and the New Forest stretches out to the west. There's a rich history, too. Henry Adams built much of Nelson's fleet on the grass above the water and the ancient slipways that launched warships still survive. A wonderful spot.

Rooms: 25 twin/doubles.
Price: £155-£205; singles £115.
Meals: Breakfast 7.30-10am weekdays, 8-10am weekends. Lunch, 2 courses, from £16.95. Dinner, 3 courses, £29.50. Bar meals also available.
Closed: Never.

From Lyndhurst, B3056 south past Beaulieu turn-off, then 1st left, signed Bucklers Hard. Hotel signed left after 1 mile.

Map No: 3

Greenwood House

Highwood Lane
Romsey
Hampshire
SO51 9AF

Tel: 01794 517990
Fax: 01794 517992
E-mail: njp@executiveretreats.co.uk
Web: www.executiveretreats.co.uk

Simon Anderson and Nicky Pope

This is a Special Place with a difference. Simon and Nicky have turned a Regency farmhouse on the edge of Romsey into a luxurious, tailor-made retreat for business people; an office from the office, if you like, but more human. Converted cellars are fully-equipped with fax, ISDN lines, copier, PC, printer and scanner; what you won't find are executives pacing up and down barking into mobile phones - it's far too subtle for that. Greenwood feels more like a stylish country house hotel; just as suited to those needing to escape their laptops. Attractive rooms make the most of the light and space. A sitting room of warm rusts and elegant creams has a large open fire and lots of magazines to browse, while breakfast is eaten communally around a lovely oak table in a deep red dining room. Bedrooms mix tapestry-style fabrics, wicker furniture, flora and fauna prints with big beds, and shiny, wood panelled bathrooms; all have fresh flowers, chocolates and fruit. Everything feels so welcoming, from the moment you step inside. You're close to ferries, trains and south coast airports; transport to and from available.

Rooms: 2 doubles; 1 double with private bathroom.
Price: £85; singles £55.
Meals: Breakfast times flexible. Lunch, 2 courses, £12.50. Dinner, 3 courses, £17.50.
Closed: 23 December-3 January.

From M27, junc. 3, M271/A3057 towards Romsey, then right on A27 to North Baddesley. Left at next r'bout, then immediately right into Highwood Lane. House 0.75 miles on right.

Map No: 3

Hotel du Vin & Bistro
Southgate Street
Winchester
Hampshire
SO23 9EF

Tel: 01962 841414
Fax: 01962 842458
E-mail:
info@winchester.hotelduvin.com
Web: www.hotelduvin.com

Manager: Nigel Buchanan

Flair, high standards and exquisite attention to detail in an easy atmosphere... and all very French. There's a bistro with old wooden floors and tables, big windows that draw in light, a garden for *al fresco* dining in summer and a mirrored champagne bar in gold and blue, with bergère sofas to loll on like kings and queens for the night. Elsewhere, sweeping expanses of cream walls covered in prints and oils and handsome furniture. Bedrooms use strikingly simple colours, fine fabrics and Egyptian linen, beds are big and tempting and bathrooms have deep baths and 'smellies' specially made on a Scottish isle. Rooms are split between the bustling main house and the quieter garden rooms; light sleepers should go for the latter. Food and wine are the *raison d'être* and staff are excellent; artisans who speak with passion about their work. Go completely *français* and play boules in the garden, or explore England's ancient capital – Winchester Castle is home to 'The Round Table of King Arthur'; Merlin crowned the 15-year-old Arthur at nearby Silchester, or so it's claimed. A place to dream of when you want a weekend away.

Rooms: 22 doubles, 1 suite.
Price: £95-£130; suite £185.
Meals: Breakfast 7-9.30am weekdays, 8-10am weekends; Continental £8.50, Full English £11.50. Lunch & dinner, 3 courses with bottle of house wine, about £40.
Closed: Never.

M3, junc. 11, signed Winchester South. At first r'bout, follow signs to St. Cross & Winchester. Hotel on left after 2 miles.

Map No: 3

Glewstone Court Hotel

Glewstone
Ross-on-Wye
Herefordshire
HR9 6AW

Tel: 01989 770367
Fax: 01989 770282
E-mail: glewstone@aol.com

Christine and Bill Reeve-Tucker

A relaxed country house - grand, yet nicely lived-in, with an authentic house-party feel. Not a place to stand on ceremony. Kick off your shoes in the sitting room bar, sink into an elegant sofa in front of the fire and let Bill pour you a large gin and tonic. Eat lunch on your lap, or at the table by the window. There's also a smartish restaurant, with a typically relaxed dress code. The centre of the house is early Georgian, with a wooden staircase that spirals up to country house bedrooms that look out onto plum, cherry, apple and pear orchards; the blossom goes on and on in spring. The honeymoon suite is enormous. Elsewhere, big bedrooms have pretty Christine-stencilled cupboards and walls, quilted bedspreads and period furniture; the *Rose* room is especially wonderful. In the garden, an ancient cedar of Lebanon towers above all it surveys. There's a fountain out there, too. Christine cooks brilliant food, much of it organic, and Bill looks after you with great style. Heaven for those in search of a small, friendly, informal country house.

Rooms: 2 junior suites, 6 doubles,
1 single.
Price: £75-£105; singles £45-£75.
Meals: Breakfast until 9.45am. Dinner,
3 courses, about £26. Bar/bistro meals
from £7.95.
Closed: 25-27 December.

*From A40 Ross-Monmouth road, right 1
mile south of Wilton r'bout, signed
Glewstone. Hotel on left after 0.5 miles.*

Penrhos Court Hotel

Kingston
Herefordshire
HR5 3LH

Tel: 01544 230720
Fax: 01544 230754
E-mail: martin@penrhos.co.uk
Web: www.penrhos.co.uk

Martin Griffiths and Daphne Lambert

Penrhos is magnificent by any standards, but as you enter the cruck hall - a stone-flagged medieval masterpiece - bear in mind that 20 or so years ago it was a pile of medieval rubble. Daphne and Martin did most of the renovation themselves, keeping even the tiny details historically accurate, and the effect is jaw-dropping: tapestries on the walls, a 14th-century snug sitting room with a wooden ceiling, a huge fireplace where they burn great knotted lengths of wood - walk in, lift up your head and see the sky. Outside, a stone barn, cow byre and puddleduck pond. The highlight is the hall where you eat at night sitting at rough-hewn slabs of oak, illuminated by candlelight. Daphne cooks between running a school of food and health and the restaurant is fully organic, with no red meat, reflecting their eco-friendly philosophy - they host a yearly 'green cuisine' festival. Bedrooms have immense character, big and bright, with upstairs views over hills; downstairs French windows look onto a pretty garden. Bring your boots and walk. A heavenly experience.

Rooms: 2 four-posters, 3 twins, 10 doubles.
Price: £90-£120; singles from £65.
Meals: Breakfast 8-9am weekdays, until 9.30am weekends. Dinner, 4 courses, £31.50.
Closed: January.

Off A44 Leominster to Kington road, 1 mile east of Kington on the right. Hotel signed 200 yards down a smooth track.

Castle House

Castle Street
Hereford
Herefordshire
HR1 2NW

Dr Albert Heijn

Tel: 01432 356321
Fax: 01432 365909
E-mail: info@castlehse.co.uk
Web: www.castlehse.co.uk

Castle House is part of one man's vision to rejuvenate Hereford. Dutch food retailer Albert Heijn chose this old market town because his wife Monique spent much of her life here. He has created a refined hotel and turned a rough part of town next to the River Wye into a stylish collection of shops, art studios and riverside bars and restaurants called the Left Bank Village. A short stroll past the graceful medieval Cathedral (home to the 13th-century *Mappi Mundi*) connects one with the other - it's all quite amazing and unexpected. The hotel is two Georgian villas converted into one grand building. Most of the bedrooms are big but all are gorgeous, with spectacular fabrics, tapestries, paintings and comfy beds. Wild flowers, a decanter of applejack brandy and Escada toiletries add the final touch. The hotel is on such a quiet street, it's hard to imagine it used to lead to Hereford Castle; only a section of moat survives today, alongside the terraced garden. Watch ducks dive for their supper as you choose yours from a gourmet menu prepared by former Savoy chef Stuart McLeod. The restaurant is even supplied by its own farm.

Rooms: 11 doubles, 4 singles.
Price: £155-£210; singles £90.
Meals: Breakfast until 10am, Continental included. Lunch, 3 courses, £18.95. Dinner, 3 courses, £29.95. Meals also served all day at the Left Bank Village.
Closed: Never.

Follow signs to Hereford city centre, then City Centre east. Right off Bath St into Union St, through St. Peters Sq to Owen's St, then right into St. Ethelbert St. Hotel on left as road veers right.

Isle of Wight

Priory Bay Hotel

Seaview
Isle of Wight
PO34 5BU

Tel: 01983 613146
Fax: 01983 616539
E-mail: reception@priorybay.co.uk
Web: www.priorybay.co.uk

Andrew Palmer

Medieval monks thought Priory Bay special, so did Tudor farmers and Georgian gentry, all helping sculpt this tranquil landscape into a rural haven. From the main house and tithe barns, parkland rolls down to a ridge of trees. The land then drops down to long, clean sands and a shallow sea. It's all owned by the hotel and as Mediterranean as Britain gets. You can hire boats, there's a summer beach café in the trees, and fishermen land their catch here, so walk down for the freshest mackerel breakfasts. The house has huge rooms that fuse classical French and contemporary English styles. The sun-filled drawing room has wonderful windows – chairs obligingly face out to sea - the dining room is muralled and there is exquisite furniture everywhere. The bedrooms are luxurious; some have fresh colours and a modern feel, others oak panelling, maybe a crow's nest balcony and telescope. They grow as much as they can, and there are nature tours in the grounds, with peregrine falcons, red squirrel and badgers and a nine-hole golf course.

Rooms: 16 twin/doubles, 10 family.
Price: £90-£190; singles from £50. Dinner, B&B £55-£100 p.p.
Meals: Breakfast until 9.30am weekdays, 10am weekends. Lunch & dinner, set menu, 3 courses, £25. Picnic hampers available.
Closed: Never.

From Seaview, B3330 south through Nettlestone, then left up road, signed to Nodes Holiday Camp. Hotel drive on left, signed.

Map No: 3

Seaview Hotel and Restaurant

High Street
Seaview
Isle of Wight
PO34 5EX

Tel: 01983 612711
Fax: 01983 613729
E-mail:
reception@seaviewhotel.co.uk
Web: www.seaviewhotel.co.uk

Nicholas and Nicola Hayward

If you know the Isle of Wight, you know Seaview. It is one of the island's institutions - smart, buzzing and down by the sea, full of thirsty sailors. Nicky and Nick bought it back in 1980 and, sea lovers that they are, they made this their ship on land. The terrace, with its railings, mast and flag, is like the prow of a boat - a great place to sit in summer. In the back bar, learn your knots, in the front bar, brush up your semaphore. Wander the stripped wood floors and pass portholes, ships' wheels, lanterns, even sails in the smart back restaurant, serving superb seafood. Bedrooms upstairs have everything you need, but it's the tiptop service that sets the place apart: beds are turned down, a full-cooked breakfast can be brought to your room and the staff couldn't be nicer - nothing here is too much trouble. Bigger rooms at the front have sea views from bay windows; smaller rooms at the back are good value, some have little balconies and all are quiet. The sea is half a minute's walk away and you can learn to sail close by. The nearby village sports club, with tennis, squash, swimming pool and steam room, is available to guests at discounted rates.

Rooms: 3 doubles, 13 twin/doubles.
Price: £70-£125; singles from £55.
Meals: Breakfast until 10am. Lunch & dinner £5-£25.
Closed: Christmas.

From Ryde, B3330 south for 1.5 miles. Hotel signed left.

Biskra Beach Hotel and Restaurant

17 St. Thomas's Street
Ryde
Isle of Wight
PO33 2DL

Tel: 01983 567913
Fax: 01983 616976
E-mail: info@biskra-hotel.com
Web: www.biskra-hotel.com

Barbara Newman and
Hamish Kinghorn

The terrace has wooden chairs and tables, canvas umbrellas, a palm tree and views across a ripple of sea back to the mainland. The beach starts on the other side of the wall while the hot tub is a full 10 paces away. Barbara, who is as easy-going as the hotel, lived in the Middle East and has infused every inch of Biskra with a casual, colonial elegance. The house, with its high ceilings and big windows, is alive with ideas: sisal matting everywhere, driftwood furniture, painted tongue-and-groove panelling, sofas to curl up on, art floating on walls, Mediterranean colours and candles in the restaurant at night. Bedrooms are just as stylish with crisp white linen, director's chairs, swathes of curtain, bathrobes and most have sea views - two have deck balconies. In the breakfast room, exquisite murals of Afghan rugs tease the senses. The food is excellent and continues to win accolades - eat on the terrace on warmer days. In winter, leave your alarm clock at home and let the fog horn wake you. Wonderful. *Cots and high chairs available.*

Rooms: 9 doubles, 5 twins.
Price: £60-£140.
Meals: Breakfast until 10am. Lunch from £5. Dinner, 3 courses, £22-£30.
Closed: Christmas Day & Boxing Day.

Entering Ryde from the west, follow signs to town centre. Take 1st left before Nat West bank. Hotel on left, signed, at bottom of hill.

The George Hotel

Quay Street
Yarmouth
Isle of Wight
PO41 0PE

Tel: 01983 760331
Fax: 01983 760425
E-mail: jacki@thegeorge.co.uk
Web: www.thegeorge.co.uk

Jacki Everest

The position here is just fabulous, with the old castle on one side, the sea at the end of a sun-trapping garden; yet walk out through the front door and you're in the heart of Yarmouth, the oldest town on the island. Handy, if you're a corrupt Governor, intent on sacking ships that pass. Admiral Sir Robert Holmes moved here for that very reason in 1668, demolishing a bit of the castle to improve his view. Inside, the grand feel still lingers, though the house has probably been rebuilt since Sir Robert left. The entrance is large, light and stone-flagged; the next-door drawing room is panelled and echoes to the sound of dice scuttling across a backgammon board. Upstairs, all the big bedrooms are panelled; one with a huge four-poster and two with timber balconies and views out to sea. Meals can be taken outside in the garden bar. You can also eat in the buzzy, cheerful, yellow and wood brasserie or the sumptuous, Michelin-starred, burgundy dining room. A very welcoming hotel and an attractive island base.

Rooms: 15 twin/doubles, 2 singles.
Price: £155-£205; singles from £115. Dinner, B&B rates available.
Meals: Breakfast 8-10am weekdays, 8.30-10.30am weekends. Lunch & dinner in brasserie, from £25. Dinner in restaurant, 4 courses, £45.
Closed: Never. Restaurants closed Sundays & Mondays.

Take Lymington ferry to Yarmouth,
then follow signs to town centre.

Map No: 3

Hotel du Vin & Bistro

Crescent Road
Royal Tunbridge Wells
Kent
TN1 2LY
Manager: Matt Callard

Tel: 01892 526455
Fax: 01892 512044
E-mail: info@tunbridgewells.hotelduvin.com
Web: www.hotelduvin.com

You enter immediately and literally into the spirit of the place - an ocean of wooden floor and high ceiling with animated chatter spilling out from the bars and bistro. This enormous hall is the hub of the house, leading to bars and bedroom stairs and, even though the bedrooms are magnificent, you'll want to get back down and join the fun. The Burgundy bar buzzes with local life; open fires and facing sofas lead inevitably to 'later' dinners. The yellow-walled, picture-crammed bistro is distinctly French, with more wooden floors, while hops tumble from the windows paying tribute to Kent. Afterwards, wander into the Havana Room - the bullet holes are fake - for a game of billiards and a cigar, or take coffee in the Dom Perignon room where huge hand-painted copies of the Impressionists hang boldly. Bedrooms come in different sizes - the biggest is *huge* - and all have fantastic bathrooms; you sleep on Egyptian linen, naturally. A modern masterpiece.

Rooms: 32 doubles.
Price: £85-£155.
Meals: Breakfast 7-9.30am weekdays, 8-10am weekends; Continental £8.50, Full English £11.50. Lunch & dinner, 3 courses with bottle of house wine, about £35.
Closed: Never.

M25, A21 south for 13 miles, then A264, signed Tunbridge Wells, into town. Right at lights into Calverley Rd, then left at mini-r'bout into Crescent Road.

Romney Bay House

Coast Road
Littlestone, New Romney
Kent
TN28 8QY

Tel: 01797 364747
Fax: 01797 367156

Helmut and Jennifer Gorlich

Designed by Clough Williams-Ellis - creator of Portmeirion - for American star Hedda Hopper, this is an atmospheric dreamscape. The whole house has a lingering 1920s house-party feel. There's an honesty bar full of colour, a drawing room with deep sofas to sink into and a pretty dining room and conservatory for wonderful Jennifer-cooked delights - don't miss tea. Everything has been thought out and is just right, a perfect home from home. You can unwind with a book in front of the fire, go for long beachside walks, or simply fall in love with the sheer romance of the place - nothing disappoints. Upstairs, there's a library lookout with a telescope (on a clear day you can see France), books and games. The bedrooms are elegant, full of everything you'll need, and with great bathrooms. There's lots of pretty furniture, half-testers and sleigh beds, and most of the rooms look out to sea. Add to this Jennifer and her undying enthusiasm, and Helmut and his great sense of humour. A very special place indeed.

Rooms: 8 doubles, 2 twins.
Price: £80-£140; singles £60-£95.
Meals: Breakfast times flexible. Light lunch at the weekend from £5.50. Cream teas £4.50. Dinner, 4 courses, £29.50.
Closed: Christmas & mid-June.

M20, junc. 10, A2070 south, then A259 east through New Romney. Right to Littlestone. At sea, left and continue for 1 mile.

Map No: 4

Wallett's Court Country House Hotel

Westcliffe, St. Margaret's at Cliffe **Tel:** 01304 852424
Dover   **Fax:** 01304 853430
Kent   **E-mail:** stay@wallettscourt.com
CT15 6EW   **Web:** www.wallettscourt.com

Chris, Lea and Gavin Oakley

Wallett's Court is *old*. Odo, half-brother of William the Conqueror, held this land in Norman times, and Jacobeans restored the house in 1627. When the Oakleys renovated in 1975, the house gave up long-held secrets. From a ceiling fell 17th-century tobacco pipes; in a hidden passageway hung 17th-century paintings. The Oakley's passion, commitment and care have all paid off and the house feels warm and genuine. Old features catch the eye: ancient red-brick walls in the drawing room, an oak staircase with worn, shallow steps in the hall. Bedrooms in the main house are big and have heaps of character; there's also an impeccably behaved ghost. There are good, quiet rooms in the barn and cottages. Above the spa complex, with indoor pool, sauna, steam room and spa, four excellent, contemporary rooms have been added recently. There's tennis, a terrace with views towards a distant sea and white cliffs for breezy walks, towering views, rolling mists and wheeling gulls within a mile. Great food, too, with puddings to diet for.

Rooms: 13 doubles, 2 twins, 1 family, split between main house, stables, barn and cottage.
Price: £90-£150; singles £75-£110.
Meals: Breakfast until 9.30am weekdays, 10am weekends. Lunch, 3 courses, £17.50. Dinner, 3 courses, £27.50.
Closed: Open all year; special Christmas breaks available.

From Dover A2/A20, A258 towards Deal, then right at Cliffe to St. Margaret's. House 1 mile on right, signed.

Map No: 4

The Ringlestone Inn

Ringlestone Hamlet	**Tel:** 01622 859900
Nr. Harrietsham	**Fax:** 01622 859966
Kent	**E-mail:** bookings@ringlestone.com
ME17 1NX	**Web:** www.ringlestone.com
Michael Millington-Buck	Manager: Michelle Stanley

Two old sisters once ran the Ringlestone; if they liked the look of you, they'd lock you in; if they didn't, they'd shoot at you. Michael and his daughter Michelle have let that tradition slip, preferring to run their 1635 ale house with a breezy conviviality. Glass tankards dangle above the bar, a woodburner throws out heat from the inglenook and old *Punch* cartoons hang on the original brick and flint walls between oak beams and stripped wooden floors. They stock 30 fruit wines and liqueurs as well as excellent local ales to sup in settles or on quirky, tiny, yet very comfy, chairs. Across the lane in the farmhouse, bedrooms are perfect: oak furniture, sublime beds, crisp linen and big, luxurious bathrooms. The food is delicious - try a Ringlestone pie - and in the garden, you can play *Pétanque* - they hold competitions here. The inn has a children's licence, they sometimes host vintage car rallies and Leeds Castle is close by. As for Michael's breakfasts, they'll keep you going for a week. Good walking, too.

Rooms: 1 four-poster, 2 twin/doubles.
Price: £89-£96; singles £79.
Meals: Breakfast 8-9.45am;
Continental £9, Full English £12.
Lunch from £5. Dinner £8-£25.
Closed: Christmas Day.

M20, junc. 8. After 0.25 miles, left at 2nd r'bout, signed Hollingbourne. Through Hollingbourne, up hill, then right at brown 'Knife and Fork' sign. Pub on right after 1.5 miles.

The Inn at Whitewell

Whitewell
Forest of Bowland, nr. Clitheroe
Lancashire
BB7 3AT

Richard Bowman

Tel: 01200 448222
Fax: 01200 448298

Richard, the Bowman of Bowland, wears an MCC tie and peers over half-moon glasses with a soft, slightly mischievous smile constantly on his face. "All those years ago" he was advised not to touch this inn with a bargepole. It must qualify as some of the worst advice ever given because you'll be hard-pressed to find anywhere - hotel or inn - as good as this; it's pure informal bliss. Peat fires, sofas, music systems, great art, a square piano... and that's only the bedrooms. They are a triumph of style; warm and fun, some with fabulous Victorian brass-piped showers, others with deep cast-iron baths - superb. The inn sits just above the river Hodder with views at the back across parkland; the long restaurant drinks it in or there's a terrace if you want to be outside. Wander inside past old sporting memorabilia hanging in a corridor, settles, rugs, beams in the terracotta-walled bar, wood floors, open fires... the works. But book early; weekends can be booked up months in advance. Fabulous.

Rooms: 4 four-posters, 1 suite, 10 twin/doubles.
Price: £82-£114; singles £57-£68.
Meals: Breakfast 7.30-9.30am. Bar meals from £5.50. Dinner, à la carte, from £23.50.
Closed: Never.

From the south, M6, junc. 31a, then B6243 east. Straight through Longridge, then follow signs for Whitewell.
9 miles to inn.

Map No: 6

Number Ten
10 Manchester Street
London
W1U 4DG

Tel: 020 7486 6669
Fax: 020 7224 0348
E-mail:
stay@10manchesterstreet.fsnet.co.uk
Web: www.10manchesterstreet.com

Manager: Neville Isaac

In a city where a good night's sleep can often cost a fortune, Number Ten has good rooms without frills at reasonable prices. The smaller doubles here cost £120 a night, which, given that you're only a five-minute walk from Oxford Street, is good value indeed. Rooms are simple and spotless, with good use of space and natural colours, comfortable beds and crisp linen. Bathrooms are fine, too, and you get all the little bits: TVs, mini hi-fis, a box of chocolates and fans in case of summer. Bay trees stand guard outside this 1919 red-brick building, while inside staff wait to usher you into the lift and to carry your bags up to your room. There's a bright and breezy sitting room with sea-grass matting and a basement breakfast room. No restaurant, but you are given an excellent London-wide restaurant guide and the best advice on the hottest night spots. Theatre tickets can be booked, taxis called. The Wallace Collection, which has reopened after years of magnificent restoration, is at the end of the road; don't miss it.

Rooms: 13 doubles, 5 small doubles, 19 twins, 9 suites.
Price: £120-£150; suites £195.
Meals: Breakfast 7-11am; Continental included, Full English £5. Lunch & dinner available locally.
Closed: Never.

Bond Street tube. Left onto Oxford Street. 3rd left into Duke Street. Straight over Manchester Square into Manchester Street and on right.

London

Portobello Gold
95-97 Portobello Road
Notting Hill
London
W11 2QB

Tel: 020 7460 4910
Fax: 020 7460 4911
E-mail: mike@portobellogold.co[m]
Web: www.portobellogold.com

Michael Bell and
Linda Johnson-Bell

Portobello Gold is a cool little place in the heart of Ladbroke Grove, one of London's trendier districts for musicians. It's a bar, a restaurant, an internet café and a place to stay. Bedrooms are basic, with small shower rooms and good beds. Ideal if the hippy in you is still active, or you're after a cheap, quirky place to stay in London, but not for those after luxury. Downstairs, sit out on the pavement in wicker chairs and watch Portobello life amble by, or hole up at the bar for a beer with the locals, just as Bill Clinton did on his last visit to Britain as US president. Tiled floors, an open fire and monthly exhibitions of photography and modern art fill the walls. At the back, the conservatory restaurant with its retractable glass roof feels comfortably jungle - dine on Irish rock oysters, sashimi, or Thai Moules to the sweet song of four canaries. Linda writes about wine, so expect to drink well, too. Michael is a cyber-visionary, hence the first-floor internet café. For a small fee, he'll put a PC in your room for all-night surfing; stay in the lounge and it's free. Ideal for the Notting Hill Carnival and Portobello antique market held every Saturday.

Rooms: 4 doubles, 1 single (2 doubles and single have ensuite showers but share separate wc).
Price: Doubles £55-£85; singles £50-£55.
Meals: Breakfast until 10am; Continental included, Full English £5.50. Bar meals from £6. Dinner, 3 courses, £20-£25.
Closed: Never.

Notting Hill tube, then north onto Pembridge road. Keep right at mini-r'bout, then 1st left into Portobello Rd. On left after 0.5 miles. Parking easy except on Saturdays.

Map No: 3

Basil Street Hotel

8 Basil Street
Knightsbridge
London
SW3 1AH

Tel: 020 7581 3311
Fax: 020 7581 3693
E-mail: info@thebasil.com
Web: www.thebasil.com

General manager: Charles Lagares

Leave the stylish hubbub of Knightsbridge behind as you walk through the doors of the Basil. Snug within the warm, civilised embrace of this elegant country house hotel, London soon seems a fond, far-off memory. Impeccably-dressed staff politely attend to you in a beautiful lobby; above hangs an ecclesiastical lantern, the hotel's logo, and a grand staircase leads upwards past an ornate Venetian mirror. The hotel, which occupies a whole block, has been in the same family since it opened in 1910 and has altered little. Upstairs, weary shoppers recharge their batteries over traditional afternoon tea in a cosy lounge. Walk down the wonderful writing corridor, with its antiques and snug cubby-holes, so popular with fashion shoots, to a smart restaurant; tables are spread nicely apart and diners are entertained in the evening by student pianists from the nearby Royal College of Music. Bedrooms are done in a regal, country house style, with all the usual comforts; ones on the Brompton Road side are noisier. The hotel is also home to the Parrot Club, London's first club for women only. *Dogs by arrangement.*

Rooms: 21 doubles, 22 twins, 4 family, 33 singles.
Price: £232.65. Singles £162.15. Special Christmas and New Year rates.
Meals: Breakfast 7-10am; Continental £11, Full English £15. Lunch, 3 courses, £18.50. Afternoon tea £12.50. Dinner, 3 courses, £25.
Closed: Never.

Knightsbridge tube station. Right out of Sloane St exit, then 1st right into Basil St. Hotel 50m on right.

Map No: 3

London

Searcy's Roof Garden Bedrooms

30 Pavilion Road
London
SW1X OHJ

Tel: 020 7584 4921
Fax: 020 7823 8694
E-mail: rgr@searcys.co.uk
Web: www.searcys.co.uk

Alexandra Saric

"It is forbidden for house maids to travel alone in the lift with a footman," reads a hand-written sign, dated 1927, in the old Victorian freight elevator that takes you up to this unusual hotel in the back streets of Knightsbridge - you literally step into the lift from the street after buzzing reception. Searcy's is a one-off; intimate, unique and owned by a 160-year-old catering company of the same name. The hotel has occupied the top three floors of this townhouse block in a quiet street in Knightsbridge since the mid-1960s. Simple, elegant bedrooms in a restrained cottage style mix with pretty floral fabrics, good beds, the odd antique and cast-iron bath; some of the bathtubs are in the same room as your bed. In the morning, eat breakfast in bed to the clip clop of the Household Cavalry, then plan your day sitting in the rooftop garden. London awaits. *Two self-catering flats also available nearby; one sleeps two people, the other three.*

Rooms: 1 suite, 4 doubles, 3 twins, 2 singles.
Price: £130-£160; singles £90-£115.
Meals: Continental breakfast delivered to room 7.30-9.30am. Restaurants nearby for lunch & dinner.
Closed: Christmas.

Knightsbridge tube station. Right out of Sloane St exit, 1st right into Basil St, then next left into Pavilion Road. Hotel 150m on right.

La Gaffe
107-111 Heath Street
Hampstead
London
NW3 6SS

Tel: 020 7435 8965
Fax: 020 7794 7592
E-mail: la-gaffe@msn.com
Web: www.lagaffe.co.uk

Lorenzo Stella

True Italian hospitality and great value await at La Gaffe. Bernardo and Androulla Stella first opened the restaurant in 1962, adding rooms in 1976. Today, it's run with the same ineffable charm by their sons, Lorenzo and Salvatore. The list of celebrities who have eaten here is too long to mention, but spaghetti western star Clint Eastwood used to be a regular in the Sixties. The hotel is made up of five former shepherds' cottages, well before Hampstead became such a desirable address. It's the highest point in London and the views from Hampstead Heath three minutes' walk away are wonderful. The village itself is full of terraced cafes, trendy boutiques and charming back streets; just the place to return to after a day exploring the city. The restaurant has a lovely unpretentious feel that's changed little over the years; expect good traditional Italian cooking. Bedrooms may be a little floral for some, but they're clean and comfortable; ones at the back look onto a quiet Georgian square. Come here for the welcome, as warm as it is genuine. *Self-catering studio, sleeps two.*

Rooms: 4 four-posters, 6 doubles, 4 twins, 4 singles.
Price: £90-£125; singles £65.
Meals: Buffet-style breakfast 7.30-9.30am. Lunch & dinner, à la carte, 2 courses, approx £15-£18.
Closed: Never.

Hampstead tube station. Right up Heath Rd. 3 mins walk on left.

Map No: 3

Bukowski Place

Seamy Side
London
E1

Tel: 020 8080808
Fax: 020 8080809
E-mail: dropout@bukowskis.co.uk
Web: www.bukowskis.co.uk

John Fante

Once known as the Hot Hotel, for reasons beyond our comprehension, this charming Georgian bijou building has been renamed with a wit that is equally beyond us. The steel shutters on the window at ground level were originally put there to prevent the gaze of prurient passers-by and the tradition has survived. Why, you may be wondering, does a book of such prodigious respectability as ours include a hotel of such dubious character. Well, the answer lies, as so often when we behave in a wayward manner, in our obsession with eclectism. In our age of anodyne, banal 'life-styles' and architectures we find ourselves driven to absurd lengths to find 'les petits coins de culture'. Here is an authentic building of another century, unchanged and still dignified – however neglected. From each window would once have hung the draped figures of the residents, gay and inviting, adding colour and seduction to the community scene. The owner would have sat by the inveigling customers to enter, a touch of intimacy so sadly lacking in our more cynical and puritanical age. Such life has ebbed away, but the place deserves our respect for trying.

Rooms: 10 garets.
Price: Free.
Meals: BYO beer and cigarettes.
Typewriters provided.
Closed: If not drunk.

Ask a tramp and bring a crowbar.

Map No: 3

Eleven Didsbury Park

Didsbury Village
Manchester
M20 5LH

Tel: 0161 4487711
Fax: 0161 4488282
E-mail: enquiries@elevendidsburypark.com
Web: www.elevendidsburypark.com

Eamonn and Sally O'Loughlin

Welcome to a warm 21st-century hotel experience - Eleven Didsbury Park celebrates the urban minimalist style without paring down your comfort in the process. Like the Hotels du Vin, it does design without the attitude, in contrast to more 'brand conscious' contemporaries hell-bent on creating a new hotel order. Eamonn has blended modern design with the sparing beauty of the Irish Georgian movement of his homeland to create a hotel full of relaxed, uncluttered style. Its simplicity delights the eye. The balance of old and new in the bedrooms sees a happy mix of the best Egyptian linen and richly coloured handmade fabrics with mirror de-misters and hi-fi gadgets. There's also a pretty garden to sit in - home to Sally's breakfast tomatoes. Didsbury Park is a lush, leafy suburb with lots to do nearby. But go and explore Manchester's mini-revival; exciting modern architecture, regenerated docklands and the Lowry Museum await. *Hot tub planned for the garden.*

Rooms: 2 suites, 4 doubles, 11 twin/doubles.
Price: £69.50-£155.50.
Meals: Breakfast 7-11.30am; Continental £8.50, Full English £10.50. Room service snacks until 10.30pm, from £2.95-£8.95. Lunch & dinner available nearby.
Closed: Never.

From Manchester city centre, A34 south for 4 miles, then right on A5145 Wimslow Rd. Didsbury Park 4th on right, house 200 yards on left.

The Norfolk Mead Hotel

Coltishall
Norwich
Norfolk
NR12 7DN

Tel: 01603 737531
Fax: 01603 737521

Jill and Don Fleming

You *can* paddle your canoe from the bottom of the garden all the way along the river Bure to the Broads, though it involves a few miles of exertion. A better idea is to stay closer to home and potter lazily about in one of the hotel's rowing boats. Norfolk Mead is in a great position, with 12 acres of lawns, mature-trees, a walled garden and swimming pool - there's even a one-acre fishing lake. Come for the owners, the food and the easy-going luxury of a lovely old Georgian country house - the sort you normally dream of. The bedrooms, all different, are super-comfortable, with the best-quality linen and every tiny, frivolous need anticipated. The food is just as good, all fresh and local, maybe samphire from Blakeney, or home-made ice-cream. A fine entrance hall with high-backed sofas and open fire unwind you immediately. Big, gracious, beautifully proportioned yet perfectly relaxing. And if that's not enough, Jill and Don's daughter, Nicky, can provide a massage or manicure in the hotel salon. Expect to be pampered.

Rooms: 5 doubles, 2 twins, 1 family suite.
Price: Doubles £80-£140; singles £70-£90. Half-board from £60 p.p.
Meals: Breakfast 8-9am weekdays, 8.30-9.30am weekends. Lunch £12. Dinner, 3 courses, £24.50.
Closed: Never.

B1150 north to Coltishall. Over humpback bridge and first right. Down drive before church. Signed.

Elderton Lodge and Langtry Restaurant

Gunton Park
Thorpe Market
Norfolk
NR11 8TZ
Mike Parsey and Pat Roofe

Tel: 01263 833547
Fax: 01263 834673
E-mail: enquiries@eldertonlodge.co.uk
Web: www.eldertonlodge.co.uk

Shades of Scotland embrace this peaceful north Norfolk shooting lodge set in a deer park with Gunton Tower graceful in the distance. Gunton Hall is just over the brow and was a favourite with Edward VII and Lilly Langtry. The local railway station was built specially to deliver their champagne - 1,000 cases at a time! Pictures of Lillie Langtry hang on the walls, as does a letter she wrote. The house echoes to her time - tasselled lamps, old rugs, leather sofas, trophies and oils - all the deep country trimmings. For new owners Mike Parsey and Pat Roofe, Norfolk is a homecoming. Mike has returned from 20 years in Africa and Pat, a pilot, has landed back where he was brought up. Elderton exudes comfort. Splash out on the more expensive rooms, as they're bigger and full of Edwardian antiques, rich fabrics and plush headboards. In most rooms, you can lie in bed and look out across parkland to the tower. Enjoy candlelit dinners in the warm and elegant restaurant and breakfast amid hanging ferns in the Victorian, tiled conservatory. Deer graze all around and there's a varied programme of 'special interest' weekends, too. *Children 6 and over welcome.*

Rooms: 2 twins, 9 doubles.
Price: £80-£115; singles from £50. Dinner, B&B from £55 p.p.
Meals: Breakfast 8-9am weekdays, 8.30-10am weekends. Lunch, 3 courses, £12.95. Dinner, 3 courses, £19.50 or à la carte.
Closed: 2 weeks in January.

From North Walsham, A149 north for 3 miles. Hotel signed left.

The Hoste Arms

The Green
Burnham Market
Norfolk
PE31 8HD

Tel: 01328 738777
Fax: 01328 730103
E-mail: thehostearms@compuserve.com
Web: www.hostearms.co.uk

Paul and Jeanne Whittome

Manager: Emma Tagg

At the risk of being excoriated for plagiarism and laziness, here's how The Hoste Arms' brochure describes itself: "Paul's partial deafness is often mistaken for rudeness. Local fishermen frequent the bar. The fine old bedrooms are occupied by anyone from film-stars to captains of industry, though thankfully most guests are none of these. In its 300-year history The Hoste has been courthouse, livestock market, art gallery, brothel. Paul, once a bouncer in a shanty pub in Australia, has not shrunk since then but has converted brilliantly from ejector to welcomer." The Hoste has deservedly won almost every prize going - *The Times* voted it their second favourite hotel in England, their 27th in the world, and gave it a 'Golden Pillow' award. The place has a genius of its own; brave and successful mixtures of bold colour, chairs to sink deep into, panelled walls, beamed fireplaces and food to be eaten in rapture, anywhere and anytime. Brilliant.

Rooms: 4 twins, 8 doubles, 1 family, 6 junior suites, 4 four-posters, 5 singles.
Price: £86-£140; singles £64-£95.
Meals: Breakfast 8-10.30am. Lunch & dinner £3.50-£25.
Closed: Never.

From King's Lynn, A149 north, then A148. After about 2 miles, left onto B1153. At Great Bircham, branch right onto B1155 to Burnham Market via Stanhoe. Inn in village.

Map No: 7

Strattons

4 Ash Close	**Tel:** 01760 723845
Swaffham	**Fax:** 01760 720458
Norfolk	**E-mail:** strattonshotel@btinternet.com
PE37 7NH	**Web:** www.strattons-hotel.co.uk

Vanessa and Les Scott

"Everything is home-made, recycled, bought locally, restored, renewed, recovered and rethought," Vanessa says of this classical Queen Anne villa. Such green nous has earned Strattons the accolade of being Britain's greenest hotel. Hidden away in its own peaceful courtyard, a minute's walk from the market square, there's a distinctly rural French feel, with gardens reassuringly unmanicured, and urns and terracotta pots in abundance. The interior is spectacular. Les and Vanessa – they met at art school – have covered every square inch with something wonderful. Bold colours, busts and sculptures, chests piled with books, bunches of dried roses, rugs on stripped floors - it feels like a small, French château. Bedrooms are exquisite; a tented bathroom, murals and stained glass, two sofas in front of a smouldering fire, tromp l'œil panelling, rich fabrics... the four-poster room is sheer heaven. Downstairs, sit by murals in the lower-ground floor bistro for Vanessa's gorgeous food. *A no-smoking house.*

Rooms: 1 twin, 4 doubles, 1 four-poster.
Price: £95-£120; four-poster £160; singles from £75.
Meals: Breakfast 7.30-9am weekdays, 8-10.30am weekends. Dinner, 4 courses, £33.
Closed: Christmas & New Year.

Ash Close runs off the north end of the market place between W H Brown estate agents and Express cleaners.

Map No: 7

The Falcon Hotel

Castle Ashby
Nr. Northampton
Northamptonshire
NN7 1LF

Tel: 01604 696200
Fax: 01604 696673
E-mail: falcon@castleashby.co.uk

Michael and Jennifer Eastick

A stone-built inn, originally a farm, which dates from 1594 and sits just across the road from the castle after which this dreamy village is named. The castle grounds are spectacular and they are open to the public; there are craft shops in the village, too. The Easticks came here recently after Michael decided he needed another change of job - he has been a farmer and a racing driver, among other things. These days he is quite content being a hotelier, making sure the cellar bar is full of beer, that the oils hang symmetrically on the smart Regency-striped walls, that the fire crackles with bounteous logs and that guests get well fed and watered in the pretty stone-walled restaurant. In summer, eat out in the garden and watch cows saunter up to the dairy while flower beds burst with colour and sheep graze beyond. Some bedrooms are in the house, others are next door and one is in the cottage - the octogenarian ex-postmistress lives in between. All are pretty, with country-cottage fabrics, bright yellows and blues, bathrobes, fresh flowers and gentle village views.

Rooms: 13 twin/doubles, 3 singles.
Price: £85-£99.50 (excluding special event weekends); singles from £69.50. Dinner, B&B from £69.50.
Meals: Breakfast 7-9.30am weekdays, 8-9.30am weekends. Lunch, 2 courses, £14.95. Dinner, 3 courses, £23.50.
Closed: Never.

Castle Ashby is signed north from the A428, 1.5 miles west of Yardley Hastings.

Map No: 3

The Pheasant Inn

Stannersburn
Kielder Water
Northumberland
NE48 1DD

Tel: 01434 240382
Fax: 01434 240382
E-mail: thepheasantinn@kielderwater.demon.co.uk
Web: www.thepheasantinn.com

Walter, Irene and Robin Kershaw

A really super little inn, the kind you hope to chance upon; not grand, not scruffy, just right. The Kershaws run it with huge passion and an instinctive understanding of its traditions. The stone walls hold 100-year-old photos of the local community; from colliery to smithy, a vital record of their past heritage remains - special indeed. The bars are wonderful; brass beer taps glow, anything wooden - ceiling, beams and tables - has been polished to perfection and the clock above the fire keeps perfect time. The attention to detail is staggering. Robin and Irene cook with relish, again nothing fancy, but more than enough to keep a smile on your face - game pies, salmon and local lamb as well as wonderful Northumbrian cheeses. Bedrooms next door in the old hay barn are as you'd expect: simple and cosy, super value for money. You are in the Northumberland National Park; hire bikes and cycle round the lake, sail on it or go horse riding. No traffic jams, no too-much-hurry and wonderful Northumbrian hospitality - they really are the nicest people.

Rooms: 4 doubles, 3 twins, 1 family.
Price: £60; singles £40. Dinner, B&B from £46 p.p.
Meals: Breakfast 8-9am. Bar meals from £6. Dinner, 3 courses, £15-£20.
Closed: Never.

From Bellingham, follow signs west to Kielder Water and Falstone for 7 miles. Hotel on left, 1 mile short of Kielder Water.

Map No: 10

The Otterburn Tower Hotel

Otterburn
Northumberland
NE19 1NS

Tel: 01830 520620
Fax: 01830 521504
E-mail: reservations@otterburntower.co.uk
Web: www.otterburntower.co.uk

John Goodfellow

The Otterburn Tower is a fortified Northumbrian country house built by a cousin of William the Conqueror in 1076 to keep the Scots at bay. It famously withstood an attack from the Scottish army at the Battle of Otterburn in 1388. These days, it deploys the distraction of luxury to keep the strain of life in the 21st century at bay - at least temporarily. The hotel is set in 32 acres on the edge of the beautiful and under-visited Northumberland National Park. The approach is dramatic, up a long, gravelled drive to a forecourt surrounded by neat, formal gardens. Inside feels more like a mini-stately home than a hotel, with wood panelling, porticoes, flagstones, panelled ceilings and giant, wooden doors. There are fireplaces in all the rooms, including an unusual one of marble, with Doric columns and carvings of Romulus (the mythical founder of Rome) and his brother Remus. Bedrooms are all different, with a smattering of antiques, traditional 'floralesque' designs and snug bathrobes. Staff are extremely friendly and the cooking is a mix of regional and French influences - try 'singin' hinnies' with afternoon tea.

Rooms: 2 four-poster, 1 half-tester, 8 doubles, 4 twin/doubles, 2 family.
Price: £90-£150; singles £60. Dinner B&B £60-£95 p.p.
Meals: Breakfast until 9.30am weekdays, 10am weekends. Afternoon tea £6.75. Dinner, set menu, 3 courses, £20.
Closed: Never.

From Newcastle, A696 to Otterburn. Hotel on right in village, signed.

Map No: 10

The Tankerville Arms Hotel

Cottage Road
Wooller
Northumberland
NE71 6AD

Anne Park

Tel: 01668 281581
Fax: 01668 281387
E-mail: enquiries@tankervillehotel.co.uk
Web: www.tankervillehotel.co.uk

A cheery Northumbrian welcome awaits at the Tankerville; honest, unpretentious, and full of warmth, the charm of this 17th-century inn is that it's not trying to be anything it isn't. Ann has been involved in running the place for more than two decades and does so in a calm, friendly way; most of the staff have been here more than five years as well. The inn lies at the foot of the Cheviot hills just inland from miles of wild and unspoilt coastline. Inside, the décor is smart and homely. A grandfather clock and Regency antiques add splendour to the reception area, while a lovely collection of paintings and prints of maps, cattle and the local landscape add character to the bar, restaurant and sitting rooms. Immaculate bedrooms are in a traditional hotel style, with shiny new bathrooms. The bar has a real fire to brighten winter nights, while an attractive garden is a nice, sheltered spot to relax in summer. Lindisfarne is well worth a visit (but do check tide times) as are the pedigree white cattle at nearby Chillingham Castle.

Rooms: 6 doubles, 6 twins, 2 family, 2 singles.
Price: £85-£90; singles £45.
Meals: Breakfast until 9.30am. Light lunch from £4.50. Dinner, 3 courses, from £14.95.
Closed: Christmas.

From Newcastle, A1 north past Morpeth, then A697 to Wooller for 30 miles. Hotel on right just north of village.

Langar Hall

Langar
Nottinghamshire
NG13 9HG

Tel: 01949 860559
Fax: 01949 861045
E-mail: langarhall-hotel@ndirect.co.uk
Web: www.langarhall.com

Imogen Skirving

Langar Hall is one of the most engaging and delightful places in this book - reason enough to come to Nottinghamshire. Imogen's exquisite style and natural *joie de vivre* make this a mecca for those in search of a warm, country house atmosphere and a place to connect with other people. The house sits at the top of a hardly noticeable hill in glorious parkland, bang next door to the church. Imo's family came here over 150 years ago. Much of what fills the house came here then and once inside, it's easy to feel intoxicated by beautiful things; statues and busts, the odd Doric column, ancient tomes in overflowing bookshelves, huge oils on the walls. Bedrooms are spectacular, some resplendent with antiques, others more contemporary with fabrics draped from beams or tromp l'oeil wallpaper. When you ring to book, you are talked through each room, much as a sommelier talks you through each wine. Magnificent food, and there's Shakespeare on the front lawn in summer. A cultural paradise.

Rooms: 1 four-poster, 1 suite, 2 twins,
8 doubles.
Price: £100-£175; singles £75-£95.
Meals: Breakfast 7-10am weekdays, 8.30-10am
weekends. Lunch, 2 courses, £10. Dinner, 3 courses,
£17.50; à la carte £30.
Closed: Never.

From Nottingham, A52 towards Grantham.
Right, signed Cropwell Bishop, then straight on
for 5 miles. House next to church on edge of village,
signed.

Map No: 6

Bath Place

4-5 Bath Place, Holywell Street
Oxford
Oxfordshire
OX1 3SU

Tel: 01865 791812
Fax: 01865 791834
E-mail:
bathplace@compuserve.com
Web: www.bathplace.co.uk

Yolanda Fawsitt

Bath Place is unlike anything else you are ever likely to come across. Close to the Bodleian Library and surrounded by four colleges, its courtyard is a throwback to Dickensian England, a warren of four cottages seemingly squashed together and pushed up into the sky. Alleyways burrow through, connecting the world to the ancient Turf pub next door. The house drips history; the last remnant of city wall stands right behind, the model for the pre-Raphaelites was born in room 11, Dorothy Sayers lived in room 5, and on it goes. Before the war, well-heeled undergrads roomed here and they still turn up sometimes on a nostalgic whim. It's a mad, wonderful, rambling place; one staircase is for mountaineers only. Bedrooms may not be grand, or that large, but you wouldn't want them to be. It's all overseen by delightful staff, the irrepressible Kathleen and her daughter Yolanda. *Pets by arrangement.*

Rooms: 10 doubles, 2 twins, 2 family suites.
Price: £95-£150; singles from £90.
Meals: Continental buffet breakfast until 9.30am weekdays, 10am weekends. Lunch & dinner available in Oxford.
Closed: Christmas & New Year.

From north Oxford ring road, down Banbury Rd, left into Parks Rd, then left at Kings Arms pub into Hollywell St. Hotel signed 100m on right. Staff will show you where to park.

Map No: 3

112

Oxfordshire

Old Parsonage Hotel

No. 1 Banbury Road
Oxford
Oxfordshire
OX2 6NN

Tel: 01865 310210
Fax: 01865 311262
E-mail: info@oldparsonage-hotel.co.uk
Web: www.oxford-hotels-restaurants.co.uk

Manager: Philip Mason-Gordon

1660 must have been a good year for cooks. Edward Selwood, the wealthy chef of nearby St. John's College, completed his house that year and the original oak door still hangs. Inside, clever use of design details and materials have kept the old-house feel and the intimacy of a private club - Oscar Wilde is reputed to have stayed here. The hall has marble floors, the original fireplace and huge pots of dried flowers. Splendid bedrooms have smart florals and checks, some in the old house have fireplaces and panelling; all have glorious bathrooms. There's a first-floor roof garden, lush with plants, for tea or sundowner, and a snug sitting room downstairs for those seeking quiet. All roads seem to lead to the Parsonage bar/restaurant, the hub of the hotel; newspapers hang on poles, walls are heavy with pictures and people float in all day long for coffee, drinks and good food. First-class service from real people - they'll do just about anything they can to help.

Rooms: 30 twin/doubles, 3 suites.
Price: £155-£190; singles £130; suites £200.
Meals: Breakfast until 11am. Lunch & dinner, 2 courses, from £15.
Closed: 24-27 December.

From A40 ring road, south at Banbury Road r'bout to Summertown and towards city centre. Hotel on right next to St. Giles church.

The Old Bank
92-94 High Street
Oxford
Oxfordshire
OX1 4BN

Tel: 01865 799599
Fax: 01865 799598
E-mail: info@oldbank-hotel.co.uk
Web: www.oxford-hotels-restaurants.co.uk

Manager: Ian Hamilton

The original safe, too heavy to remove, now guards the wine cellar. Built of mellow golden stone, the hotel is in the heart of old Oxford, flanked by colleges and cobbled streets. Rooms at the top have views across the fabled skyline of dreaming spires, towers and domes, a sublime panorama of architectural splendour. Downstairs, the big old tellers' hall has been turned into a 'hip' bar and restaurant - the hub of the hotel - with stone floors, a zinc-topped bar, huge modern oils on the walls and big arched windows that look out onto the High Street. In summer, eat on the deck at the back, beneath umbrellas or the shade of lime trees in a tiny private garden. Bedrooms are superb and just as contemporary, stylishly clean-cut with natural pastel colours, the best linen, velvet and silk; some have big bay windows or views to the back, and they're full of 21st-century gadgetry. A five-minute stroll will take you through Merton College, The Meadows and down to the river. Perfect.

Rooms: 1 suite, 42 twin/doubles.
Price: £155-£300; singles from £135.
Meals: Breakfast 7-10am; Continental £8, Full English £11. Lunch & dinner £8.75-£25.
Closed: 25-26 December.

Cross Magdalen Bridge towards city centre. Keep left through 1st set of lights, then 1st left into Merton St. Follow road right, then 1st right into Magpie Lane. Car park 2nd right.

Map No: 3

The Feathers Hotel
Market Street
Woodstock
Oxfordshire
OX20 1SX

Tel: 01993 812291
Fax: 01993 813158
E-mail: enquiries@feathers.co.uk
Web: www.feathers.co.uk

Peter Bate

Once a draper's, then a butcher's, this serenely English townhouse hotel has stayed true to its roots and now has a Michelin-starred restaurant and rooms lavished with fine fabrics. The four 17th-century houses have labyrinthine corridors that lead to the four original staircases, which have the odd mind-your-head-beam. Elsewhere, smouldering fires, stone floors, oils and antiques, an elegant upstairs sitting room, a pretty terraced bar and garden, and Johann the parrot. Window boxes to fit the season help frame glimpses of Woodstock outside. The restaurant is part library, half-panelled with soft yellow walls and low ceilings. Bedrooms are beautiful; some are smaller than others, but most have marble bathrooms and all have period furniture, towelling bathrobes, purified water and home-made shortbread - one suite has a steam bath. Play backgammon in the study while devouring sinful teas. Hot-air ballooning and chauffeured-punting can both be arranged, or stroll to Blenheim Palace along Woodstock's pretty streets.

Rooms: 8 doubles, 8 twins, 4 suites, 1 single.
Price: £135-£185; suites £235-£290; singles from £99.
Meals: Breakfast 7.30-9.45am. Lunch, 2 courses, from £17.50. Dinner, 3 courses, about £38. Tasting menu, 6 courses, £65, includes champagne & port.
Closed: Never.

From Oxford, A44 north to Woodstock.
In town, left after traffic lights. Hotel on left.

Falkland Arms

Great Tew
Chipping Norton
Oxfordshire
OX7 4DB

Tel: 01608 683653
Fax: 01608 683656
E-mail: sjcourage@btconnect.com
Web: www.falklandarms.org.uk

Paul Barlow-Heal and Sarah-Jane Courage

In a perfect Cotswold village, the perfect English pub. Five hundred years on and the fire still roars in the stone-flagged bar under a low-slung timbered ceiling that drips with jugs, mugs and tankards. Here, the hop is treated with reverence; ales are changed weekly and old pump clips hang from the bar. Tradition runs deep; they stock endless tins of snuff with great names like Irish High Toast and Dr. Kalmans. In summer, Morris Men stumble on the lane outside and life spills out onto the terrace at the front, and into the big garden behind. This lively pub is utterly down-to-earth and in very good hands. The dining room is tiny and intimate with beams and stone walls; every traditional dish is home-cooked. The bedrooms are snug and cosy, not grand, but fun. Brass beds and four-posters, maybe a heavy bit of oak and an uneven floor - you'll sleep well. The house remains blissfully free of modern trappings, nowhere more so than in the bar, where mobile phones meet with swift and decisive action.

Rooms: 5 doubles, 1 single.
Price: £65-£80; singles £40.
Meals: Breakfast 9am. Lunch from £4. Dinner from £8.
Closed: 24-27 December, 31 December & 1 January. Pub open all year round.

From Chipping Norton, A361, then right onto B4022. Pub is signed.

Burford House

99 High Street
Burford
Oxfordshire
OX18 4QA

Jane and Simon Henty

Tel: 01993 823151
Fax: 01993 823240
E-mail: stay@burfordhouse.co.uk
Web: www.burford-house.co.uk

Burford House is small enough for Simon and Jane to influence every corner; this is also their home. It's a delight, small and intensely personal, redecorated with elegant good taste without any loss of character; oak beams, good fabrics, antiques, simple colours, log fires, immaculate bedrooms and a little garden for afternoon teas, all in this exquisite Cotswold town, with a sense of fun that avoids any hint of stuffiness. There's an honesty bar, with home-made sloe gin and cranberry vodka to be sipped from cut-glass tumblers, no less. Handwritten menus promise ravishing breakfasts and tempting lunches. Both are happy in the kitchen; Simon cooks, Jane bakes. Classical music wafts about the place, fresh flowers are everywhere, as is Jumble the cat. It's a serenely comfortable place; unwind, then unwind a little more. Guests return time after time.

Rooms: 2 four-posters, 2 twins, 3 doubles.
Price: £95-£125; singles from £75.
Meals: Breakfast until 9am weekdays, 9.30am weekends. Light lunch & afternoon teas available only. Dinner available in Burford.
Closed: 2 weeks in January/February. Restaurant closed Mondays.

In centre of Burford.

The Lamb Inn

Sheep Street
Burford
Oxfordshire
OX18 4LR

Tel: 01993 823155
Fax: 01993 822228
Web: www.lamb-burford.co.uk

Caroline and Richard De Wolf

Surely the best hotel address ever - especially with the owners' name. This honourable inn must be one of the finest in the country. It dates in part from 1420 when it used to be a dormy house. In the old bar, the footsteps of monks and thirsty locals have worn a gentle groove into the original stone floor. Make a grand tour and you'll come across four fires, two sitting rooms, rambling corridors, rugs to warm stone floors, mullioned windows, old parchments and a porter's chair with a high enough back "to keep the draught off a giant's neck." In the conservatory restaurant, ferns hang above the wooden floor, with a couple of Doric columns thrown in for good measure. The food is sheer perfection. Bedrooms are just as good, with plump-cushioned armchairs, heavy oak beams, brass beds, half-testers, four-posters and antiques of every hue and colour. The whole place has a mellow magic, rather like its owners. Richard and Caroline have been here 19 years; the locals, sensibly, won't let them leave until they match the 40 years chalked up by the previous owners.

Rooms: 1 four-poster, 10 doubles, 4 twins.
Price: £110-£130; singles from £70.
Meals: Breakfast 8-9.30am. Dinner, 3 courses, £27.
Closed: Christmas Day & Boxing Day.

From Oxford, A40 west to Burford. Sheep St 1st left down High St.

Map No: 3

The Stonor Arms

Stonor
Oxfordshire
RG9 6HE

Tel: 01491 638866
Fax: 01491 638863
E-mail: stonorarms.hotel@virgin.net
Web: www.stonor-arms.co.uk

Sophia Williams

It is hard to believe you are so close to London - the Stonor, lying on the edge of the Chiltern Hills, has the feel of deep country. Footpaths lead out to hills and forest, red kites circle above the deer park at Stonor House (open to the public), and lanes lead up to pretty villages. Key notes at the hotel are the tiptop service, the elegance and the relaxed informality. Close to Henley-on-Thames, the hotel has strong links with the regatta; the grand, stone-flagged bar has oars on the ceiling and old rowing photos, and leather sofas and armchairs in which to sit and enjoy it all. In summer, life spills out into the pretty walled garden, candle-lit and flood-lit at night. Antique-furnished bedrooms tend to be huge and come with all the extras: bathrobes, turndown service, morning papers delivered to your room, and peace and quiet. In good weather, eat breakfast in the garden, or simply have it in bed. A place to spoil yourself.

Rooms: 3 doubles, 7 twin/doubles.
Price: £145-£175; singles £120.
Meals: Breakfast 7-10am weekdays, 8-10am weekends. Bar meals from £7. Dinner, 3 courses, £25-£30.
Closed: Restaurant closed Sunday nights.

M40, junc. 6, B4009 to Watlington, then B480 towards Nettlebed. After 2 miles, left, signed Stonor. Inn in village.

Map No: 3

Thamesmead House Hotel

Remenham Lane
Henley-on-Thames
Oxfordshire
RG9 2LR

Tel: 01491 574745
Fax: 01491 579944
E-mail: thamesmead@supanet.com
Web:
www.thamesmeadhousehotel.co.uk

Patricia Thorburn-Muirhead

Patricia's eye for a news story has proved equally adept at creating a wonderful place to stay in the home of the Royal Regatta. The former arts' correspondent has transformed a "seedy" 1960s Edwardian guest house into a chic getaway just a short amble from the centre of Henley-on-Thames; the walk over the famous five-arched bridge (1786) is easily the best introduction to this charming town. Soak up lazy, idyllic river views in both directions, then walk along towpaths or mess about in a rowing boat. Thamesmead is small but perfectly formed. Elegant bedrooms are decorated in a comfortably crisp Scandinavian style; mustard yellows, terracotta and soothing blues, big Oxford pillowcases to sink into, modern art on the walls, an extraordinary fossil fireplace in one, and painted wood panelling in the bathrooms. The breakfast/tea room is relaxing, with Thompson furniture from Kilburn, North Yorkshire - spot the distinctive carved mouse motif - and French windows that let in lots of light, and maybe a gentle summer's breeze. Presiding over all is the erudite and fun-loving Patricia, a Dubliner to the core.

Rooms: 4 doubles, 1 twin/double, 1 single.
Price: £115-£140; singles £95-£115.
Meals: Buffet-style breakfast until 9am weekdays, 10am weekends. Afternoon tea by arrangement. Lunch & dinner available in Henley.
Closed: Never.

From M4, junc. 8/9, A404 (M) to Burchett's Green, then left on A4130, signed Henley (5 miles). Before bridge, turn right just after Little Angel pub. House on left.

Map No: 3

120

Pen-y-Dyffryn Country Hotel

Rhydycroesau
Nr. Oswestry
Shropshire
SY10 7JD

Tel: 01691 653700
Fax: 01691 650066
E-mail: stay@peny.co.uk
Web: www.peny.co.uk

Miles and Audrey Hunter

Staggeringly beautiful scenery surrounds this old rectory, commissioned in 1845 by its first rector, Robert Williams, who compiled the first Celtic dictionary. He was said to be a stuffy character, the very opposite of Miles and Audrey, whose relaxed and easy-going manner suffuse the house with unpretentious charm. The entrance hall doubles as a bar; the bar itself an old *chiffonier* - "a posh sideboard," says Miles, with menus tucked away in the drawers. The bedrooms are 'comfy old house', with good fabrics and some have hand-painted furniture. One little double has its own flight of stairs, while the two 'old stable' rooms are big and contemporary, with private terraces; nearly all the rooms have spectacular views. There's a sitting room to curl up in, a restaurant for all tastes, organic beers and wines and a front terrace to sip long drinks and savour that view. The five acres of Pen-y-Dyffryn start at the top of the hill and roll down to Wales; the river at the foot of the beautiful valley marks the natural border.

Rooms: 4 twins, 4 doubles, 1 single, 1 family.
Price: £88-£115; singles £68.
Meals: Breakfast 8-9.30am. Dinner, 3 courses, £23.
Closed: Christmas & 1-14 January.

From A5, head to Oswestry. Leave town on B4580, signed Llansilin. Hotel 3 miles on left just before Rhydycroesau.

Shropshire

Mr Underhill's at Dinham Weir

Dinham Bridge　　　　**Tel:**　01584 874431
Ludlow　　　　　　　**Fax:**　01584 874431
Shropshire　　　　　**Web:** www.mr-underhills.co.uk
SY8 1EH

Chris and Judy Bradley

With Chris and Judy at the helm, Mr Underhill's started life in Suffolk, travelled 18,000 frustrating miles around England, looking for a new home, and finally found one at the foot of Ludlow Castle. It brought its Michelin star - a movable feast? – and it was worth the bother: its position right on the river Teme is dreamy. In summer, eat outside in the new courtyard garden and watch the river flow by. The restaurant is long, light and airy, modern, warm and fun, and there's lots of glass to help you enjoy the view. The bright bedrooms are upstairs at the other end of the house - the only noise you'll hear is the river - and though some are smallish, good design by Judy has made them feel bigger. They're almost Shaker in style: simple fabrics, crisp linen, king-size beds - one a canopied four-poster without the posts - and river views. All are good and restful. Back downstairs, you're bound to meet two British blue kittens, the heirs to Frodo's empire after whose alias, as Tolkien-lovers will confirm, the restaurant is named. Good people with huge commitment.

Rooms: 6 doubles.
Price: £75-£120; singles £65-£85.
Meals: Breakfast until 9am weekdays, 9.30am weekends. Dinner £27.50-£30.
Closed: Never.

Drive into centre of Ludlow, heading for castle. Take road called 'Dinham' to left of castle and follow down short hill, turning right at bottom before crossing river. On left, signed.

Map No: 6　　　　　　　122

The Hundred House Hotel

Norton
Nr. Shifnal
Shropshire
TF11 9EE

Tel: 01952 730353
Fax: 01952 730355
E-mail: hphundredhouse@messages.co.uk
Web: www.hundredhouse.co.uk

Henry, Sylvia, David and Stuart Phillips

A watering hole in the true sense, where the traditions of a good inn live on. Henry is an innkeeper of the 'old school', with a great sense of humour - he once kept chickens, but they didn't keep him. He and Sylvia came here 15 years ago and made it absolutely charming, inside and out. Enter a world of blazing log fires, old brick walls, panelling and terracotta-tiled floors. Dried flowers hang from the beams, blackboard menus trumpet roast rib of beef, Moroccan lamb or Italian pork, and in the restaurant, Sylvia's wild and wonderful collage art hangs on wild and wonderful walls; one is gold. Quirky bedrooms come in different shapes and sizes. Patchwork quilts on brass beds, a half-tester in the purple and gold room, carafes of shampoo and bubble bath in the bathrooms. Some of the rooms even have swings, while pillows are sprinkled with lavender water, presumably home-made, judging by the outstanding herb and flower gardens outside - they're open to the public. Wander out with your pint and share a quiet moment with a few stone lions.

Rooms: 5 doubles, 2 twins, 2 family, 1 single.
Price: £95-£120; singles £69. Dinner, B&B from £65 p.p.
Meals: Breakfast 7-9am weekdays, 8.30-10.30am weekends. Dinner & lunch in brasserie from £3.50. Dinner, 3 courses, £28.
Closed: Never.

On A422 in village of Norton between Shifnal and Bridgnorth.

Map No: 6

The Crown Hotel

Exford
Somerset
TA24 7PP

Tel: 01643 831554
Fax: 01643 831665
E-mail: info@crownhotelexmoor.co.uk
Web: www.crownhotelexmoor.co.uk

Hugo and Pamela Jeune

Entering the mildly eccentric world of Hugo and Pamela Jeune is guaranteed to be entertaining; don't be surprised to find Pamela's horse propping up the bar. This is their latest venture, following on from their success at the Rising Sun in Lynmouth. They're generous hosts, tuned in to what guests want. Pamela is a trained scientist with a big heart: "People work so hard these days, they deserve to be spoilt." Hugo wears a wry smile beneath a shock of white hair and sharpens his wits playing bridge with seasoned oldies who clout him over the head if he makes a foolish bid. The hotel is in the middle of Exmoor; unspoilt horsey country that's justly compared to the easy-going pace of rural Ireland. The building itself is Exmoor's oldest coaching inn, set in the pretty village of Exford; from the front, its angled eaves and peaking roof do look like a crown. Bedrooms are gradually being transformed - Molton Brown toiletries and other special touches are already making a difference, as is chef Gary Fisher's imaginative cooking.

Rooms: 8 doubles, 4 twins, 3 singles; 2 doubles, both with private bathroom.
Price: £95-£110; singles £47.50. Dinner B&B £70-£77.50.
Meals: Breakfast times flexible. Lunch, 3 courses, £18.50. Dinner, 3 courses, £25. Bar meals from £3.95.
Closed: Never.

M5, junc. 25, A38 to Taunton, A358 towards Minehead, then B3224 to Exford, via Wheddon Cross. Hotel by village green.

Map No: 2

Porlock Vale House

Porlock Weir
Somerset
TA24 8NY

Tel: 01643 862338
Fax: 01643 863338
E-mail: info@porlockvale.co.uk
Web: www.porlockvale.co.uk

Kim and Helen Youd

Exmoor National Park runs into the sea here, tiny lanes ramble down into lush valleys while headlands rise to meet the waves. At the hotel, spurn two feet and wheels, saddle up a horse and ride off into the sunset. Well, not quite, but this is also an exceptional riding school, so come to jump, to brush up your dressage, or to hack across the moors. All levels from beginner to Olympic medalist welcome, so don't be shy. You don't have to ride; come instead to sit out on the terrace and watch the deer eat the garden (they do), or walk down across fields and paddle in Porlock Bay. Whatever you do, you'll enjoy coming back to the simple splendour of this relaxed country house. Good, hearty food in the dining room, crackling log fires and leather sofas in the hall, books and games scattered about the place. Bedrooms are big, bright and comfortable with sofas if there's room; most have sea views and the bigger rooms are huge. Make sure you see the beautiful Edwardian stables; you may find the blacksmith at work in the yard, and the smell of polished leather in the tack room is just fantastic. Smashing people, too.

Rooms: 9 doubles, 5 twins, 1 single.
Price: £70-£105; singles £35-£85. Dinner B&B £55-£75 p.p., single £65-£85.
Meals: Breakfast 8.30-9.45am weekdays, 9-10.15am weekends. Lunch from £5. Dinner, 3 courses, £20.
Closed: Mid-week in January.

West past Minehead on A39, then right in Porlock, signed Porlock Weir. Through West Porlock, hotel signed right.

The White House

Long Street   **Tel:**   01984 632306
Williton
Somerset
TA4 4QW

Kay and Dick Smith

Jazz muscians make perfection look easy, their skills seem born from pleasure rather than hard work; so it is with the White House. Dick played double bass in a jazz band for many years before he and Kay decided to imbue a restaurant with rooms on the Somerset/Devon border with the same ethos. That was more than 30 years ago and the results have mellowed wonderfully. The downstairs bar feels beautifully marooned somewhere in the tropics, with its huge cheese plant and a bar of one single hewn lump of wood; bring your Panama hat. Across the corridor, an elegant living room with paintings, modern sofas and lots of light evokes 60s cool. They have a lovely eye for bits and bobs; the beautifully worn butcher's block at the top of the stairs is one of the nicest surprises. Bedrooms in this Georgian villa are all distinctive: the odd antique, stuffed birds, maybe a showbiz mirror in the bathroom. Best of all is the restaurant, the mellow stone walls and aged wooden tables have a seasoned warmth. Food here is exceptional - "flavours are ringingly clear and fresh" was how one reviewer described the experience. A real find.

Rooms: Main house: 3 doubles,
2 twins, all en suite; 1 double with
private bathroom; Annexe: 1 double,
1 twin, 1 single, 1 family.
Price: £84-£108; singles £49-£67.
Meals: Breakfast times flexible. Dinner,
3 courses, £34.
Closed: End of October-mid-May.

*From Bridgwater, A39 to Williton.
Entering village, house on right.*

Langley House Hotel and Restaurant

Langley Marsh
Wiveliscombe, Taunton
Somerset
TA4 2UF

Tel: 01984 623318
Fax: 01984 624573

Stuart and Sue Warnock

The entrance hall was once an alleyway between two 15th-century farm cottages. In 1720 two became one and it turned into a gentleman's residence, the gentleman being good enough to have it panelled. The atmosphere inside is warm, elegant and full of comfort. The drawing room is the highlight; wooden floors, thick rugs and scarlet walls makes it feels more like home, all visible signs of a hotel banished. Likewise the bedrooms. Some are casually grand, others cosy, but all have that old country house feel. This is the Warnocks' first excursion into hotels but they are full of enthusiasm and plan to make a real go of the place; they take over from Anne and Peter Wilson, who built up an enviable foodie reputation during 16 years at the helm. There's a garden, too, with a half-acre, walled kitchen garden where they grow as much as they can. Behind it sheep graze on the hillside and buzzards fly off to Exmoor five miles away.

Rooms: 1 four-poster, 1 family suite, 2 twin/doubles, 4 doubles.
Price: £95-£127.50; singles from £77.50.
Meals: Breakfast until 9.30am. Dinner, 3 courses, £27.50; 4 courses, £32.50.
Closed: Never.

From Taunton, B3227 to Wiveliscombe town centre, then right signed Langley Marsh. Hotel on right after 0.5 miles.

Map No: 2

Bindon Country House Hotel
Langford Budville
Wellington
Somerset
TA21 0RU

Tel: 01823 400070
Fax: 01823 400071
E-mail: stay@bindon.com
Web: www.bindon.com

Lynn and Mark Jaffa

An extraordinary, beautiful building that hides on the edge of woodland where wild flowers flourish. Four years ago this was a derelict mansion, now it is merely a mansion, thanks to Mark and Lynn who laboured long and hard to get things just right. Enter through the large glass front door and wonder at the crispness of the tiled entrance hall, the stained glass, the huge wall tapestries, the plaster-moulded ceilings, the oak galleried staircase, the glass-domed roof. Keep going into the snug panelled bar, past the wrought-iron candlesticks, for coffee served with piping hot milk and delicious home-made biscuits. In summer, the hall doors open up and you can move outside to sit by the magnificent stone balustrading and gaze out over the rose garden and down to the uninhabited dovecote. Bright bedrooms come in different sizes; two oval rooms at the front of the house are *huge*, with window seats, tremendous wallpaper, a high brass bed or a Victorian cast-iron bath. The food is gorgeous and the pool is luxuriously heated.

Rooms: 1 four-poster, 11 twin/doubles.
Price: £95-£195; singles £85. Dinner B&B from £60 p.p. (min 2 nights).
Meals: Breakfast 7.30-9.30am weekdays, 8-10am weekends. Lunch, 2 courses, £12.95. Dinner, 5 courses, £29.95.
Closed: Never.

North out of Wellington on B3187. After 1.5 miles, left at sharp S-bend, signed Langford Budville. In village, right towards Wiveliscombe, then 1st right again. House signed on right after 1.5 miles.

Glencot House
Glencot Lane
Wookey Hole, Nr. Wells
Somerset
BA5 1BH

Tel: 01749 677160
Fax: 01749 670210
E-mail: glencot@ukonline.co.uk

Jenny Attia

Jacobean elegance spills from this beautiful late-Victorian mansion into its 18-acre parkland setting. Inside, it's just as you would expect; four-poster beds, carved ceilings, walnut panelling, magical hallways filled with ancient furniture and bric-a-brac, plants and flowers everywhere. The drawing room is the magnet of the house; you'll meet the other guests here, all staring at the ceiling. The room is panelled top-to-toe with a mix of four woods and there's an inglenook fireplace the size of a room; in winter the flames leap six feet high. Hard to believe it's all en suite, with mod-cons, too. Glencot was rescued from a state of dilapidation by Jenny and her husband; long hours of toil have brought it back to life. Don't miss the garden: a magnificent terrace with stunning stone balustrade and wide, gracious steps sweeps you down to the river Axe. There are fountains too, a waterfall and an old stone bridge to take you over to the cricket pitch where the village team plays in summer. *Pets by arrangement.*

Rooms: 5 four-posters, 2 doubles, 3 twins, 3 singles.
Price: £88-£110; singles from £67.
Meals: Breakfast 7.30-9.30am weekdays, 8-9.45am weekends. Dinner, 3 courses, from £26.50. Packed lunch by arrangement.
Closed: Never.

From Wells, follow signs to Wookey Hole. Sharp left at finger post 100m after pink cottage. House on right in Glencot Lane.

Map No: 2

Little Barwick House

Barwick Village
Yeovil
Somerset
BA22 9TD

Tel: 01935 423902
Fax: 01935 420908

Emma and Tim Ford

This restaurant with rooms places real emphasis on producing superb food in a relaxed atmosphere. Emma and Tim belong to a vanguard of British hoteliers bringing depth of experience to a new-found freedom to experiment and do their own thing. Flair, bravery and masses of ability are all in evidence here, set off by a sense of vocation and commitment that seems rare these days. Step out of your car and immediately the smell of something irresistible wafts your way. They make whatever they can - marmalades, chutneys, sorbets, ice-creams, breads, shortbreads, jams - even pasta. The house isn't bad, either. Emma has blended the graceful Georgian interior with a fresh, contemporary feel, using natural colours on the walls, stripped floorboards and polished stone floors. Anything stuffy or frilly has been banished. In winter, a three-day stay is incredible value; spoil yourself at breakfast with house champagne by the glass.

Rooms: 2 twins, 4 doubles.
Price: £93-£103. Dinner, B&B from £66.50 p.p.
Meals: Breakfast times flexible. Lunch from £12.50. Dinner, 3 courses, £27.95. Restaurant closed Sunday & Monday nights.
Closed: 2 weeks in January.

From Yeovil, A37 south. Left at 1st r'bout by Red House pub. Down hill, past church, house signed left after 200m.

Map No: 2

130

The George
Norton St. Philip
Bath
Somerset
BA3 6LH

Tel: 01373 834224
Fax: 01373 834861
E-mail:
info@thegeorgeinn-nsp.co.uk
Web: www.thegeorgeinn-nsp.co.uk

David and Tania Satchell

Once an ostler would have calmed your snorting steed after its urgent canter across the Downs, directing you under the massive stone arch, across the cobbled courtyard and into the snug bar where logs crackled and wenches served ale under the darkened oak beams. The George must have been like that; today it is a luxurious inn, brilliantly converted. The building is one of Somerset's finest, a 12th-century inn in continuous use - an English record. There are 16th-century wall paintings, timber and stone everywhere, an ancient balconied corridor above the courtyard, and rear views across the cricket pitch to the church. The village street passes in front, but quietly at night, and the village, too, is handsome. Bedrooms are magnificently redone with timber reproduction beds and furniture, bare floorboards in some, plain woollen carpet in corridors, luxury in all... impeccable.

Rooms: 3 four-posters, 4 doubles, 1 twin.
Price: £80-£90; singles £60.
Meals: Breakfast until 10am. Bar meals £3.95-£7.95. Dinner, 3 courses, about £18.
Closed: Never.

From Bath, A36 south, then A366 west for 1 mile. Inn in middle of village.

Ye Olde Dog and Partridge

High Street	**Tel:** 01283 813030
Tutbury, Burton-upon-Trent	**Fax:** 01283 813178
Staffordshire	**E-mail:** info@dogandpartridge.net
DE13 9LS	**Web:** www.dogandpartridge.net
Barbara Tunnicliffe	Manager: Kerry Turner

Surely and steadily, this old coaching inn is raising the standard of accommodation in the Midlands. By introducing the odd stylish touch here and there, Barbara has gradually steered Ye Olde Dog and Partridge from 'run of the mill' to 'talk of the village' and beyond. Built in 1440, the building was converted to an inn in 1754. The most recent addition has been a stylish brasserie, with big arched mirrors, wooden floor, studded-leather chairs and a brass-topped bar; the food here provides a modern alternative to the carvery menu in the main bar. The inn's bedrooms have also received a makeover; smart fabrics, exposed wall beams, big beds and bathrooms, with chrome fittings and exposed stonework, all add character. The other rooms are in a Georgian townhouse next door; comfortable enough and in line for an upgrade, too. Five minutes' walk away is Tutbury Castle where Mary Queen of Scots was first imprisoned in England. Chatsworth House and the Peak District are a short drive.

Rooms: Inn: 6 doubles; Georgian house: 2 four-posters, 1 tester, 5 doubles, 1 twin, 3 twin/doubles, 2 family.
Price: £70-£99; singles £45-£55.
Meals: Breakfast until 7-9am weekdays, 7.45-9.45am weekends. Light lunch from £4. Dinner, 3 courses, £12-£20.
Closed: Open for food only on Christmas Day & Boxing Day.

From M1 junc. 24, A50 towards Stoke for about 20 miles, then left on A511 to Tutbury (4 miles). Inn on left in High St.

Map No: 6

The Black Lion
The Green
Long Melford
Suffolk
CO10 9DN

Tel: 01787 312356
Fax: 01787 374557
Web: www.blacklionhotel.net

Craig Jarvis

This splendid Georgian house overlooking Long Melford village green has had plenty of time to get things right. It has been a hotel since 1661, back when Oliver Cromwell's short-lived English republic was falling apart and Charles II was about to be restored to the throne. The handsome Georgian proportions came later, but little else has changed, like the village itself. New owner Craig Jarvis has turned The Black Lion into a fabulous place to stay, with a mixture of old and new that feels more country house than hotel. A range of four-poster, half-tester and Victorian brass beds give smart bedrooms an individual touch, while a cosy bar, with lovely rich colours, paintings and old leather armchairs, is an ideal tonic after a stroll round the many antique shops. The dining room is more contemporary, the pristine linen and high-backed chairs a clear indication that food is taken seriously here; it draws on European and Thai influences. Stay here for Constable country and Cambridge. *Children's toys available.*

Rooms: 7 doubles, 2 twins, 1 family.
Price: £93-£124; singles £71-£88 (not available on Friday & Saturday nights).
Meals: Breakfast until 9.30am weekdays, 10am weekends. Lunch & dinner approx. £20-£30.
Closed: Never.

Hotel on the green in Long Melford.

The Great House

Market Place
Lavenham
Suffolk
CO10 9QZ

Tel: 01787 247431
Fax: 01787 248007
E-mail: info@greathouse.co.uk
Web: www.greathouse.co.uk

Régis and Martine Crépy

A little pocket of France run by a charming couple with French staff. They have pulled off a trick rare in the UK, creating a superb hotel that feels like a home. The 18th-century front hides a 15th-century house, full of surprises and utterly lovely. Each of the bedrooms has antique desks and chests of drawers to offset the superb marble of the perfect bathrooms. Some have views over the bustling, historic market place, one has a big Jacobean oak four-poster, an island surrounded by a sea of rugs, another is a huge beamed double up in the roof with sofas and armchairs. Most rooms have their own private sitting room as well. You can't escape the beams, the fresh flowers, the sheer generosity and good taste of it all. Nowhere is this more true than in the restaurant, the very essence of France in the middle of Suffolk. The cheese board alone is a work of art; the sheer splendour of the food brings guests back again and again. Catch the early sun in the courtyard for breakfast or wait awhile and eat *al fresco* on warm and lazy summer nights. A fabulous little place.

Rooms: 5 doubles.
Price: £80-£150; singles from £55. Dinner, B&B from £62.95 p.p.
Meals: Breakfast 7.30-9.30am. Lunch from £11. Dinner from £21.95; restaurant closed Mondays.
Closed: January.

Lavenham is on A1141. The Great House is in the market place. Take Market Lane, at the corner of newsagents, signed Guildhall.

Map No: 4

The White Hart Inn

High Street
Nayland, Nr. Colchester
Suffolk
CO6 4JF

Michel Roux

Tel: 01206 263382
Fax: 01206 263638
E-mail: nayhart@aol.com
Web: www.whitehart-nayland.co.uk

Manager: Franck Deletang

Michel Roux's 'other place' is exquisite on all counts; the way things are done here is second to none. The service is remarkable, the staff fired by a sense of proud vocation - a rarity in Britain these days. The inn dates from the 15th century and has kept its timber-framed walls and beams. The inside has been opened up a bit - not so much as to remove the 'ramble', but just enough to give it a light, airy feel. Here you feast on "scrumptious food" to quote an enraptured guest, and sup from a vast collection of New World wines. "People like to travel when they drink," says Michel. Exemplary bedrooms have a striking yet simple country elegance; yellow walls and checked fabrics, crisp linen and thick blankets, beams (two have almost vaulted ceilings), piles of cushions, sofas or armchairs. The single has wonderful art, some have wildly-sloping floors and one has original murals that may be the work of Constable's brother. All have excellent bathrooms. Superb.

Rooms: 4 doubles, 1 twin/double, 1 single.
Price: £71.50; singles £66.
Meals: Breakfast 8-10am. Lunch, 2 courses from £11. Dinner, 3 courses, about £26.50. Restaurant closed Mondays.
Closed: Never.

Nayland signed right 6 miles north of Colchester on the A134 (no access from A12). Hotel in village centre.

Ravenwood Hall

Rougham Green
Bury St. Edmunds
Suffolk
IP30 9JA

Craig Jarvis

Tel: 01359 270345
Fax: 01359 270788
E-mail: enquiries@ravenwoodhall.co.uk
Web: www.ravenwoodhall.co.uk

At Ravenwood, it's easy to transport yourself back to the Tudor period and imagine the mellifluous sound of lute music drifting from a leafy bower, as courtiers in doublet and hose escort ladies of elegant persuasion through formal gardens. It was from such a gentle reverie that I awoke to the sound of ice tinkling in a crystal cut glass of gin and tonic. The scent of honeysuckle spiced the early evening air, its heavy fragrance warmed by the hot summer's day. Such pleasure. Ravenwood dates from Henry VIII's reign - the surviving oak carvings and 16th-century wall paintings are said to be national treasures - and it's surrounded by seven gorgeous acres of lawn, woodland, and fields of goats and horses. Inside, newspapers and books lie waiting to be read, there's assorted memorabilia and the oil paintings deserve closer scrutiny. It feels more family home than hotel; there's even a friendly cat. Bedrooms are clean and comfortable with some good antiques, while the more formal oak panelled restaurant has a magnificent inglenook fireplace that blazes in winter. English to a T. *Ideal for Newmarket races.*

Rooms: Main house: 6 doubles,
1 twin/double; Mews: 6 doubles,
1 twin/double.
Price: £93-£129; singles £71-£95 (not available Friday and Saturday nights).
Meals: Breakfast 7.30-9.30am weekdays, 8.30-10am weekends. Lunch & dinner in restaurant, 3 courses £28.95. Bar meals from £6.50.
Closed: Never.

From Bury St. Edmunds, A14 east for about 4 miles, then right, signed to hotel, down lane for 3 miles. Left after 30mph sign, entrance on right.

Ounce House

Northgate Street
Bury St. Edmunds
Suffolk
IP33 1HP

Tel: 01284 761779
Fax: 01284 768315
E-mail: pott@globalnet.co.uk
Web: www.ouncehouse.co.uk

Simon and Jenny Pott

An extremely handsome 1870 red-brick townhouse minutes from the heart of one of England's prettiest ancient towns. Bury St. Edmunds has a rich history; the Romans were here, its Norman abbey attracted pilgrims by the cartload, and the wool trade made it rich in the 1700s. A gentle, one-hour stroll takes you past 650 years of architectural wonder - special indeed. Ounce House is more house than hotel, pristine and full of fine antiques. Enjoy sumptuous breakfasts around a mighty-sized mahogany dining table and slump in leather armchairs around a wildly ornate carved fireplace. Light floods in all day through the double doors between the drawing room and dining room. Elsewhere, a snug library has an honesty bar, while fine, homely bedrooms are packed with books, mahogany furniture, local art and piles of magazines; the room at the back of the house has a pretty view of the garden. The Potts can arrange tickets to the local theatre, pick you up from the train station, or help you decide between the 35 restaurants within five minutes of the house. Take your pick.

Rooms: 2 doubles, 1 twin.
Price: £85-£95; singles £60-£70.
Meals: Breakfast times flexible.
Lunch & dinner available locally.
Closed: Never.

Leave A14 at northern junction for Bury St. Edmunds and follow signs to centre. At 1st r'bout, left into Northgate St. House on right at top of hill.

The Dolphin
Peace Place
Thorpeness, Nr. Aldeburgh
Suffolk
IP16 4NA

Tel: 01728 454994
Fax: 01728 454300
E-mail: info@thorpeness.co.uk
Web: www.thorpeness.co.uk

Tim Rowan-Robinson

Thorpeness is a one-off, the perfect antidote to 21st-century holidays. The village was the turn-of-century brainchild of G.S. Ogilvie, who set out to create a holiday resort for children, free of piers and promenades, with safety assured. His master stroke is the Meare - a 64-acre lake, never more than three feet deep, inspired by Ogilvie's friend, J.M. Barrie, creator of *Peter Pan*. Children can row, sail and canoe their way up creaks and discover islands that may have a lurking (wooden) crocodile round the corner. The Dolphin - in the middle of the village - is a great little inn. It has three very good bedrooms in cottage style with old pine furniture, soft colours and spotless bathrooms. Downstairs, there are two lively bars, open fires, wooden floors in the dining room and outside, a terrace and lawn for barbecues and *al fresco* dinners. Play tennis at the Country Club, there's a great golf course, an unspoilt sand and pebble beach, a summer theatre company and even a 'house in the clouds'. A paradise for families and excellent value for money.

Rooms: 3 twin/doubles.
Price: £60-£65; singles £45.
Meals: Breakfast until 9.30am weekdays, 10am weekends. Lunch & dinner, 2 courses, from £10. Packed lunch by arrangement.
Closed: Christmas Day.

From A12 at Farnham, take A1094 to Aldeburgh seafront. Turn left and follow coast road for 2 miles into Thorpeness. Inn on right, signed.

The Crown

High Street
Southwold
Suffolk
IP18 6DP

Michael Bartholomew

Tel: 01502 722275
Fax: 01502 727263
E-mail: crown.hotel@adnams.co.uk
Web: www.adnams.co.uk

"Rooted in our place, we have always been proud to do different and to do it well". Thus spake Adnams, the brewery, local owners of The Crown. Southwold is almost an island, bounded on all sides by creeks, marshes, the River Blyth and the sea. Almost unchanged for a century, it has a strong Dutch element in the brickwork of the older houses, a gleaming white lighthouse, numerous pubs and a small museum. Scores of notable figures have come here to retreat from the frenzy of the outside world; most popular of all, the Sailors' Reading Room, tiny, snug, heart-warming, nostalgic. As for The Crown, well you'll just have to come and see; pub, wine bar, restaurant and small hotel, with a terrific wine list, imaginative food and a bustling atmosphere of cheerful informality. Look in vain for poor taste. Bedrooms are small, comfortable and 'decent' - nothing over the top, but that is the hotel's mood. Perfect... as is the beer.

Rooms: 5 doubles, 3 twins, 2 family, 2 singles. 1 twin, 1 double, with private bathrooms.
Price: £82; family £100-£110; singles from £57.
Meals: Breakfast 8-10am. Light lunch in bar from £3.95. Dinner in restaurant, from £22.50-£27.50.
Closed: Never.

From A12, A1095 to Southwold.
Inn on High Street.

The Millstream Hotel and Restaurant

Bosham Lane
Bosham
Sussex
PO18 8HL

Tel: 01243 573234
Fax: 01243 573459
E-mail: info@millstream-hotel.co.uk
Web: www.millstream-hotel.co.uk

Antony Wallace

Bosham (pronounced bozzum) has a busy past: a fishing port in Roman times, the launching pad for Harold's Norman expedition and the place where King Canute got his feet wet, or so it's claimed. These days the tide really has turned and Bosham is now a very gentle, very English summer paradise for sailors, its tidal waters their playground. Half a mile from the water - if that - the Millstream has become a sanctuary for landlubbers and the occasional old sea dog who prefers the comforts of land at night. You can't blame him; the Millstream has the feel of 'the place to be'. In summer, the front garden fills with parasoled tables for cream teas. Inside, a tapestry acts as a bar shutter. There is a long, light, yellow sitting room with good comfortable furniture and a big, equally light dining room for good, well-priced food; everywhere, the sound of chatter. Bedrooms are kept fairly simple: pretty fabrics, pastel colours, comfy beds, good lighting and spotless bathrooms. Chichester Festival Theatre is close, and worth a trip. Or come and learn to sail.

Rooms: 10 twins, 17 doubles, 3 suites, 5 singles.
Price: £120-£160; singles from £75. Dinner, B&B from £60 p.p.
Meals: Breakfast until 9.30am. Lunch, 2 courses, £11.95. Dinner, 3 courses, £23.
Closed: Never.

From Chichester, A259 west through Fishbourne. At Swan r'bout, follow brown hotel signs left, then right at T-junction. Hotel on right in village.

Map No: 3

The Old Railway Station

Station Road   **Tel:** 01798 342346
Petworth   **Fax:** 01798 342346
Sussex   **E-mail:** mlr@old-station.co.uk
GU28 OJF   **Web:** www.old-station.co.uk
Lou Rapley

Without doubt the most beautiful railway station in Britain... and though disused, this is one platform where you'd be happy to wait a while; built in 1894, royalty used to pass through on their way to Goodwood. Lou has renovated immaculately, bringing back the Edwardian grandeur: stripped wooden floors, tasselled lamps, busts, writing desks, a gramophone, old black and white pictures, shuttered windows, rising ferns and a 20-foot vaulted ceiling. Breakfast in winter is accompanied by an open fire; in summer, have your bacon and eggs on the platform. The biggest problem here is deciding where to sleep. The Pullman carriages are exceptional - you almost expect to bump into Poirot - and were last used to transport the Admiralty to the Queen's coronation. Rooms in the station have tongue-and-groove walls, marble bathrooms and maybe a brass bed; all have a colonial freshness. Great food at the pub up the drive. Ideal for stressed commuters and lovers of luxury. *Children over 10 welcome. Weekends essential to book three months in advance.*

Rooms: 5 doubles, 1 twin.
Price: £84-£116; singles £62-£75.
Meals: Breakfast 8-10am. Lunch & dinner available locally.
Closed: Never.

A285 1.5 miles south of Petworth. Turn into Badgers pub forecourt, then follow drive on right down to Old Railway Station.

Bailiffscourt Hotel

Climping
Sussex
BN17 5RW

Tel: 01903 723511
Fax: 01903 723107
E-mail: bailiffscourt@hshotels.co.uk
Web: www.hshotels.co.uk

Sandy and Anne Goodman

Manager: Axel Bambach

Everything about Bailiffscourt is exhilarating. It is beautiful to the eye, the architect having searched high and low for soft, golden Somerset sandstone. The gardens and grounds are a simple paradise and as you stroll in peace from barn to coach house, you feel as if you are walking around an ancient monastery. Inside, rooms are big and have a perfect medieval atmosphere, set off brilliantly by bold colours, rich fabrics and large tapestries on the walls. There are mullioned windows, heavy, ancient beams, even an entire ceiling of wood in the restaurant. Bedrooms are perfect too, with carved four-posters, oak chests, waterfalls of cushions, 600-year-old doors, fabulous bathrooms and decanters of sherry. Best of all is the truth - Bailiffscourt, incredibly, is a 'genuine fake', built in the 1930s from innumerable medieval bits and bobs; one of the buildings was moved here brick by brick - only the 13th-century chapel is authentic. It is quite magnificent; there's even a beach at the end of the garden. Come and revel in it all.

Rooms: 31 doubles.
Price: £150-£320; singles from £135.
Meals: Breakfast 7.30-9.30am weekdays, 8-10am weekends. Lunch from £14.50. Dinner £35.
Closed: Never.

From Littlehampton, A259 west. At the brown sign for Bailiffscourt, turn left into Climping St and continue up lane to hotel.

Map No: 3

142

Sussex Arts Club

7 Ship Street
Brighton
Sussex
BN1 1AD

Tel: 01273 727371
E-mail: sxarts@hotmail.com
Web: www.sussexarts.com

Mary Sassi

"Shabbily chic, not *The Ritz,* but we loved it," said one review. A place to move at your own pace: pour a glass of orange juice, grab the papers and stretch out on the *chaise longue.* In the Singaporean Raffles-style bar, find members standing six deep at weekends - come early for the leather sofas. The nearby domed ballroom is a venue for salsa, blues, poetry, talks - and the Friday night disco. Upstairs, past the photos of luminaries who have stayed, and returned, a small theatre/conference room for the occasional production, then, ever upwards, great bedrooms. Your climb will be rewarded - choose a brass four-poster, or maybe a low-slung French bed, surrounded by marble-topped side tables, Art Deco furniture, summery colours, and thick rugs. One room has a pet seagull - on the outside - and there's the tiny *Tinker* single, too. Don't come with any pre-set notions of it being grand, think dynamic, laid-back, effortless fun. Turn right out of the front door and land on the beach, or left for strolls past antique shops in Brighton's famous Lanes.

Rooms: 1 four-poster, 5 doubles, 1 single.
Price: £80-£100; single £50.
Meals: Breakfast bar, available till noon. Lunch & dinner available nearby.
Closed: Never.

From Palace Pier, west along seafront. Ship Street is 200m on right, just after The Old Ship Hotel. Nearby car parks from £8 a day.

Ockenden Manor

Ockenden Lane
Cuckfield
Sussex
RH17 5LD

Sandy and Anne Goodman

Tel: 01444 416111
Fax: 01444 415549
E-mail: ockenden@hshotels.co.uk
Web: www.hshotels.co.uk

Manager: Kerry Turner

The first thing you notice about Ockenden is how handsome it is, with a soft sandstone grandeur, tall brick chimneys, magnolia trees and runaway lawns. Inside, the aesthetic treat continues, much of it the indirect legacy of fire as the house burnt down in 1608 and was rebuilt soon after. The oak panelling is all original, stretching from floor to ceiling in the dining room. The detail is more recent, added by Anne and Sandy: decanters of port, cut-glass crystal glasses, green leather armchairs and good prints in the bar. There's a crisp, elegant drawing room full of stunning furniture, much of it under vases of fresh flowers. Bedrooms are split between the original house and the 1990 addition, but all have a smart country house look helped along by lots more antiques and, predominantly, Colefax and Fowler and Zoffany materials. You'll find oil paintings, bathrobes in spotless bathrooms, and starched linen sheets to sleep on; some of the bedrooms are panelled. Close to Gatwick, but much more than an airport stopover.

Rooms: 6 four-posters, 11 doubles, 4 twins, 1 single.
Price: £127-£265; singles from £99.
Meals: Breakfast until 10am; Continental included, Full English £5. Lunch, 2 courses, from £10. Dinner, 3 courses, from £31.
Closed: Never.

A23 south from M23, then B2115 south-east to Cuckfield. In village, right, opposite Talbot Inn, into Ockenden Lane. Hotel signed.

Map No: 3

144

The Griffin Inn

Fletching
Nr. Uckfield
Sussex
TN22 3SS

Tel: 01825 722890
Fax: 01825 722810
Web: www.thegriffininn.co.uk

Bridget, Nigel and James Pullan

On a chilly Tuesday morning in January, the locals were queuing up outside before opening time. This is not surprising - The Griffin, voted best dining pub in Sussex, is the sort of local you'd move to the village for. Run with gentle passion by the Pullan family as a true 'local', warmed by six smouldering fires with obligatory 500-year-old beams, settles, red carpets and panelling, its sense of perfection comes from the occasional touch of scruffiness - this inn has been allowed to age. Black and white photos on the walls, a small club room for racing on Saturdays and, in summer, two cricket teams. Bedrooms are perfect, tremendous value for money and full of crisp, uncluttered country-inn elegance. You might have a free-standing Victorian bath, the shower heads are huge, there are bathrobes, rag-rolled walls, lots of old wood furniture, beams and uneven floors; rooms in the coach house are quieter. In summer jazz bands play in the garden, the backdrop being a 10-mile view across Ashdown Forest to Sheffield Park and there are spit roast barbecues, too. Wonderful.

Rooms: 7 four-posters, 1 twin.
Price: £70-£120.
Meals: Breakfast 8am-9.30am weekdays, 10am weekends. Lunch from £7. Dinner, 3 courses, £20.
Closed: Christmas Day.

From East Grinstead, A22 south. Turn right at Nutley, signed Fletching, and straight on for 2 miles into village.

Map No: 4

Stone House

Rushlake Green
Heathfield
Sussex
TN21 9QJ

Tel: 01435 830553
Fax: 01435 830726
Web: www.stonehousesussex.co.uk

Peter and Jane Dunn

One of the bedrooms has a huge en suite bathroom with enough room for a sofa and two chairs around the marble bath, but does that make it a suite? Jane thought not. The bedroom is big, has a beautiful four-poster, floods with light and, like all the rooms, has sumptuous furniture and seemingly ancient fabrics, all typical of the generosity of both house and owners. Stone House has been in the Dunn family for a mere 500 years and Peter and Jane have kept the feel of home. Downstairs, amid the splendour of the drawing room, there's still room for lots of old family photos; across the hall in the library, logs piled high wait to be tossed on the fire. Weave down a corridor to ancient oak panelling in the dining room for Jane's cooking - she's a Master Chef. Having eaten, walk out to the superb, half-acre, walled kitchen garden and see where it's all grown - they're 99% self-sufficient in summer. There are 1,000 acres to explore and you can fish for carp. Indulgent picnic hampers for Glyndebourne, including chairs and tables, are an added treat.

Rooms: 1 suite, 3 twin/doubles, 2 four-posters, 1 double/single.
Price: £100-£215; singles £65-£80.
Meals: Breakfast 8.30-9.45am. Lunch £24.95, by arrangement. Dinner £24.95.
Closed: 24 December-2 January.

From Heathfield, B2096 then 4th turning on right, signed Rushlake Green. Continue to village, then 1st left by the green. House signed to left.

Map No: 4

146

Little Hemingfold Hotel

Telham	**Tel:** 01424 774338
Battle	**Fax:** 01424 775351
Sussex	
TN33 0TT	

Allison and Paul Slater

The south east of England is much underrated in terms of rural beauty, but drive up the bumpy track that leads to Little Hemingfold and you could be miles from the middle of nowhere. People who want to get away to the simplicity of deep country will love it here. It's comfortably rustic, a little like renting a remote country cottage, though here you don't have to cook or clean, with open fires, bergère sofas and armchairs, books and games, lots of flowers and floods of light. Breakfast in the yellow dining room is under beams; at night the candles come out for delicious home-cooked dinners. The bedrooms are all over the place, some in the main house, others across the small, pretty courtyard. They are fairly earthy, four having woodburning stoves - again that feel of deep country - with a four-poster perhaps, maybe a sofa, glazed-brick walls and simple bathrooms. Outside, a two-acre lake to row and fish or swim in, a grass tennis court - the moles got the better of the croquet lawn - woodland to walk in and lots of peace and quiet.

Rooms: 10 twin/doubles; 2 family with private bathroom.
Price: £84-£95; singles £42-£77. Dinner, B&B £58-£97.50 p.p.
Meals: Breakfast 8.30-9.30am. Dinner, 4 courses, £24.50.
Closed: 2 January-15 February.

From Battle, A2100 towards Hastings for 1.5 miles. Hotel signed left by 'sharp left' road sign, 0.5 miles up farm track.

Jeake's House
Mermaid Street
Rye
Sussex
TN31 7ET

Tel: 01797 222828
Fax: 01797 222623
E-mail:
jeakeshouse@btinternet.com

Jenny Hadfield

Rye, one of the Cinque Ports, is a perfect town for whiling away an afternoon; wander aimlessly and you'll come across the tidal river, old fishing boats, arts and crafts shops and galleries. Jeake's House is hidden away at the top of the hill - the heart of old Rye - on an ancient cobbled street. The house has a colourful past as wool store, school and home of American poet Conrad Potter Aiken. The dining room is an old Baptist chapel, now painted deep red and full of plants, busts, books, clocks and mirrors. It is galleried and you can make a grand entrance, walking down for breakfast. Jenny is engagingly easy-going and has created a lovely atmosphere. Rooms are pretty, not fussy, with good furniture and all are excellent value. There are old four-posters and a big attic room up a mind-your-head stairway, beams and timber frames and views over roof tops and chimneys to open country. Downstairs, there's a small library for rainy days and a fire in the hearth in winter. A super little hotel. *Children over 12 welcome.*

Rooms: 10 doubles, 1 honeymoon suite; 1 double, 1 single, sharing bathroom.
Price: £63-£103; singles £31.50-£65.
Meals: Breakfast 8-9.30am, 8.30-10am Sundays. Lunch & dinner available locally.
Closed: Never.

Entering Rye, follow 'Town Centre' signs under arch into High St, then 3rd left at Lloyds Bank and 1st right into Mermaid St. House on left, signed. Private parking nearby, £3 a day.

The Howard Arms

Lower Green
Ilmington
Warwickshire
CV36 4LT
Robert and Gill Greenstock

Tel: 01608 682226
Fax: 01608 682226
E-mail: howard.arms@virgin.net
Web: www.howardarms.com

Once upon a time Robert and Gill ran the Cotswold House Hotel in Chipping Campden with a mix of flair, quirkiness and professionalism. After a deserved sabbatical, they cast their fairy dust over The Howard, with magical results. The place buzzes with good-humoured babble, well-kept beer pours from a genial, flagstoned bar and an irresistible dining room at the far end has unexpected elegance for a pub, with great swathes of bold colour and some noble paintings. Gorgeous bedrooms are set discreetly apart from the joyful throng, blending period style and modern luxury beautifully; the double oozes old world charm, the twin is more folksy, with American art and patchwork quilts, while the half-tester is almost a mini-suite, full of classy antiques; all are individual, all are huge by pub standards. The village is a surprise, too, literally tucked under a lone hill, with an unusual church surrounded by an extended village green and orchards. Spend the day walking to the buzzing of bees, then retire to The Howard - people come from afar to sample the food, which changes weekly. The theatre at Stratford beckons, too.

Rooms: 1 twin, 1 double, 1 half-tester.
Price: £74-£84; singles from £45.
Meals: Breakfast 8.30-9.30am. Lunch & supper £7-£19.
Closed: Christmas Day.

*From Moreton-in-Marsh, north on A429 for about 5 miles, then left, signed Darlingscott and Ilmington.
Pub in village centre.*

Map No: 3

The Fox and Goose

Armscote
Nr. Stratford-upon-Avon
Warwickshire
CV37 8DD

Tel: 01608 682293
Fax: 01608 682293
Web: www.foxandgoose.co.uk

Sue Gray

Sue is one of those irrepressible innkeepers with an instinctive feel for what works. She took on a pub that had seen better days, stripped it back to its walls, pulled up the carpets, put in earthy wooden floors, then coated the walls with Farrow and Ball paints. The whole place is fresh, informal, vibrant - a 'happening' place. Purple, crushed velvet stools in the stone-flagged bar, shutters on all the windows, an open fire and woodburner, and heavy oak beams - fixtures and fittings from the 17th century, blended with 21st-century style. She also added an excellent dining room for food that's "not too fancy, but very well cooked" - maybe Thai chicken, rib-eye steaks or home-made pasta; on Sundays take your pick from goose, beef and lamb, all roasted to perfection. Bedrooms above the restaurant are spectacular, though fairly compact. Big, comfy beds have 'jester hat' padded headboards; there are bold colours - blues, reds and yellows - stripped wooden floors and CD players. Grab a disc from reception, light the candles in the bathroom, fill the tub, take in your glass of wine...

Rooms: 4 doubles.
Price: £80; singles £40.
Meals: Breakfast 8.30am-midday.
Lunch & dinner £4.50-£25.
Closed: Christmas Day & New Year's Day.

From Stratford-upon-Avon, A3400 south for 8 miles, then right for Armscote just after Newbold-on-Stour. In village.

The Red Lion

High Street
Lacock
Wiltshire
SN15 2LQ

Tel: 01249 730456
Fax: 01249 730766

Chris and Sarah Chappell

Lacock, built around the 13th-century abbey, is a beautifully preserved National Trust village; when the BBC filmed part of *Pride and Prejudice* here, the dashing Mr Darcy was sensible enough to stop at The Red Lion for refreshments. The inn dates from the early 1700s and is beamed and airy, with big open fires and tankards that hang from the bar. There are rugs on stone flagging in one bar, bare wood floors in the other, so take your pick, order a drink and sit down to some fine home-cooked food, amid timber frames, old settles and hanging Victorian birdcages. In summer, eat outside in the garden, with country views towards the abbey. Climb the shallow tread of the stairs to excellent bedrooms with a Georgian style: old oak dressers, half-testers, crowns above beds, antique furniture, a beam or two. Breakfast - the full Wiltshire - is eaten in a pretty, first-floor room that looks out onto the High Street.

Rooms: 3 doubles, 1 twin.
Price: £65-£75; singles from £45.
Meals: Breakfast 8-8.30am weekdays, 9-9.30am weekends. Lunch from £6. Dinner, 3 courses, about £15.
Closed: Never.

Lacock is signed just off A350 between Chippenham and Melksham. Inn on High Street.

The Compasses Inn

Lower Chicksgrove
Tisbury
Wiltshire
SP3 6NB

Tel: 01722 714318
Fax: 01722 714318

Jon and Caren Bold

Your first impression is of having arrived at the perfect English pub; so is the second impression. The setting is almost over-the-top: crinkly-roaded village of thatched cottages and beamed walls. The pub seems to have settled into the ground, bedroom windows peering just above the lawn. You instinctively duck into the sudden darkness of the bar, to have your nostalgia nourished by a long wooden room, flagstones, cubicles, piano, fireplace - the works. Jon and Caren are fresher and more modern than their pub, and are a charming counterpoint to the suitably dark and cosy interior. Bedrooms are as perfect as the pub, each leading off an attractive, carpeted lobby and furnished simply, properly, cosily. Pine beds, coloured duvets, plain carpets, nothing grand and nothing ugly. Beyond the windows is the sweet serenity of Wiltshire. And the food is far better than you'd expect of a pub. Modest, ineffably pretty, and great value.

Rooms: 3 doubles, 1 twin.
Price: £55; singles £40.
Meals: Breakfast times flexible. Lunch & dinner £3-£25.
Closed: Restaurant closed Sundays. Bar and restaurant closed on Mondays.

From Salisbury, A30 west, 3rd right after Fovant, signed Lower Chicksgrove, then 1st left down single track road to village.

Map No: 2

Howard's House

Teffont Evias
Nr. Salisbury
Wiltshire
SP3 5RJ

Paul Firmin

Tel: 01722 716392 or 716821
Fax: 01722 716820
E-mail: paul.firmin@virgin.net
Web: www.howardshousehotel.co.uk

Howard's House has the ingredients of an English idyll: a quiet village, gently rising hills, a soaring church spire and the occasional splutter of a tractor; it's the last house in the village, with one toe in deep country. It's as English inside with a stone-flagged hall, stone-mullioned windows, open fires in winter, the scent of flowers from the garden in summer. There's masses of space - *no* clutter in this house - and every room seems to be swimming in light. The style is of elegant simplicity: warm pastel colours in all the rooms with a sprinkling of good floral fabrics and lots of fresh flowers. The bedrooms are faultless, bright and crisp, with fresh fruit and home-made biscuits, bathrobes and big, white towels. Some have views of the garden - more English perfection - which stretches out past terrace, fountain and croquet pitch to fields and hills beyond. It's all utterly immaculate as is the lauded modern British cooking. The sort of place where the sun shines, even in January.

Rooms: 1 four-poster, 1 twin/double, 1 family, 6 doubles.
Price: £135-£155; singles from £85.
Meals: Breakfast until 10am. Dinner, 3 courses, £19.95. A la carte from £24.95.
Closed: Occasionally.

A350, then B3089 east to Teffont. Turn right at sharp left-hand bend in village, following brown hotel sign. Hotel on right after 0.5 miles.

Map No: 2

The Mill at Harvington

Anchor Lane
Harvington, Evesham
Worcestershire
WR11 5NR

Tel: 01386 870688
Fax: 01386 870688
E-mail: millatharvington@aol.com

Simon and Jane Greenhalgh

Not a bad house for a miller; he baked Birmingham's bread until 1898 when the river froze over, breaking the mill's waterwheels, a fate from which it never recovered. But he left a legacy: Russian pine beams - imported for the great weight they could support - with shipping marks branded in Cyrillic. The house dates from the 1700s though you enter through the 'Chestnut Tree', a bright 1990s addition with glass walls and a trim wooden roof. Like the rest of the house, it looks out onto the huge lawned garden that runs down to the river Avon. In summer, a liberal sprinkle of parasoled tables; pick one up and plonk it wherever you like, then sit back and watch canal boats chug by. Alternatively, sink into deep sofas in the sitting room or hang your head out of one of the bedroom windows - they all look 'the right way'. Rooms are "comfortable, not luxurious" says Simon, who always wears a bow-tie; good fabrics, drapes and king-size beds prove his point. *Children over 10 welcome.*

Rooms: 5 twins, 16 doubles.
Price: £86-£121.
Meals: Breakfast until 9.30am. Dinner, 3 courses, £23. Light lunch also available.
Closed: 24-29 December.

A46 north of Evesham, then B4088 to Norton. In village, right, signed Bidford. After 1.5 miles, hotel signed right over bridge. Drive on left after about half a mile.

The Weavers Shed
Knowl Road
Golcar, Huddersfield
Yorkshire
HD7 4AN

Tel: 01484 654284
Fax: 01484 650980
E-mail: stephen@weavers-shed.demon.co.uk

Stephen and Tracy Jackson

Stephen's reputation for producing sublime food goes from strength to strength at The Weavers Shed, a restaurant with rooms firmly fixed on the wish lists of foodies all over the country. His passion stretches as far as planting a one-acre kitchen garden; it now provides most of his vegetables, herbs and fruit. You may get warm mousse of scallops, Lunesdale duckling and warm rhubarb tartlet, the latter home-grown, of course. The old mill owner's house sits at the top of the hill, with cobbles in the courtyard and its own lamp post by the door. Inside, whitewashed walls are speckled with menus from famous restaurants, a small garden basks beyond the windows and, at the bar, malts and eaux de vie stand behind a piece of wood that look as if it came from an ancient church, but actually came from the Co-op. Earthy stone arches and plinths in the Sardinian-tiled restaurant at the back give the feel of a Tuscan farmhouse. Elsewhere, gilt mirrors and comfy sofas and big, bright, brilliantly priced bedrooms that hit the spot with complimentary sherry, dried flowers, bathrobes and wicker chairs.

Rooms: 1 four-poster, 3 doubles, 1 twin/double.
Price: £60-£70; singles from £45.
Meals: Breakfast 7-9am weekdays, 8-10am weekends. Lunch (Tues-Fri) from £9.95. Dinner (Tues-Sat) about £25.
Closed: Christmas & New Year.

From Huddersfield, A62 west for 2 miles, then right, signed Milnsbridge and Golcar. Left at Kwiksave, signed on right at top of hill.

Weaver's
15 West Lane
Haworth
Yorkshire
BD22 8DU

Tel: 01535 643822
Fax: 01535 644832
E-mail: weavers@amserve.net
Web: www.weaversmallhotel.co.uk

Colin and Jane Rushworth

If you don't know what a Clun or a Lonk is, use it as an excuse to make a trip to this unusual restaurant with rooms - the answer is somewhere on the walls. There's a rambling eccentricity downstairs, where nothing has a place, but everything is exactly where it should be. The front bar is intimate and has the feel of an old French café with heavy wood, marble-topped tables, atmospheric lighting and comfy chairs. The lively restaurant at the back is where Jane, who cooks, serves the best and most unpretentious food imaginable; maybe smoked haddock soup, Pennine meat-and-potato pie and home-made ice cream. The value is outstanding and people come back time and again. Bedrooms upstairs are just as surprising and ooze more understated originality: French beds, dashes of bright colour, the odd bust and antique furniture - everything seems just right. Rooms at the back overlook the Brontë Parsonage. Colin runs front of house and is a real Yorkshire character: straight-talking, down-to-earth, with a good sense of humour. Worth a long detour.

Rooms: 2 twin/doubles, 1 single, all with private bathrooms.
Price: £75; singles £50.
Meals: Breakfast 7.30-9.30am. Set menus £10.50-£15.50; à la carte to £25; bar suppers about £12.50. Restaurant closed Sundays & Mondays.
Closed: 2 weeks after Christmas & 1 week in June.

From A629, B6142 to Haworth. Follow Brontë Parsonage Museum signs. Use their car park; Weaver's backs onto it. Ignore signs for Brontë village.

Map No: 6

The Red Lion

By the Bridge at Burnsall
Nr. Skipton
Yorkshire
BD23 6BU

Tel: 01756 720204
Fax: 01756 720292
E-mail: redlion@daelnet.co.uk
Web: www.redlion.co.uk

Elizabeth and Andrew Grayshon

This old-fashioned inn mixes old-world charm and fun - even the ghost in the 12th-century cellars has a sense of humour, occasionally turning the beer taps off. The Red Lion is an inn for all ages; the sitting room, with cosy old armchairs and sofas and a woodburning stove, is strewn with both guide books and children's books. Family-friendly and family run, son-in-law Jim cooks seriously good food, while Elizabeth keeps a matriarchal eye on things. The net result is a cosy, unpretentious inn, thoroughly comfortable, humming with happy locals. Bedrooms in the main building have beams and slanting, low ceilings, while rooms in the next door annexe are larger; one has an open fire and a big brass bed, and the family rooms have highchairs and baby listeners. This was originally a ferryman's inn. Now the river runs wide and shallow under the bridge, through an English landscape of great beauty, and past a sleepy village. The Burnsall fell race in August - eight minutes up, four minutes down - starts outside the front door.

Rooms: 4 twin/doubles, 5 doubles, 1 family, 1 single,
Price: £95-£120; singles from £47.50. Dinner, B&B from £70 p.p.
Meals: Breakfast until 9.30am. Dinner in restaurant, £24.95. Bar meals from £7.50.
Closed: Never.

From Harrogate, A59 west to Bolton Bridge, then B6160 to Burnsall. Hotel next to bridge.

Map No: 6

The Devonshire Fell

Burnsall
Yorkshire
BD23 6BT

Tel: 01756 729000
Fax: 01756 729009
E-mail: sales@thedevonshirearms.co.uk
Web: www.devonshirefell.com

Manager: Sarah Graham-Harrison

Devonshire Fell doesn't do indifference; it provokes a reaction the moment you enter. From the outside, it looks every bit the sober Victorian hotel for travelling gentlemen as originally intended and you walk in, expecting solid Yorkshire décor. Instead, you're plunged into colour, as if a rainbow has been let loose indoors - mauve walls, vivid modern art, shocking pink armchairs, wicker chairs of various tones. Pick your favourite colour and settle in. The pine-floored bar leads to a smart modern bistro in a light, sunny conservatory, with Poole pottery and Hockney paintings. Those who love colour will also enjoy the bedrooms. They're pure doll's house and lots of fun; the showers even sprinkle you with soft rainwater from the Yorkshire Dales. The hotel's signature is a goldfish cistern in the ladies toilet, while the gents has a ceiling-to-floor waterfall that springs to life as you approach. This unexpected shrine to modernity is a joint collaboration between the Marquis and Marchioness of Hartington, owners of the Devonshire estate; he supplied the paintings and she chose the interior. An unexpected one-off.

Rooms: 2 suites, 6 twin/doubles, 4 doubles.
Price: £110-£140; singles £70-£90.
Meals: Breakfast until 9.30am weekdays, until 10am weekends. Lunch, set menu, 3 courses, £15.95. Bar meals from £1.75. Dinner, à la carte, 3 courses from £24.75.
Closed: Never.

From Harrogate, A59 west for about 15 miles, then right onto B6160, signed Burnsall and Bolton Abbey. Hotel in village.

Map No: 6

The Boar's Head Hotel

Ripley Castle Estate
Harrogate
Yorkshire
HG3 3AY

Tel: 01423 771888
Fax: 01423 771509
E-mail: reservations@boarsheadripley.co.uk
Web: www.ripleycastle.co.uk

Sir Thomas and Lady Emma Ingilby

When the Ingilbys decided to reopen The Boar's Head, the attic at the castle got a shakedown and the spare furniture was sent round. The vicar even came to bless the beer taps - you'll find them in Boris' bar, Boris being the eponymous head. Elegant fun is the net result and there's something for everyone. The décor has been brilliantly created by Lady Ingilby. The sitting rooms and hall have crisp yellow Regency wallpaper, big old oils, roaring fires and gilt mirrors. The restaurant is a deep, moody crimson, candlelit at night, and you drink from blue glass. There are games, newspapers to peruse, menus to drool over and a parasoled garden for summer drinks. Up the staircase, past more ancestors, bright bedrooms have delicate floral fabrics, flowers and maybe a sofa, some antique furniture, tumbling crowns above big beds or a rag-rolled bathroom. In the coachman's loft in the courtyard you'll find the odd beam and pretty pine panelling. You can visit the castle gardens as a guest of the hotel; there are umbrellas and wellies for rainy days, too.

Rooms: 21 twin/king doubles, 4 doubles.
Price: £120; singles £99-£120. Dinner B&B £80 p.p. (minimum 2 nights); singles £100.
Meals: Breakfast 7.30-9.30am. Dinner, 3 courses, £27.50-£35. Bistro main courses from £6.95.
Closed: Never.

North from Harrogate on A61. Ripley signed, left at r'bout after 3 miles.

The Abbey Inn

Byland Abbey
Coxwold
Yorkshire
YO61 4BD

Tel: 01347 868204
Fax: 01347 868678
E-mail: jane@nordli.freeserve.co.uk
Web: www.bylandabbeyinn.co.uk

Jane and Martin Nordli

The monks of Ampleforth who built this farmhouse would surely approve of its current devotion to good food; whether they'd be as accepting of its unashamed devotion to luxury is another matter. But one monk's frown is another man's path to righteousness. The Abbey is a delightful oasis next to a ruined 12th-century abbey - lit up at night – that indulges the senses. They measure success in smiles up here; Jane loves to see the look on people's faces as they enter the Piggery restaurant, a big flagstoned space lit by a skylight, full of Jacobean-style chairs and antique tables, that demands your joyful attention. Bedrooms are jaw-dropping, too. *Abbot's Retreat* has a huge four-poster while a bust of Julius Caesar in the gorgeous black- and white-tiled bathroom strikes a nice, decadent note - order a bottle of bubbly and jump in the double-ended bath. *Priors Lynn* has the best view - right down the aisle of the abbey; all have bathrobes, aromatherapy oils, fruit, home-made biscuits and a "treasure chest" of wine. Come and enjoy it all.

Rooms: 3 doubles.
Price: £70-£110.
Meals: Breakfast until 10am. Dinner, à la carte, 2 courses from £11.50. Light lunch available. Restaurant closed Sunday nights & Monday lunchtimes.
Closed: Never.

From A1, junc. 49, A168 towards Thirsk for about 10 miles, then A19 towards York at r'bout. Left after 2 miles, signed Coxwold. Left in village, signed Byland Abbey. Inn opposite abbey.

The Yorke Arms

Ramsgill-in-Nidderdale
Nr. Harrogate
Yorkshire
HG3 5RL

Tel: 01423 755243
Fax: 01423 755330
E-mail: enquiries@yorke-arms.co.uk
Web: www.yorke-arms.co.uk

Bill and Frances Atkins

It takes a lot of nous to establish one of the best restaurants in Britain, let alone up a small country lane in the middle of the Yorkshire Dales, but Bill and Frances have really made their mark. The Yorke Arms is near perfection; exquisite food, wonderful rooms and beautiful countryside make it irresistible. The oldest part was built by monks in the 11th century, the rest added in 1750 when it became a coaching inn. Inside is absolutely charming, with polished flagstone floors, low oak beams, comfy armchairs, open fires and antique tables; in summer, eat under a pergola to the sound of a burbling beck. Classy rooms upstairs continue the theme; attention to detail guaranteed. Bill's affable nature makes him a natural front of house, while Frances scintillates the palette in the kitchen, using fish from the east and west coasts and meat and game from the Dales. Wander from the hamlet of Ramsgill to nearby Gouthwaite reservoir; formed during the Industrial Revolution to supply the city of Bradford with water, or work up an appetite visiting Brimham Rocks, or Stump Cross caverns. *Kennels for pets £5 per night.*

Rooms: 7 doubles, 4 twin/doubles, 3 singles.
Price: Dinner B&B £85-£105 p.p. Higher rate for single Saturday bookings.
Meals: Breakfast 8-9am, later by arrangement. Lunch & dinner, 3 courses, about £25-£30; restaurant closed to non-residents on Sunday evenings.
Closed: Occasionally in February & November.

From Ripley, B6165 to Pateley Bridge. Over bridge at bottom of High St, then right into Low Wath Rd to Ramsgill (about 4 miles).

Map No: 6

The Blue Lion

East Witton
Nr. Leyburn
Yorkshire
DL8 4SN
Paul and Helen Klein

Tel: 01969 624273
Fax: 01969 624189
E-mail: bluelion@breathemail.net
Web: www.bluelion.co.uk

The Blue Lion is one of those names that follow you round a county, with everyone asking if you've been there. There's good reason for this - the superlative food served in this dreamy inn have made it a favourite with locals. Paul and Helen came here 10 years ago, mixing the traditions of a country pub with the elegance of a country house. Aproned staff, polished beer taps, stone-flagged floors and smouldering fires. In the bar, newspapers hang on poles and there are big settles to sit at, while huge bunches of dried flowers hang from beams and splashes of flowers erupt from vases. The two restaurants have boarded floors and shuttered Georgian windows, two coal fires, gilt mirrors and candles everywhere. Bedrooms are split between the main house - comfortable rather than luxurious, with dashes of colour, big padded headboards and wooden beds - and the stables - exposed beams, old pine furniture, regal colours and maybe a brass bed. A place to come for a spot of indulgence. Jervaulx Abbey is a mile away.

Rooms: 9 doubles, 2 twins, 1 family.
Price: £69-£89; singles £54.
Meals: Breakfast 8-10am. Bar meals from £7. Dinner, 3 courses, about £25.
Closed: Never.

East Witton is 3 miles south of Leyburn on A6108. Inn in village.

Simonstone Hall

Hawes
Yorkshire
DL8 3LY

Tel: 01969 667255
Fax: 01969 667741
E-mail: e-mail@simonstonehall.demon.co.uk
Web: www.simonstonehall.com

Manager: Jill Peterson

Drool over the picture of Simonstone, knowing it's just as good inside. This is a glorious country house, built in the 1770s as a shooting lodge for the Earl of Wharncliffe. The drawing room is magnificent - gracious and elegant - with a wildly ornate fireplace, painted panelled walls and a flurry of antiques. Its triumph is the huge stone-mullioned window through which Wensleydale unravels - a place to stand rooted to the spot. Elsewhere, find stone-flagged floors, stained-glass windows and old oils and trophies. There's a big warm traditional bar - almost a pub - with hanging fishing nets, clocks and mirrors, and if you don't want to eat in the panelled dining room, have excellent bar meals here. Bedrooms are superb. It's well worth splashing out and going for the grander ones - they indulge you completely: four-posters, mullioned windows, stone fireplaces, oils - the full aristocratic Monty. Even have breakfast on the terrace with those fabulous views.

Rooms: 2 suites, 7 doubles,
4 twin/doubles, 5 four-posters.
Price: £90-£180; four-posters £200;
singles from £60.
Meals: Breakfast 8.30-10am.
Lunch & dinner £5-£25.
Closed: Never.

From Hawes, follow signs north for Muker for about 2 miles. Hotel on left, at foot of Buttertubs Pass.

Map No: 6

Wales

The afternoon can know
what the morning never suspected.

Swedish proverb

Windsor Lodge

Mount Pleasant
Swansea
SA1 6EG

Tel: 01792 642158
Fax: 01792 648996
Web: www.windsor-lodge.co.uk

Ron and Pam Rumble

Windsor Lodge's brochure shows a smiling former US president Jimmy Carter, enjoying himself in the dining room; just one of the many known faces this fabulous and unexpected treasure in the heart of Swansea has attracted over the years. They come because Pat and Ron know how to look after you. She is an absolute sweetie and he has the flamboyance of someone who loves competing in classic car rallies. The hotel's highlight is the drawing room; you're surrounded by lovebirds on hand-blocked wallpaper that looks as good as the day it was hung more than two decades ago; a black and white David Hicks carpet, comfy sofas, a gilded mirror, wooden blinds and fresh lilies complete the Art Deco feel, which spills into a nearby bar. An intimate dining room is full of stylish prints vying for space; the food is excellent. Bedrooms vary from large and elegant to small and quirky, all with lovely tiled bathrooms – the curious should ask to see the amazing "cockpit" bath. Carry on up the hill to the Gower Peninsula, one of Wales' best-kept secrets.

Rooms: 9 doubles, 1 twin, 1 family, 8 singles.
Price: £60-£68; singles £49.50-£60.
Meals: Breakfast 7-11am. Dinner, 3 courses, £20-£25. Lunch & packed lunch by arrangement.
Closed: Christmas Day & Boxing Day.

From M4, junc. 42, A483 into city centre, right after Sainsbury's, up Wind St, past Argos, left at railway station, right at 2nd set of traffic lights. Hotel up hill on left. Parking.

Map No: 1

Penally Abbey

Penally
Nr. Tenby
Pembrokeshire
SA70 7PY

Tel: 01834 843033
Fax: 01834 844714
E-mail: info@penally-abbey.com
Web: www.penally-abbey.com

Steve and Elleen Warren

It's not often a hotel exceeds your expectations, but then there aren't many places like Penally. It's not a grand hotel and doesn't pretend to be. It just does well the simple things that make a stay memorable. Steve's gentle, unflappable manner suits front of house: chatting to guests one minute, taking orders and mixing a drink at a small bar the next - he makes it look so easy. There's an unhurried charm about the whole place. You won't feel rushed into doing anything. The building is a former 1790s abbey; there's also a ruined 13th-century church called St. Diniel's, suggesting even earlier roots – and lit up at night. A beautiful garden looks across Carmarthen Bay; the beach is a 10-minute walk and great for pebble collectors - beautiful coastal walks lead from here. Bedrooms are all different; most in the main house have gorgeous four-posters and antiques, while those in the Tuscan-style coachhouse are more cottagey. Elleen cooks in a self-taught French style, much of it picked up in the kitchen of a French château many years back. The Tenby sea bass was exquisite.

Rooms: 8 four-posters, 3 doubles, 1 twin.
Price: £112-£136. Singles £98. Dinner B&B £86-126 p.p. Special winter rates available.
Meals: Breakfast 8.30-10am. Dinner, 3 courses, £28. Lunch by arrangement.
Closed: Never.

From Tenby, A4139 towards Pembroke. Right into Penally after 1.5 miles. Hotel signed at village green. Train station 5 mins walk.

Cnapan

East Street
Newport
Pembrokeshire
SA42 0SY

Tel: 01239 820575
Fax: 01239 820878
E-mail: cnapan@online-holidays.net
Web: www.online-holidays.net/cnapan/

John and Elund Lloyd, Michael and Judith Cooper

The welcome is immediate and wonderful - you'll feel like an old friend by the time you've walked through the front door; locals love it here too. Michael and Judith were on duty the Saturday afternoon I arrived up to their eyeballs supervising a *cawl* lunch to raise money for the twinning committee, but they still made me feel my arrival was the best thing to have happened to them all day. Michael answered the door with a big welcoming smile and, immediately, Judith pulled her hands out of a mixing bowl in the kitchen, gave them a wipe and came over to shake my hand. The house has all you'll need to feel comfortable and cosseted: bright rooms and lots of books, fresh flowers, traditional stone walls and pine dressers. And sea views to boot. Bedrooms are homely without a whisper of bad taste. "It's only our house - you can take it or leave it," said Judith. We recommend you take it.

Rooms: 1 family, 1 double, 3 twins.
Price: £62; singles £38.
Meals: Breakfast 8.30-9.30am. Lunch (high season only) from £6.50. Dinner, 3 courses, £20. Restaurant closed Tuesday nights, Easter-October.
Closed: January & February.

Newport on A487 between Fishguard and Cardigan. Cnapan 1st pink house on right coming from north.

Map No: 1

Three Main Street

Fishguard
Pembrokeshire
SA65 9HG

Tel: 01348 874275
Fax: 01348 874017

Inez Ford and Marion Evans

A beautiful Georgian townhouse, a restaurant with rooms and less than a minute's walk from Fishguard's market square. Marion and Inez have made a bit of a splash in Wales building up a reputation for sublime food and the style and generosity of spirit with which they serve it. Rugs and stripped wooden floors, candles, hand written menus and classical music or jazz all combine to give a warm and relaxed, slightly bohemian feel to the place. Big bedrooms have a hint of Art Deco and are homely with fresh flowers, rugs, sofas, good furniture, maybe a walnut bed. The whole place is extremely comfortable - superb value for money - but the pounding heart of Three Main Street is the kitchen whence comes exceptional food. Inez makes the pastries and puddings while Marion looks after the starters and main courses - maybe baked goats cheese on toasted *brioche*, sea bass baked with garlic, chilled lemon and lime soufflé. Take to the nearby coastal path and walk off your sin amid the divine Welsh landscape. Day trips to Ireland are also possible; it's only an hour and a half away by Sea Lynx.

Rooms: 2 doubles, 1 twin.
Price: £65-£75; singles £50.
Meals: Breakfast 8-10am. Lunch, Easter-October, £10. Dinner, 2 courses, £24; 3 courses, £30.
Closed: February. Restaurant closed Sundays & Mondays.

Main Street runs off town square in town centre. All roads lead to it.

Map No: 1

167

Conrah Country House

Chancery
Aberystwyth
Ceredigion
SY23 4DF
Pat and John Heading

Tel: 01970 617941
Fax: 01970 624546
E-mail: enquiries@conrah.co.uk
Web: www.conrah.co.uk

The Conrah is very much a family affair. Pat and John have been here more than 20 years and in that time their son Paul and their daughter Sarah have literally grown into the business, too. This delightful hotel is known throughout Wales for the warmth of its welcome – they had just won another award when I visited, and long may it continue. Arrive down a leafy avenue that opens into a view north across fields towards Cader Idris and Snowdonia. The ha-ha or raised terrace at the front is the longest in Wales; designed to stop livestock ruining the lawn without interrupting the view, it's also the likely reaction to seeing someone walk off it by accident. The house is Edwardian, built in 1911 after a fire destroyed the original Georgian mansion. Rooms in the main house are comfortable and enjoy the view, but for something really special try the three terrific new courtyard rooms; bold, beamed and full of style, with tantalising glimpses of the garden, you almost feel in a different hotel. The more energetic can follow footpaths to the sea; far enough to work up an appetite for the menu - award-winning, of course.

Rooms: Main house: 6 doubles, 4 twins, 1 single; Magnolia courtyard: 2 doubles, 1 twin.
Price: from £110-£140; singles £70-£85. Dinner B&B £85-£100 p.p. (minimum 2 nights).
Meals: Breakfast until 9.30am. Lunch, à la carte, from £3.75. Dinner, 2 courses £24; 3 courses £27.
Closed: 2 weeks at Christmas.

From Aberystwyth, A487 south towards Cardigan for 3 miles. Hotel signed on right.

The Bell at Skenfrith
Skenfrith
Monmouthshire
NP7 8UH

Tel: 01600 750235
Fax: 01600 750525
E-mail:
enquiries@thebellatskenfrith.com
Web: www.thebellatskenfrith.com

William and Janet Hutchings

Indulge all the senses at this swish gastro-pub on the Welsh-English border. Follow remote country lanes to a blissful village setting, with a ruined Norman castle and a meandering river, crossed by an old hump-backed bridge. Lie back on a grassy riverbank outside this old fishing inn and just take it all in. Inside is smartly done, but run with warmth - Janet treats staff like members of the family. Expect the best of everything - coffee comes from an authentic cappuccino machine, food is mostly organic and the wine - superb. William got the first issue of Decanter magazine for his 11th birthday, so be adventurous and ask his advice. Bedrooms are luxurious, with piqué bed linen, Jura limestone, Farrow and Ball colours, home-made biscuits, fresh flowers and a hi-tech console by the bed which lets you listen to music in the bath. Fully refreshed, drink at a long bar, or flop in a big sofa next to a blazing fire. Eat in an elegant, formal dining room, with linen napkins and sparkling wine glasses, or at wooden tables in the bar, looking onto the garden terrace. Toast the occasion with perry, English 'champagne' and much underrated.

Rooms: 2 four-posters, 2 attic suites (twin), 3 doubles, 1 twin.
Price: £85-£140; singles from £65.
Meals: Breakfast times flexible. Bar lunch, 2 courses, from £12. Packed lunch from £5. Cream tea £3.95. Dinner, 2-3 courses, £25-£30.
Closed: Never.

From Monmouth, B4233 to Rockfield, then B4347 for 5 miles; right on B4521, signed Ross-on-Wye. Skenfrith 1 mile. Inn on right before bridge.

Map No: 2

169

Llanthony Priory

Llanthony
Abergavenny
Monmouthshire
NP7 7NN

Tel: 01873 890487
Fax: 01873 890844
Web: www.llanthony.co.uk/abbey

Ivor and Noreen Prentice

Llathony is a remarkable place, a heady historical mix of religion, brigands, orgies, monastic endeavour and home-brewed beer; its history even tells of a repentant knight who never removed his armour once he'd set eyes on this enchanting place. It lies in the beautiful Vale of Ewyes (pronounced 'Uis'), hidden up a twisting single track road. Stand in the once-cloistered courtyard and wonder at the sagas that have shaped it since the 6th century; the magnificent ruined Augustinian Priory alone took over half a century to build (1175-1230). The long dining room was formerly the prior's outer parlour; the view of the valley and garden is superlative. Bedrooms are in the surviving west front - the topmost is 62 steps up a spiral stone staircase, with a tantalising view through a tiny arched window to the slype, the only place monks could talk. Rooms are simply furnished, with antique beds and lots of character; allow for the lack of bathrooms as this is a protected building. Walks begin in all directions - Offa's Dyke runs along the ridge behind. Afterwards, drink to your exertions in the fabulous cellar bar, with its vaulted ceilings and worn stone steps. *Minimum 2 nights' stay at weekends.*

Rooms: 5: 2 four-posters, 3 half-testers, sharing 1 bath/shower, 1 w.c.
Price: £55-£130; singles (Sun-Thurs only) £28.
Meals: Breakfast until 9.30am. Bar lunches £3.50-£5.20. Dinner, 3 courses, approx. £15.
Closed: Open Fridays & Saturdays only November-Easter, except Christmas week. Closed Mondays all year.

From Abergavenny, A465 north to Llanvihangel Crucorney. Left on slip road into village, then left signed Llanthony for 6 miles. Entrance on right.

Gliffaes Country House Hotel

Crickhowell
Powys
NP8 1RH

Tel: 01874 730371
Fax: 01874 730463
E-mail: calls@gliffaeshotel.com
Web: www.gliffaeshotel.com

Nick and Peta Brabner, James and Susie Suter

Gliffaes is matchless - a perfect place - grand yet as casual and warm as home. It's a house for all seasons - not even driving rain could mask its beauty. In summer, stroll along the rhododendron-flanked drive and wander the 33 acres of stunning gardens and woodland or just bask in the sun on the high, buttressed terrace while the river Usk cuts through the valley 150 feet below. In winter, stay inside amid gleaming, polished floors, panelled walls and fires burning in extravagantly ornate fireplaces - one looks like the Acropolis. Tea is a feast of scones and cakes laid out on a long table at one end of the sitting room. The house could be a garden shed and you'd still love it - as long as the Brabners and Suters remained at the helm. They've been welcoming guests for over 50 years - the fourth generation, aged six and eight, are ready for some rope-learning - and they run their home with instinctive generosity. Bedrooms are excellent, the cooking British with a Mediterranean influence and a hint of the Orient, and you can fish seriously, too.

Rooms: 16 twin/doubles, 6 singles.
Price: £65-£140; singles from £53.
Meals: Breakfast 8-9.30am. Light lunch from £2.50. Dinner, 3 courses, £24.50.
Closed: Never.

From Crickhowell, A40 west for 2.5 miles. Gliffaes is signed left. Wind up hill for exactly 1 mile.

Three Cocks Hotel

Three Cocks
Brecon
Powys
LD3 0SL

Tel: 01497 847215
Fax: 01497 847339
Web: www.threecockshotel.com

Michael, Marie-Jeanne and Thomas Winstone

"You don't have to walk through it; the house just creaks on its own," says Michael of this 500-year-old coaching inn built around a tree. Michael and Marie-Jeanne are exceptionally friendly, bringing energy and experience from Belgium where they ran a restaurant for ten years. They obviously know their Belgian onions. Michael, who is English, but Belgian by marriage, and his son Thomas produce incredible Belgian dishes - i.e. French without the portion control - in the stonewalled restaurant that's peppered with some fine old Dutch oils. The house is hugely welcoming with a bright red carpet, stone walls, a crackling fire, heavy rugs and lots of lovely Belgian beer. It's a very sociable place; the warm and simple bedrooms are TV-free, so people stay up late chatting in the limed-oak panelled drawing room downstairs. When you do make it to bed, you'll find beams, sloping floors, timbered walls, thick old eiderdowns and comfy beds. At breakfast, the feasting continues with home-baked bread that melts in the mouth.

Rooms: 4 doubles, 2 twins; 1 twin with private bath.
Price: £70.
Meals: Breakfast 8-9am weekdays, 8.30-9.30am weekends. Dinner, 4 courses, £28.
Closed: 1 December-14 February.

On A438 Brecon-Hereford road. 27 miles from Hereford, 11 miles from Brecon, 4 miles from Hay-on-Wye.

Llangoed Hall

Llyswen
Brecon
Powys
LD3 0YP

Tel: 01874 754525
Fax: 01874 754545
Web: www.llangoedhall.com

Sir Bernard Ashley

Welcome to one of the most refined hotels in Britain. Sir Bernard Ashley has transformed Llangoed's impressive manor house proportions with brand new designs inspired by his wife Laura Ashley, doyenne of the stylish floral print. She always dreamed of doing up this Clough Williams-Ellis house but sadly died in a freak fall. Sir Bernard stepped in after her death, saving the house from certain demolition. The latest refurbishment gives the classic Ashley style a modern lift without losing the lavish Edwardian house party style; amazing curios include model railway memorabilia and a breakfast room devoted to Whistler lithographs, while old Penguin editions and Robert's radios add period detail. Bedrooms are big and traditional, some with lovely views. Wander in beautiful formal gardens that include a maze big enough to get lost in, or follow a path to the River Wye and picnic on a small beach. Afternoon tea served on a tiered silver tray was pure indulgence. Special, indeed.

Rooms: 3 suites, 20 double/twins.
Price: £145-£320. Dinner, B&B
£105 p.p., minimum 2 nights.
Meals: Breakfast 7.30-10am. Lunch,
3 courses, from £16.50. Afternoon tea £6-£12.50.
Dinner, 3 courses, £37.50-£42.50.
Closed: Never.

From Brecon, A470 towards Builth Wells for about 6 miles, then left staying on A470 to Llyswen. Left in village at T-junc, hotel entrance 1.5 miles further on right.

Map No: 2

The Felin Fach Griffin

Felin Fach
Brecon
Powys
LD3 0UB

Tel: 01874 620111
Fax: 01874 620120
E-mail: enquiries@eatdrinksleep.ltd.uk
Web: www.eatdrinksleep.ltd.uk

Charles Inkin and Huw Evans-Bevan

Add a dash of London to a liberal dose of the Brecon Beacons and you have The Felin Fach Griffin, a bold new venture that mixes the style of a smart city bistro with the easy-going bonhomie of good country living. Huw and Charles have converted a derelict farmhouse into a place to stay that's full of casual elegance. Young, smiley staff radiate warmth - they genuinely seem to be enjoying themselves. Downstairs fans out from a bar into several eating and sitting areas, with stripped pine and old oak furniture, even a pair of skis. Make for three monster leather sofas around a raised hearth and settle in. You can eat dinner at a smartly-laid table, or opt for the rustic charm of a small backroom bar. Charles cooks like an angel; steak and chips topped with a Béarnaise sauce was done to perfection. Breakfast is served around one table in a morning room; make your own toast on an Aga as you like it. Bedrooms are done in a simple Scandinavian style with a few designer touches; cute cylindrical bedside tables and a carved antique four-poster came from India. A place to relax rather than to be cool. *Dogs welcome by arrangement.*

Rooms: 3 four-posters, 2 doubles, 2 twin/doubles.
Price: £59.50-£73; singles £40.
Meals: Breakfast times flexible. Lunch, 2 courses, approx. £10. Dinner, 3 courses, approx. £15.
Closed: Christmas Day, New Year's Day & last 2 weeks in January.

From Brecon, A470 towards Builth Wells to Felin Fach (4.5 miles). Inn on left.

Map No: 2

The Lake Country House

Llangammarch Wells
Powys
LD4 4BS

Tel: 01591 620202
Fax: 01591 620457
E-mail: info@lakecountryhouse.co.uk
Web: www.lakecountryhouse.co.uk

Jean-Pierre Mifsud

The very essence of a real country house, not stuffy at all, but grand and cosseting nevertheless. Afternoon tea is served in the drawing room where seven beautiful rugs warm a brightly-polished wooden floor and five chandeliers hang from the ceiling. The hotel opened 100 years ago and the leather-bound fishing logs and visitor's books go back to 1894. A feel of the 1920s lingers. Fires come to life in front of your eyes, seemingly unaided by human hands, walking sticks wait at the door, grand pianos, antiques and grandfather clocks lie about the place and snooker balls clink in the distance. The same grandeur marks the bedrooms, most of which are suites: trompe l'œil wallpaper, rich fabrics, good lighting, stacks of antiques, crowns above the beds, a turndown service - the works. Jean-Pierre runs his home with gentle charm, happy to share his knowledge of this deeply rural slice of Wales. The grounds hold a lake to fish - you can hire rods - a nine-hole golf course, the river Ifron where kingfishers swoop and acres of peace and quiet. Horse riding can also be arranged.

Rooms: 10 suites, 8 twin/doubles.
Price: £135-£210; singles £90.
Meals: Breakfast 9-10am. Lunch, 3 courses, £18.50. Dinner, 3 courses, £35.
Closed: Never.

From Builth Wells, A483 west for 7 miles to Garth. Hotel signed from village.

Carlton House
Dolycoed Road
Llanwrtyd Wells
Powys
LD5 4RA

Tel: 01591 610248
Fax: 01591 610242
E-mail:
info@carltonrestaurant.co.uk
Web: www.carltonrestaurant.co.uk

Alan and Mary Ann Gilchrist

In the late 1800s, Victorians fêted spa towns, drawn in the belief that natural springs could cure everything from a troubled soul to a wart on the toe. The English spa towns are probably familiar but what about the Welsh spa scene? Here in the prettiest spa town of them all, one of the most talented chefs in Wales has been igniting the tastebuds of shakers and movers in the food industry for some time. Carlton House in Llanwrtyd Wells is an unexpected pleasure buried in the lush valleys of mid-Wales. The Gilchrists are old pro's, and great company. Alan is an engaging and unflappable host, while Mary Ann combines creative instinct with the freshest produce; entirely self-taught, she only decides what to cook hours before she dons her apron. Their 1900 townhouse was built when the town was a thriving resort and there's a wonderful feeling of several black and white movies rolled into one as you walk up the gun metal galleried staircase to rooms full of eccentric charm. Pony-trekking, bike-riding and good walking bring bustle to the town today, and their new brasserie across the road is a fun place in the evening.

Rooms: 4 doubles, 2 twin/doubles, 1 single.
Price: £60-£75; singles £30-£45. Dinner B&B £49.50 p.p. (minimum 2 nights).
Meals: Breakfast until 9.30am. Dinner, set menu, 3 courses, £24-£32. Packed lunches approx. £3.50.
Closed: Last 2 weeks December. Open for New Year.

From Builth Wells, A483 to Llanwrtyd Wells (12 miles). 1st right in town. House 50 yds on right.

Panteidal Organic Garden Restaurant

Aberdyfi
Gwynedd
LL35 0RG

Tel: 01654 767322
Fax: 01654 767322
E-mail: office@panteidalorganics.co.uk
Web: www.panteidalorganics.co.uk

Sheila Mathias

Organic in every sense, Panteidal shines like a beacon in a woodland oasis overlooking the Dyfi estuary. It started life as an organic nursery, then began serving afternoon teas outdoors; a shop selling chemical-free produce followed, then an old barn was converted into a full-blown restaurant, and now there are three gorgeous rooms to stay in. Masterminding it all is the ever-cheerful Sheila, a long-time and passionate devotee of organic cooking: "I would be flattened if I was asked to cook with anything else." You understand why once you've tried the food. My salad tasted remarkable, full of flavours I'd forgotten about, perhaps never even tasted before. It's then you realise supermarkets have been 'flattening' us for years into accepting that green stuff isn't supposed to taste of anything. The organic wine was also superb. The restaurant opens into an oriental-style garden with gravel paths winding around *Acer* trees, a frosted fir, ponds and wonderful, rusty metal cockerel sculptures from Zimbabwe. Bedrooms in the farmhouse are impeccable, with big, big beds and beautiful views. Downstairs, relax in plush, comfortable sitting rooms. Lovely.

Rooms: 3 doubles.
Price: £75; singles £50.
Meals: Breakfast until 11am. Dinner, 2-3 courses, £21-£25.
Closed: Never.

From Dolgellau, A470 north towards Porthmadog, then A493, signed Aberdyfi. Restaurant on right after 6 miles.

Map No: 5

177

Ty bach ar y polyn
Mr Jones's allotment
Conwy
TO1 LET

Tel: 12121212
E-mail: jack@feefiefoe.fum
Web: www.feefiefoe.fum

Jack Beanstalk

'Ridiculous'. you may think, but look at the space. It is amazing what one can squeeze into the least promising of spaces if you have a gifted architect and an even more gifted interior designer. The climb up that rickety little entrance ladder is unpromising, but what matter if you are greeted with such inspired aesthetics in the main sitting room? Those glass-topped tables upstage their more exotic Swedish imitators, and the airport chairs are supranational – there to give you a sense of arrival and departure. Few hotel owners go to the lengths of providing you with the instant satisfaction available from those two giant drink dispensers. Fie to those who decry their ugliness; they are a fine example of function taking precedence over form. The discreet ceiling lights, hidden behind the plastic panels, are the last word in post-modernist tat, so appreciate them. This strange little hotel is evidence, if nothing else, of our eclectic approach to hotels – a gentle challenge to the grander places in the book.

Rooms: Pick a seat. Squidgy travel bags or folded jumpers make good pillows.
Price: Hours and hours of waiting.
Meals: Crumbs off the giant's table. Drink machines only exact change.
Closed: When Jack is off on his adventures.

In Conwy, head for the giant beanstalk – you can't miss it. Hotel at base.

Penhelig Arms

Aberdyfi
Gwynedd
LL35 0LT

Tel: 01654 767215
Fax: 01654 767690
E-mail: penheligarms@saqnet.co.uk

Robert and Sally Hughes

The value here is second to none - friendly folk, easy elegance, a popular fish restaurant and such a perfect position overlooking the Dyfi estuary (pronounced 'dovey'); all but one room has long views. Robert has just opened four gorgeous new rooms in a purpose-built annexe above the inn - two have balconies, two sun terraces; all reached by probably the most curious modern water feature in Wales. The view from the terraced sitting area is outstanding. Bedrooms match the mood perfectly, some big, some small, and not a nasty thing in sight. Yet you'd trade it all for the welcome. Penhelig is a vibrant hub of the community. Within minutes of arriving, our inspector was coffee tasting with Robert, while he waved to people passing by and greeted friends coming in. The local catch of the day determines what's on the menu - fish doesn't get much fresher than this - and the wine list is stocked with delicious glug under £15 a bottle. The restaurant is a mixture of sea-grass and rugs, long views, cool colours and lots of natural light. Across the hall, a door opens to a hugely intimate and cosy bar of wood and stone. Unwind with a good ale in front of the fire, surrounded by pictures of local fishermen's boats.

Rooms: Inn: 4 twin/doubles,
5 doubles and 1 single; Bodhelig
annexe: 4 doubles.
Price: £70-£92; singles £42. Dinner,
B&B, £52-£68 p.p.
Meals: Breakfast until 9.30am. Lunch
& dinner, bar or restaurant, £2.75-£22.
Closed: Christmas Day & Boxing Day.

From Dolgellau, A470 north towards
Porthmadog, then A493 to Aberdyfi.
Inn on right entering village.
Parking opposite.

Penmaenuchaf Hall

Penmaenpool
Dolgellau
Gwynedd
LL40 1YB

Tel: 01341 422129
Fax: 01341 422787
E-mail: relax@penhall.co.uk

Mark Watson and Lorraine Fielding

The track that leads up to the Hall is bumpy, but it's worth it for the views. You can stand at the front of the house, on the Victorian stone balustrade, and gaze down on the tidal ebb and flow of the Mawddach estuary, or walk around to the back to blazing banks of rhododendrons, azaleas and camellias, a rising forest behind. When you manage to reach the front door, you'll be equally delighted. The house is pristine: rugs, wooden floors and oak panelling, flowers erupting from jugs and bowls, leather sofas and armchairs, open fires and sea-grass, and, everywhere, those views. Some of the rooms have cushioned window seats, a sort of aesthetic pre-emptive strike. Upstairs bedrooms - more views, of course - come in different shapes and sizes, the big being *huge*, the small being warm and cosy. One room up in the eaves has a fine bergère bed. Fish in the hotel's 13 miles of river, while back in the garden, they grow as much as they can. There's Mark's sense of humour, too. *Children over six welcome and pets by arrangement.*

Rooms: 1 four-poster, 5 twins, 8 doubles.
Price: £110-£170; singles from £70.
Meals: Breakfast until 9.30am weekdays, 10am weekends. Lunch £3.50-£15.50. Dinner, 4 courses, £27.50.
Closed: 10 days in early January.

From Dolgellau, A493 west for about 1.5 miles. House signed left.

Borthwnog Hall

Bontddu
Dolgellau
Gwynedd
LL40 2TT

Tel: 01341 430271
Fax: 01341 430682
E-mail: borthwnoghall@enterprise.net
Web: homepages.enterprise.net/borthwnoghall

Derek and Vicki Hawes

The hills behind the house are full of gold. Bontddu's mine has provided royal wedding rings and you can still pan the streams that feed the Mawddach estuary. This blue-shuttered house dates back to the late 17th century to a shoemaker who made his money making shoes for cattle - they needed them to get over the mountains to market. Later, it became the manor house of the Borthwnog estate before the Victorians added the balcony that runs along the front; two light-flooded bedrooms open onto it. All the bedrooms are good. There's a suite at the back, with antique mahogany beds and crimson bedspreads, but take a balcony room if they're available; one is enormous with three sets of French windows, the other is snugger, with a big brass bed and compact en suite shower. Vicki and Derek have continued the spirit of evolution by opening a small art gallery - you can buy paintings, books and pottery - and a small restaurant. As for the view, it needs no description.

Rooms: 1 suite, 1 twin/double, 1 double.
Price: £75-£110. Dinner, B&B £55-£70 p.p.
Meals: Breakfast until 9am. Dinner, 3 courses, £20. Packed lunch by arrangement.
Closed: 23-27 December.

A470 north through Dolgellau, then west for 2 miles on A496.
House on left, signed.

Llwyndû Farmhouse and Restaurant

Llanaber	**Tel:** 01341 280144
Barmouth	**Fax:** 01341 281236
Gwynedd	**E-mail:** intouch@llwyndu-farmhouse.co.uk
LL42 1RR	**Web:** www.llwyndu-farmhouse.co.uk

Peter and Paula Thompson

It's a good mile down the steepish hill to the gracious sweep of Cardigan Bay, but it looks as though you could hurdle the wall and jump straight into it; an old stone wall frames the view perfectly. The beach is long and wide, a good place to walk, as are the Rhinog mountains which take to the skies behind. And walkers will love Llwyndû. It's warm and earthy, generously simple, with bold colours on ancient stone walls, spiral stone stairways that lead nowhere, a woodburner in the big inglenook and a likely priest's hole cupboard. Peter, an historian turned cook, has brought life to the simple, everyday story of the house and its past owners; you can read up on it. Old wills hang on the walls, the proof of fables. Bedrooms are split between the main house and the converted granary; there are two four-posters, beams, bold Peter-painted stone walls, good bathrooms and bunk beds for children. All this in four pretty acres, with great views up and down, and cats, dogs and a horse that comes home for the holidays.

Rooms: 2 four-posters, 2 family, 2 doubles, 1 twin.
Price: £64-£74.
Meals: Breakfast 8.30-9.30am. Packed lunch £4-£5. Dinner, 3 courses, £17.95-£21.95. Restaurant closed Sunday nights.
Closed: Christmas Day & Boxing Day.

From Barmouth, A496 north. Pass through Llanaber. Farmhouse signed right where street lights and 40mph limit end.

Map No: 5

Lake Vyrnwy Hotel

Llanwddyn
Montgomeryshire
SY10 0LY

Tel: 01691 870692
Fax: 01691 870259
E-mail: res@lakevyrnwy.com
Web: www.lakevyrnwy.com

The Bisiker Family

This little pocket of Wales is wonderfully remote. Pine forests and ancient grazing land meet on the hills and run down to a lake, man-made in 1890 to provide Liverpool's water. Victorian tourists flocked here to see the dam, then the biggest in Europe. Lake Vyrnwy (pronounced 'Vernwee') started life as a shooting and fishing lodge, and tales of the 1930s echo. Ruth, who ran it back then, still comes in to do the flowers. The view is stupendous, the lake stretching five miles; a playground for rolling mists and sunburst into the distance. Walk, cycle, canoe, sail or fish on it. Bedrooms are excellent - only a few don't have a lake view - but the award-winning restaurant, the yellow drawing room, the leather-armchaired library and the terraced bar amply make up for that. Over the years, the Bisikers have restored the hotel to its old glory, with wooden floors, a grand piano, heavy oak furniture, even a postbox in the entrance hall. A place to return to again and again.

Rooms: 35: 2 four-posters, 32 twin/doubles, 1 suite.
Price: £115-£185; singles from £85. Dinner, B&B £75-£107.50 p.p.; singles £100.
Meals: Breakfast 8.30-10am. Lunch, 3 courses, £15.95. Dinner, 3 courses, £27.50. Bar meals also available.
Closed: Never.

A490 from Welshpool, then B4393 to Lake Vyrnwy. Brown signs from A5 at Shrewsbury as well.

Plas Bodegroes
Pwllheli
Gwynedd
LL53 5TH

Tel: 01758 612363
Fax: 01758 701247
E-mail: gunna@bodegroes.co.uk
Web: www.bodegroes.co.uk

Chris and Gunna Chown

Close to the end of the world and worth every single second it takes to get here. Chris and Gunna are inspirational, their home a temple of cool elegance, the food possibly the best in Wales. Fronted by an avenue of 200-year-old beech trees, this Georgian manor house is wrapped in climbing roses, wildly roaming wisteria and ferns. The veranda circles the house as do the long French windows that lighten every room; open one up, grab a chair and sit out reading a book. Not a formal place - come to relax and be yourself. Bedrooms are wonderful, the courtyard rooms especially good; exposed wooden ceilings and a crisp clean style give the feel of a smart Scandinavian forest hideaway. Best of all is the dining room, almost a work of art in itself, cool and crisp with modern art and Venetian carnival masks on the walls - a great place to eat Chris's ambrosial food. If you can tear yourself away, explore the Llyn peninsula: sandy beaches, towering sea cliffs, country walks. Snowdon is also close. Gunna and Chris will direct you.

Rooms: 1 four-poster, 7 doubles,
2 twins, 1 single.
Price: £70-£120; singles £35-£80.
Dinner, B&B from £55 p.p.
Meals: Breakfast 8-9.30am weekdays,
8-10am weekends. Sunday lunch
£13.50. Dinner, 3 courses, £25-£30.
Closed: 1 December-1 March. Closed
on Mondays.

*From Pwllheli, A497 towards Nefyn.
House signed on left after 1 mile.*

Map No: 5

Scotland

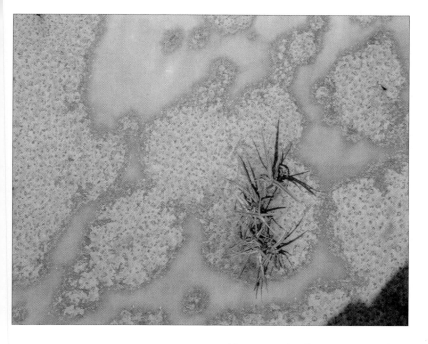

Always watch where you are going.
Otherwise, you may step on a piece of the
Forest that was left out by mistake.

Winnie-the-Pooh

The Roxburghe Hotel and Golf Course

Heiton
Nr. Kelso
Borders
TD5 8JZ

Tel: 01573 450331
Fax: 01573 450611
E-mail: hotel@roxburghe.net
Web: www.roxburghe.net

The Duke of Roxburghe   Manager: Stephen Browning

Not quite a castle, but a big, old pile none the less. Bonnie Prince Charlie came here in 1745, but the house that stood then was rebuilt in the same Jacobean style after a 1770 fire. It is now a grand country house hotel with all the trimmings: the richest of fabrics in opulent bedrooms; the most intricate of carved fireplaces in the sitting room; the deepest of sofas in the grand drawing room. High ceilings, roaring fires, an ocean of floor to navigate in reception, marble bathrooms, the best linen... tremendous stuff. Noble pursuits include archery, falconry, fishing... and golf. Roxburghe's course is one of Scotland's finest and considered one of the top 100 courses in Britain; there to be discovered as it's still relatively unknown. Cavernous bunkers, huge undulating greens and, of course, the odd moment of terror provide thrilling entertainment. You don't even have to be a golfer to enjoy it. The course cuts through glorious country, rolls down through parkland to the river Teviot and passes by a 19th-century viaduct railway bridge - a breathtaking sight. Nearby, Floors Castle, the Duke's family seat and the oldest inhabited castle in Scotland, is open to the public.

Rooms: 2 suites, 4 four-posters,
6 doubles, 5 twins, 3 twin/doubles,
2 singles.
Price: £120-£255; singles £120.
Meals: Breakfast 7.30-9.30am, 8-10am
Sundays. Brasserie lunch from £5.50.
Dinner, 3 courses, table d'hôte £25;
à la carte approx £35.
Closed: 24-29 December.

From Kelso, A698 south. Hotel signed right after 2 miles, at southern end of Heiton village.

Map No: 10

Dan Dare's Diner
Twilight Zone
Borders
UF0 7FX

Tel: 0800 424242
Fax: 0800 002001
E-mail: aliens@ufo.cos.mos
Web: www.ufo.cos.mos

The Jetson family

In our relentless search for the utterly unique and the incredibly implausible, it was inevitable we'd bump into the extra terrestrial sooner or later. The Jetsons, now retired from their successful seventies cartoon series, have converted this former unidentified flying object into a revolving restaurant with rooms; apparently the alien craft got stuck on this white pole during a failed attempt to invade the earth. No-one quite knows what happened to the crew though local bed and breakfast owners say a lot of well-spoken Americans with 'Pentagon' written on their brief cases stayed in the area afterwards. Dan Dare's Diner is a splendid example of the early mother ship design with huge windows that draw in the universe. It's also haunted – guests have independently reported seeing a green man, a dalek, Ming the Merciless and Miss Piggy in an astronaut's suit. Modern cottage-style 'pods' – bedrooms to the more earthbound – entice the eye, with flock-wallpaper, tarmac floors, crocheted slippers and lovely views of five continents. Dinner is unreal; eat a galaxy of ingredients as the restaurant spins at the speed of light to the enchanting sound of Chewbacca singing Verdi. Out of this world in every way.

Rooms: 1 king pod, 1 queen pod, 1 tripod, 1 pea pod.
Price: Dinner Bed & Abduction 1 soul p.p. Special weekend abductions available.
Meals: Breakfast for several light years. Dinner, set NASA menu.
Closed: During a supernova.

Left at Esso garage, through quaint village, then right at inn down country lane to field. Shout: "I've come to see the little green men." Restaurant will appear.

Cavens Country House Hotel

Kirkbean
By Dumfries
Dumfries and Galloway
DG2 8AA

Tel: 01387 880234
Fax: 01387 880467
E-mail: enquiries@cavens-hotel.co.uk
Web: www.cavens-hotel.co.uk

Jane and Angus Fordyce

"*In Ardus Fortis*" (strength in adversity) runs Angus's family motto; it's an appropriate one given their tussle to turn Cavens into a splendid country house hotel; battle tales with grotty nylon, Formica and Anaglypta made our inspector's hair stand on end. Thankfully, rich fabrics, gorgeous colours and elegant antiques won the day. It's hard to appreciate the extent of their labours, but easy to enjoy the fruits next to an open fire in the lovely Green Room, with a single malt in hand, relishing a gorgeous view over the Solway Firth. This house was built in 1752 by Sir Richard Oswald, a wealthy tobacco importer, who owned as much as the eye can see from the window, and more; they plan to knock down a later extension and restore the original front door. Classic country house-style bedrooms have views over the six-acre garden and beyond; one has a great arched ceiling, with bottle green walls. Angus has a hotel background and also produces excellent home-cooked food with a Scottish/French twist. You're in safe hands.

Rooms: 5 doubles, 1 twin, 1 family.
Price: £80-£106.
Meals: Breakfast until 10am. Dinner, 4 courses, £25. Packed lunch by arrangement.
Closed: Never.

From Dumfries, A710 to Kirkbean (12 miles). Hotel signed in village.

The Witchery by the Castle

Castlehill
Royal Mile
Edinburgh
EH1 2NF

James Thomson

Tel: 0131 225 5613
Fax: 0131 220 4392
E-mail: mail@thewitchery.com
Web: www.thewitchery.com

The two restaurants and two suites which James Thomson has carved out of a 16th-century tenement ought, really, to be a theatre - Jacobean drama would work best. The spiral staircase and the candles, the stone floor and the tapestries, the shadows and the shining wood delight the senses; this is unequivocally a passionate and magical setting. The kitchen, too, is stiff with culinary skill and aims for maximum entrapment - try hot smoked salmon with leeks and hollandaise sauce. The two suites are full of romantic panache, overlaid with sumptuous architectural bric-a-brac, ranging from the medieval to the quasi-Byzantine which James - a stately member of the Tartan Army - has plucked from European flea-markets. The bathroom of the *Old Rectory* features pillars from London's Trocadero Theatre and gilded panelling from St Giles' Cathedral. The *Inner Sanctum* encompasses one of Queen Victoria's chairs and Art Deco taps from an Edinburgh hairdresser. Both have enough drapes and alcoves to conceal a medium-sized cast of conspirators and lovers. Beyond the front door, Edinburgh awaits.

Rooms: 2 suites, 1 four-poster.
Price: From £195.
Meals: Breakfast until 11am. Set lunch, 2 courses, £9.95. Dinner, à la carte, 3 courses approx. £30.
Closed: Christmas Day & Boxing Day.

Find Edinburgh Castle. Witchery 20m from main castle gate.

Map No: 9

Knockinaam Lodge

Portpatrick
Wigtownshire
Dumfries and Galloway
DG9 9AD

Tel: 01776 810471
Fax: 01776 810435

Michael Bricker and Pauline Ashworth

The writer, John Buchan, knew of this 1869 shooting lodge and described it in *The Thirty-Nine Steps* as the house to which Hannay fled. It's still a good place to hide out, hunkered down with hills on three sides and the sea at the end of the vast lawn. In spring, the grounds transform as hundreds of thousands of bluebells appear while sunsets can be awesome with the Irish Sea streaked red. Knockinaam is as good as its setting; a supremely comfortable country house. A Michelin star in the dining room, breakfasts fit for kings, a wine list for the gods and 144 malts in the panelled bar. Everywhere, crisp, uncluttered elegance. Big windows flood gracious rooms with light, an open fire smoulders in the panelled drawing room, an antique Queen Anne sofa takes the strain. Bedrooms have the best fabrics, big beds, pillows and cushions piled high; two have sea views. Michael and Pauline, easy-going perfectionists, came over from Canada to make this peaceful land of Galloway their home; as Michael will tell you, the weather here is much better than you'd think - his daily log for 2000 reveals 130 days of summer sunshine.

Rooms: 8 doubles, 2 twins, 1 single.
Price: Dinner, B&B £90-£170 p.p.
Meals: Breakfast 8.15-9.30am. Bar lunch from £3.50. Lunch, 3 courses, £29. Dinner, 4 courses, included; non-residents £39.
Closed: Never.

From A77 or A75, follow signs for Portpatrick. 2 miles west of Lochans, left at smokehouse, then 1st left, 1st right and straight on, signed 'Knockinaam.'

Royal Hotel
Tighnabruaich
Argyll and Bute
PA21 2BE

Tel: 01700 811239
Fax: 01700 811300
E-mail: info@royalhotel.org.uk
Web: www.royalhotel.org.uk

Roger and Bea McKie

In that never-ending search for a tourist-free destination, Tighnabruaich is near the top of our list, an end-of-the-road village, lost to the world and without great need of it. The Royal is its relaxed and informal hub. Yachtsman tie up to moorings and drop in for lunch, the shinty team pop down for a pint after a game and fishermen land fresh mussels and langoustine straight from the sea for Roger to cook. Roger and Bea - ex-pat Scots - came back up from Cheltenham with an eye to "buying something run-down so they could..." run it up? That's very much what they've done. There's a fresh, designer-feel downstairs, where Bea has rag-rolled a bold orange onto the walls. Wooden floors, rugs and jazz in the brasserie, a small locals' bar at the back and a big, bright restaurant with great views of the Kyles of Bute. Upstairs, bedrooms are big, warm, comfy and homely - just what you'd hope for - and all but one has glorious sea views. There's a nearby tennis court where you can lose balls in the sea and Bute is a short ferry-ride away.

Rooms: 10 doubles, 1 twin.
Price: £78-£158. Dinner, B&B from £65 p.p.
Meals: Breakfast 9-10.30am. Dinner, 3 courses, £26.95. Meals in brasserie from £8.
Closed: Christmas Day.

From Glasgow, A82 north, A83 west, A815 south, A886 south, A8003 south, then B8000 north into village. Hotel on seafront.

Map No: 8

The Creggans Inn

Strachur
Argyll and Bute
PA27 8BX

Tel: 01369 860279
Fax: 01369 860637
E-mail: info@creggans-inn.co.uk
Web: www.creggans-inn.co.uk

Thomas, Onny and Alex Robertson Manager: Paul Armstrong

Like all the best inns, history and legend have blurred into one over the years. Mary Queen of Scots is said to have landed outside, 200 or so years before the original inn arrived. More recently, Creggans was owned by the late Scottish author Fitzroy MacLean. Now it's in the capable hands of the Robertson family. They used to run a smaller place on the Isle of Mull which we also loved. This is a bigger venture, but they're already making an impression, adding style to tired rooms and flair to the kitchen. The dining room has a lovely modern feel, with wooden floors, designer furniture, and beautiful views over Loch Fyne, source of truly great breakfast kippers. Most bedrooms have the loch view and are decorated with Jane Churchill wallpaper and Liberty fabrics, all very swish and comfortable; the rest lack the same pizzazz but it's only a matter of time. The newly-refurbished MacPhunn's bar is named after a local fella who survived a hanging and lived happily ever after. Friendly locals are full of life, too, and it's the only bar serving real ale for miles. Great walks start from the inn.

Rooms: 1 suite, 6 doubles, 3 twins, 4 twin/doubles.
Price: £110-£237; singles £55-£138.50. Dinner B&B £70-£103 p.p. Special rates for 2 or more nights.
Meals: Breakfast until 9.30am. Bar lunch £4-£10. Dinner, 3 courses, £28.50.
Closed: Never.

From Glasgow, A82 to Tarbert, A83 towards Inverary for 13 miles, then left on A815 to Strachur (10 miles). Hotel on left before village.

Map No: 8

Ardanaiseig

Kilchrenan
By Taynuilt
Argyll and Bute
PA35 1HE

Tel: 01866 833333
Fax: 01866 833222
E-mail: ardanaiseig@clara.net
Web: www.ardanaiseig.com

Robert Francis

"All you need to stay in love," was how one guest described this seductive place. The pleasure of the journey to Ardanaiseig unfolds with lingering suspense. From the village of Kilchrenan, an even smaller single track road leads into a mighty landscape of loch and mountain. Wind through heath and ancient woodland, then down an avenue of beech trees and through a collection of rare and exotic rhododendron to, finally, the house; built in 1834 in the baronial style right on the shores of Loch Awe. According to Celtic legend, the lake has magical properties after Bheithir, goddess of ageless beauty, let the well of eternal youth on nearby Ben Cruchan accidentally spill over. Guests enthuse about the light here - over breakfast, watch mists swirl over the faint silhouettes of islands in the lake. Dreamy. The hotel is impeccably done in an eclectic style inspired by its art dealer owner. Bedrooms have quirky flair; the *Tervine* is wonderfully over the top; others are more restrained. An enchanting hideaway run with friendly professionalism.

Rooms: 8 doubles, 8 twin/doubles.
Price: £78-£250; singles £69-£155. Dinner B&B £59-£148 p.p. (minimum 3 nights); single £89-£178.
Meals: Breakfast 8-10am. Light lunch from £2.75. Afternoon teas £2-£10. Dinner, 5 courses, £38.50.
Closed: January-mid-February.

From Glasgow, A82 then A85 to Taynuilt. Left before village on B845, signed Kilchrenan. Left in village at Kilchrenan pub down single track lane for 3.9 miles. Hotel at end down drive.

Map No: 8   192

Tigh an Truish

Clachan
Isle of Seil
Argyll and Bute
PA34 4QZ

Tel: 01852 300242

Miranda and Gustl Brunner

There is nothing grand about this honest old inn, but it's fun, and just one card in the Brunner pack. Cross the 'Bridge over the Atlantic', and you enter their world: pub, petrol station, postbox and photo gallery - it's all theirs, all ten paces apart, a small enclave of engagingly odd, mild eccentricity. Tigh an Truish means 'house of trousers' - it goes back to when Scots had to leave their kilts behind to go onto the mainland. Miranda rules the inn with a rod of pure sponge. It's full of life; you may get a *ceilidh*, definitely a pint and good home-cooked food. Her brother farms oysters and may drop some off, fresh from the seabed; otherwise you'll have to settle for *moules marinières*, half a lobster or venison. There are two big, modestly comfy bedrooms, both with enough room for sofas and chairs. You also get a kitchen - tiny, tiled and functional, and a fridge stocked with breakfast essentials. Look out for the Gustl-made furniture, especially the strange but remarkably comfortable bar bench. Bag another small island, Luing, while you're here; Miranda will give you the best advice.

Rooms: 1 double, 1 twin.
Price: £40-£45.
Meals: Breakfast times flexible. Bar meals available (April-October) from £5.
Closed: Christmas & New Year.

A816 south from Oban, then B844 towards Easdale. After 3 miles, cross bridge and house on right opposite petrol station.

Barcaldine House

Barcaldine
Oban
Argyll and Bute
PA37 1SG

Tel: 01631 720219
Fax: 01631 720219
E-mail: barcaldine@breathe.co.uk
Web: www.countrymansions.com

Wendy Graham and Gary Smith

House-party in true Scottish style at this baronial mansion just north of Oban. Barcaldine is a bastion of the Campbell clan; seven generations lived here, starting with Red Patrick who built the original house in 1709 to escape the confines of the family castle - clansmen across the Highlands were doing the same as devilish intrigue replaced full-scale war. The house is full of lived-in elegance; take afternoon tea in the splendid Wedgewood-style drawing room with white cameo reliefs, wooden floors and comfy sofas, or retire after dinner to the wood-panelled snooker room on the first floor and sit in worn leather armchairs under a fabulous vaulted ceiling, surrounded by antler trophies. Bedrooms are lovely: floral designs, the odd antique, fresh flowers, maybe a roll-top bath for long soaks after a day's exertions, maybe a friendly ghost - there are two according to legend: the Blue Lady and an unknown Highlander. Wendy looks after guests with helpful enthusiasm, while Gary cooks with pride; his scones are delicious. Walks start from the back of the house.

Rooms: 4 doubles, 3 twins.
Price: £70-£90.
Meals: Breakfast until 9.30am. Packed lunch £5. Dinner, à la carte, 3 courses £20-£25.
Closed: Never.

From Fort William, A82 to North Ballachulish, then A828 to Barcaldine. Entering village, house on left up drive, signed.

Map No: 8

Ardsheal House

Kentallen of Appin
Argyll and Bute
PA38 4BX

Tel: 01631 740227
Fax: 01631 740342
E-mail: info@ardsheal.co.uk
Web: www.ardsheal.co.uk

Neil and Philippa Sutherland

At the end of a two-mile, private, bumpy drive and just a stroll from Loch Linnhe, you'll find Ardsheal, a grand old Scottish mansion in 11 acres of peaceful gardens and impressively ancient woodlands. The Sutherlands are relaxed and friendly and have kept the grandeur, while expunging any leftover stuffiness - if there was any. You can ask Neil - he grew up here. The hall is awesome, oak-panelled, with roaring fire, leather armchairs and a barrel window giving a porthole view of Loch Linnhe. Equally awesome is the billiard room; walls, floors, ceiling, all are wood, and there's a big bay window looking out to sea with an old naval telescope to scour the horizon. You shouldn't be too surprised to hear that the bedrooms are grand, too, in that old 'country house' style. There's a Javanese four-poster, lots of period furniture, and rooms at the front have 'the view'. There's also a conservatory dining room. Philippa, fun and bubbly, does most of the cooking. More home than hotel, it's terrific value and you can walk to the loch for a swim.

Rooms: 1 four-poster, 3 doubles,
3 twin/doubles, 1 single.
Price: From £90; singles from £45.
Meals: Breakfast 8.30-9.30am. Dinner,
4 courses, £25.
Closed: Occasionally.

*From Oban A85 north, then A828.
Continue for about 25 miles to
Kentallen; house drive signed left
just after town sign.*

Map No: 8

Ballachulish House

Ballachulish
Argyll and Bute
PA39 4JX

Tel: 01855 811266
Fax: 01855 811498
E-mail: mclaughlins@btconnect.com
Web: www.ballachulishhouse.com

Marie and Micheal McLaughlin

The sight of this charming Scottish laird's house coming into view after a long day's trek in the mountains is as special for today's traveller as it was for ancient clansmen. Tucked under mighty Glencoe mountain, scene of 1692's massacre of the recalcitrant MacDonald clan, Ballachulish appears part fortress, part country house; a welcome sanctuary from the elements - flop those weary bones into a comfortable chair by an open fire and savour the warm glow of endeavour. The McLaughlins have retained the simplicity that characterised the house when it was built in the 18th century. Bedrooms with big sleigh beds, the odd combed ceiling and nice touches like fresh fruit are discreetly elegant. Most have mountain views across a part-walled garden of herb beds, stone fountain, orchard, and beautiful specimen trees, while two rooms at the front have loch views. Both sitting rooms have honesty bars, while a tiled iron range in the dining room, inscribed with the words "Lang may your lum reek" raises a smile. Food is wonderful, and the range of Scottish cheeses unsurpassed. *Children over 10 welcome.*

Rooms: 1 suite, 3 twins, 4 doubles, 1 single.
Price: £60-£140; singles £50-£60.
Meals: Breakfast 9.30am. Dinner, 5 courses, £30.
Closed: Never.

A82 from Glasgow, then A828 to Oban. Under Ballachulish Bridge, house 100m further on left, past golf course, signed.

Blairquhan Castle

Straiton
Maybole
Ayrshire
KA19 7LZ

James Hunter Blair

Tel: 01655 770239
Fax: 01655 770278
E-mail: enquiries@blairquhan.co.uk
Web: www.blairquhan.co.uk

A baronial castle, lived in for generations by the same family, on the most gorgeous estate in Ayrshire - Blairquhan is as authentic as it gets and James Hunter Blair, its present incumbent, couldn't be more charming. His great-great-grandfather Sir David Hunter Blair commissioned architect William Burn to build this magnificent Regency building. It's never been altered and many original fixtures and fittings still remain; you'll find the date 1824 woven into blankets on the four-posters. Huge rooms on both floors lead off a wonderful galleried saloon, with ornate plasterwork, marble busts, family portraits, and a domed atrium high above. The stately home feel continues into the dining room; guests sit around a long, mahogany table surrounded by more ancestors. Your house-party starts in a comfy living room with a welcoming open fire; afternoon tea is served here on arrival and you can help yourself from a trolley bar before dinner. James is an engaging host - discover his collection of Scottish colourists, the family museum, roam in 2,000 acres, or visit the pretty village of Straiton. Marvellous.

Rooms: 4 four-posters, 1 doubles,
5 twins, 5 singles.
Price: £230; singles £115.
Meals: Breakfast times flexible. Lunch from £20.
Dinner, 4 courses, £75, including wine and drinks.
Closed: Christmas.

From Maybole, south on B7023 through Crosshill, left onto B741 towards Straiton for 2 miles. Estate wall, lodge and gates on left, signed.

Culzean Castle

The National Trust for Scotland
Maybole
Ayrshire
KA19 8LE

Tel: 01655 884455
Fax: 01655 884503
E-mail: culzean@nts.org.uk
Web: www.culzeancastle.net

Jonathan Cardale

Culzean Castle, by Robert Adam, is awe-inspiring by any castle standards. The top floor, with six bedrooms, is probably the most interesting hotel address in Scotland, especially loved by Americans because it was presented to General Eisenhower for his lifetime use. The rooms are exquisitely decorated in elegant country house rather than castle style with inimitable views of the wild coast to the Isle of Arran and Ailsa Craig. The sitting room is spectacular, oval in shape and jutting out above the cliffs with a sheer drop down to breaking rollers. To single one room out for praise is unfair; Culzean (pronounced Cullane) is a thrilling architectural masterpiece, both inside and out, and you can expect the very best of everything. Guests can tour the castle before the public invades at 11am and there are 560 acres of country park to explore with deer park, vinery, swan pond, orangery, exotic stone pagoda and cliff walks. You'll find fresh flowers from the walled garden everywhere and *Cordon Bleu* cooking from Susan Cardale. A National Trust for Scotland showpiece.

Rooms: 1 four-poster, 3 twin/doubles, 1 double; 1 twin with private bath.
Price: £200-£375; singles from £140.
Meals: Breakfast times flexible. Dinner, 4 courses, £45 including house wine, by arrangement.
Closed: 1 November-31 March.

From A77 in Maybole, A719 for 4 miles following signs for Culzean castle.

Map No: 9

198

The Inn at Lathones

Lathones
By Largoward, St. Andrews
Fife and Teeside
KY9 1JE

Nick White

Tel: 01334 840494
Fax: 01334 840694
E-mail: lathones@theinn.co.uk
Web: www.theinn.co.uk

Manager: Lynn Bell

Once upon a time in the Kingdom of Fife, two people fell in love, married and lived happily ever after in this old inn; beer flowed, food was plentiful, customers burst into song, even a dwarf highwayman occasionally dropped in after 'work'. When the landlady died in 1736, legend says the wedding stone above the fireplace in the lounge cracked, so strong was their love. Today, she and her horse haunt the wonderful Stables - the oldest part of the inn, with its garlands of hops and bottle-green ceiling - but in the friendliest manner. No wonder, really, as Lathones could charm the most cantankerous ghost. Superb food, the draw of an open fire, leather sofas to sink into, and a warm Scottish welcome await here. Walk into the bar to find bottles of grappa and eau de vie asking to be sampled, while Marc Guibert's menu is mouth-watering; try local grilled sea bass followed by a clootie dumpling served with fresh strawberry. Comfortable, traditional-style bedrooms are split between a coachhouse and an old blacksmith's house either side of the inn. Historic St. Andrews and the East Neuk of Fife fishing villages are close.

Rooms: 2 masters, 10 twin/doubles, 2 singles.
Price: £110-£140; singles £65-£85.
Meals: Breakfast 7.30-10am weekdays, 8-10am weekends. Lunch, 2 courses, £9. Packed lunch from £5. Dinner, à la carte, from £20.95.
Closed: 3 weeks in January.

From Kirkcaldy or St. Andrews, A915 to Largoward. Inn 1 mile north on roadside.

The Peat Inn

Peat Inn
By Cupar
Fife and Teeside
KY15 5LH

Tel: 01334 840206
Fax: 01334 840530
E-mail: reception@thepeatinn.co.uk
Web: www.thepeatinn.co.uk

David and Patricia Wilson

Just up the road at St. Andrews is the home of golf; here you get the home of modern Scottish cooking. David came here about 30 years ago; in that time, he has put The Peat Inn on the gastronomic *Mappa Mundi*, and inspired a whole generation of Scottish chefs to follow his lead and cook brilliantly, using local suppliers and growers wherever possible. He is irrepressible; when I arrived at nine o'clock one morning I found him making pastry in the kitchen, his passion as strong today as it ever was. Take it as read that his restaurant is the perfect place for a feast. Eat amid gilt mirrors, sprays of fresh flowers, stone walls, the odd four-foot high statue and tapestries on the walls. In the front snug bar, a fire burns in an ancient fireplace amid smart sofas piled high with cushions; sit down with a glass of champagne while your table is prepared. Bedrooms are just as good and bring a fine night's sleep; all are split-level suites with sleigh beds, four-posters, marble bathrooms, home-made biscuits and bowls of fruit. Expect to be spoiled in every way.

Rooms: 8 suites.
Price: £145; singles £95.
Meals: Breakfast 8-10am. Lunch, 3 courses, £19.50. Dinner, 3 courses, £30-£38.
Closed: Rooms and restaurant both closed Sundays and Mondays.

From Edinburgh, A90 north, then A92 for Dundee. Right onto A91 and into Cupar. There, B940 for Crail to inn.

Creagan House

Strathyre
Callander
Perth and Kinross
FK18 8ND

Tel: 01877 384638
Fax: 01877 384319
E-mail:
eatandstay@creaganhouse.co.uk
Web: www.creaganhouse.co.uk

Gordon and Cherry Gunn

Cosy, convivial and occasionally quirky... there is something very special about sitting at a long, polished slab of oak in a baronial dining room, reading a small treatise entitled *The Iconography of the Creagan Toast Rack* while waiting for your bacon and eggs. Cherry and Gordon plough great reserves of energy and dedication into their restaurant with rooms; warm and friendly with exceptional food and a remarkable homely simplicity, it's a great place to be. Bedrooms up in the eaves have Sanderson wallpaper and bed covers, old wood furniture and no TVs. "You don't come to Creagan to watch a box," Cherry rightly points out. Downstairs is a small bar with brass hangings and a beam 'acquired' from the Oban railway line; better still, it's stocked with 42 malts and a good whisky guide to help you choose. There are no airs and graces here, just the attention you only get in places that are small and owner-run. Why not 'bag a Munro' - walking sticks at the front door will help you up Ben Shean.

Rooms: 4 doubles, 1 twin.
Price: £85; singles £52.50.
Meals: Breakfast 8-9.30am. Dinner, 3 courses, £23.75.
Closed: February.

From Stirling, A84 north through Callander on to Strathyre. Hotel 0.25 miles north of village on right, signed.

Map No: 9

Monachyle Mhor

Balquhidder
Lochearnhead
Perth and Kinross
FK19 8PQ

Tel: 01877 384622
Fax: 01877 384305
E-mail: info@monachylemhor.com
Web: www.monachylemhor.com

Rob, Jean, Tom and Angela Lewis

They started here as farmers, went on to do B&B and ended up with a hotel. It's a warm, friendly and eclectic place, packed with interest, full of music ranging wonderfully from jazz to opera, and run by a spirited family: son Tom cooks fabulously, while Rob and Jean chat, serve and make everybody feel thoroughly welcome. Rob and another son still run the farm, so walk as much as you like; you're nearly at the end of the road where it gets dynamic and interesting. The place seems to evolve at its own pace: a vegetable garden has just been put in. Huge, funky barn bedrooms make bold use of space and colour and contemporary brown and cream fabrics will you to bed. There's a snug, traditional bar with open fire. Ideal to return to after exploring the hills that rise to one side. Loch Voil stretches away on the other; walk round, or boat across. The truly lazy can simply slump in a chair on the parasoled terrace and just take it all in with glass in hand.

Rooms: 5 doubles, 2 twins, 3 suites.
Price: £80-£100; singles from £50.
Meals: Breakfast until 9.30am. Dinner, 3 courses, £32.50. Sunday lunch £19.50. Packed lunch by arrangement.
Closed: Never.

Turn off A84 at Kings House Hotel, following signs to Balquhidder. Continue along Loch Voil. Monachyle is up drive on right, signed.

Map No: 9

The Four Seasons Hotel

St. Fillans
Perth and Kinross
PH6 2NF

Tel: 01764 685333
Fax: 01764 685444
E-mail: info@thefourseasonshotel.co.uk
Web: www.thefourseasonshotel.co.uk

Andrew Low

This is a great position with forest rising immediately behind and Loch Earn stretching out seven miles distant. It all comes into play; ski, sail, canoe or fish on the loch - even learn to fly on it - or simply take to the hills for fabulous walks. The hotel has simple chalets on the lower slopes and each has long views, through pine trees, across water. Andrew is a great traveller, a Scot born 'down south' who has come home, and his love and enthusiasm for this heavenly spot are contagious. He has refurbished the interior completely, bringing bright colours to the walls, a gentle elegance to the rooms, superb food to the tables and a relaxed spirit to the whole place. Sit out on the small terrace underneath cherry trees for evening drinks and stare out across the loch or stay in front of the fire with a warming malt - The Four Seasons is well-named. Bedrooms in the house are excellent - smart, with plush carpets, huge beds and those at the front have loch views. Fish successfully and they'll cook your catch for supper. A super place.

Rooms: 7 doubles, 5 twins; 6 family chalets, each sleeps 4.
Price: £74-£98; singles from £35; Dinner, B&B from £56 p.p.
Meals: Breakfast 8-9.30am, Monday-Saturday, 8.30-10.30am Sundays. Bar meals from £8. Dinner, 4 courses, £26.95.
Closed: January & February.

St. Fillans is on the eastern tip of Loch Earn on A85, 12 miles west of Creiff, 25 miles north of Stirling.

Map No: 9

Loch Tummel Inn

Strathtummel
By Pitlochry
Perth and Kinross
PH16 5RP

Tel: 01882 634272
Fax: 01882 634272

Liz and Michael Marsden

"When you get here, you can stop travelling," says Michael. "People need to be still and remember what their childhood senses are for - just look, listen, smell and let it all seep in." These wise sentiments sum up the simple, honest pleasures in store at this lovely old coaching inn on a remote stretch of road overlooking Loch Tummel. Michael is in his element here; he and his wife Liz moved up from Sussex eight years ago. He's very much the consummate host orchestrating proceedings from behind the bar, and a firm believer in preserving the art of conversation; there's no piped music, your mobile phone won't work, and televisions are only provided on request. Idiosyncratic bedrooms have earthy, rustic charm, with checked bedspreads, china and good bathrooms; soak in a bath of soft hill water in one room next to a log fire while gazing at snow-capped mountains. There's also a sweet bothy room, with an open fire, where guests can retreat for some privacy. Breakfast is served in a converted hayloft with loch views, while the bar serves good local food, including salmon smoked on the premises. Perthshire in autumn is stunning.

Rooms: 3 doubles, 1 family; 1 double, 1 single, both with private bathroom.
Price: £70-£90; singles £45-£60.
Meals: Breakfast until 9.30am. Bar lunch from £2.95. Dinner, 2 courses, from £11.
Closed: Winter.

From Perth, A9 north, then turn off after Pitlochry, signed Killicrankie. Left over Garry Bridge onto B8019. Inn 8 miles on right.

Map No: 9

204

Killiecrankie Hotel

Pass of Killiecrankie
By Pitlochry
Perth and Kinross
PH16 5LG
Colin and Carole Anderson

Tel: 01796 473220
Fax: 01796 472451
E-mail: enquiries@killiecrankiehotel.co.uk
Web: www.killiecrankiehotel.co.uk

Pitlochry is known in Scotland as the gateway to the Highlands. Keep going north a couple of miles and you come to Killiecrankie, where, blissfully, nothing particular happens at all. The glorious glens here are home to castles and distilleries, fine lochs and mountain paths, a place to unwind with a dram or a rod. The Killiecrankie is an excellent base for such work. Colin and Carole have been here for 13 years and share their knowledge of the area with unhurried generosity, talking you through a walk or letting you know the best picnic spots on Loch Tummel. Whatever exertions you get up to by day, return to the cosseting luxuries of the hotel by night: piping hot baths, drinks in the panelled bar, sublime food in the restaurant, Scrabble in the sitting room, a final stroll around the four-acre garden and then upstairs to pretty bedrooms for undisturbed sleep. The hills on one side of the house are an RSPB sanctuary, so you may see buzzard or falcon circling. Golf and fishing can also be arranged.

Rooms: 6 twin/doubles, 2 doubles, 2 singles.
Price: Dinner, B&B £71-£91 p.p.
Meals: Breakfast 8-9.30am, 8.30-9.30am Sundays. Lunch from £8. Dinner, 4 courses, included; non-residents £32.
Closed: January & February.

From Pitlochry, A9 north for 1 mile, then B8079, signed Killiecrankie. Straight ahead for 2 miles. Hotel signed on right.

Map No: 9

Darroch Learg

Braemar Road
Ballater
Aberdeenshire and Moray
AB35 5UX

Tel: 013397 55443
Fax: 013397 55252
E-mail: nigel@darrochlearg.co.uk

Nigel and Fiona Franks

There's an easy professionalism and self-confidence about this Victorian hotel in the fir district of Deeside, home to the royal family in the summer months. The Franks family has been here 40 years, honing good, considerate hospitality into an art form. Darroch Learg loosely translates from Gaelic as 'an oak copse on a sunny hillside' and the hotel, built of granite in the 1888, is in a lovely raised position to the west of Ballater. Lovely views stretch across the Dee Valley to Lochnagar mountain, snow-capped for much of the year. The main house is turreted and done in a baronial style; smart but unpretentious. Bedrooms have a Regency feel; all subtly different, with warm colours, local watercolours, thick curtains to keep out the chill of winter, fresh flowers, and modern bathrooms full of luxurious Molton Brown toiletries - most rooms have the view, too. Downstairs, an intimate conservatory-style dining room, with lamps at each table, pulls in the view; chef David Mutter's modern Scottish cooking has won various awards, ably supported by a keen wine list. "You feel good staying here," wrote our inspector.

Rooms: Main house: 2 four-posters, 3 doubles, 6 twin/doubles, 1 single; Oakhall: 2 doubles, 3 twin/doubles.
Price: £124-£154; singles £62-£82. Dinner B&B £65-£105 p.p.; single £90.
Meals: Breakfast 8-9.30am weekdays, 8-10am weekends. Sunday lunch £18.50. Dinner, 3 courses, £34.
Closed: Christmas week & last 3 weeks in January.

From Perth, A93 north to Ballater. Entering village, hotel first building on left above road.

Map No: 13

Minmore House

Glenlivet
Banffshire
Aberdeenshire and Moray
AB37 9DB

Tel: 01807 590378
Fax: 01807 590472
E-mail: minmorehouse@ukonline.co.uk
Web: www.minmorehousehotel.com

Victor and Lynne Janssen

Driving up from Balmoral in the late afternoon sun, it struck me that the colour green had probably been created here. The east of Scotland often plays second fiddle to its 'other half', but this lush cattle-grazing land is every inch as beautiful as the west. Minmore is a great wee pad run breezily by Victor and Lynne. They used to live in South Africa where they had a restaurant - and once cooked for Prince Philip. Their kingdom here stretches to 10 spotless bedrooms, all cosy and warm, not grand, just downright comfortable; a pretty sitting room where guests swap highland tales and, best of all, a carved wood bar, half-panelled, with scarlet chairs, a resident Jack Russell, the odd trophy and oodles of Glenlivet light flooding in. Oh, and 104 malts. The garden has free-range chickens and a good swimming pool, while the famous Glenlivet distillery is just up the road. Hire bicycles locally and follow tracks deep into the Ladder Hills where buzzard, falcon, even eagles soar. Afterwards, unwind with an Indian head massage or reflexology treatment.

Rooms: 1 four-poster, 4 doubles, 3 twins, 2 singles.
Price: £110; singles £55. Dinner, B&B £82.50 p.p.
Meals: Breakfast 8-9.30am. Light lunch £8-£15. Full picnic £10. Dinner, 4 courses, £30.
Closed: Limited opening in winter.

From Aviemore, A95 north to Bridge of Avon, then south on B9008 to Glenlivet. House at top of hill, 400m before distillery.

Argyll Hotel

Isle of Iona
Argyll and Bute
PA76 6SJ

Tel: 01681 700334
Fax: 01681 700510
E-mail: reception@argyllhoteliona.co.uk
Web: www.argyllhoteliona.co.uk

Claire Bachellerie and Daniel Morgan

When the boat stops at six o'clock in the evening, the Argyll is a good spot to be marooned. Walk over to the west coast, about a mile away, for awesome sunsets - there's nothing between you and America. Daniel and Claire, a young and gentle couple, have preserved the old, cosy island feel, adding their own sweet touches, too. Rooms are spot-on and full of simple, homely comforts; piles of old paperbacks, armchairs, comfy beds and boiling hot water bursting from bathroom taps - you won't think you're being deprived of a thing. Sitting rooms have open fires, there's a pretty conservatory and the dining room has a lovely old-fashioned feel. Food is wholesome, home-cooked and mostly organic, with seasonal vegetables from the garden. Outside, Iona is magical, a mystical dreamscape, home to a hermit's cave, the Abbey and sandy beaches; St. Columba landed on one of them, bringing Christianity to Scotland in 563 AD. Mark, maintenance man, friend and sailor, will take you under sail to Fingal's Cave, seal colonies and dolphins. A perfect place for those who want solitude to be fun.

Rooms: 5 doubles, 2 twins, 1 family,
6 singles; 1 double with separate bath.
Price: £52-£96; singles £37-£46. Dinner, B&B £31-£67 p.p.
Meals: Breakfast 8.15-10am. Light lunch & cream teas also available. Dinner, à la carte, 3 courses approx. £20.
Closed: 1 November-1 April.

Oban ferry to Craignure on Mull, then west to Fionnphort for Iona ferry. Cars are not allowed on Iona but can be left safely at Fionnphort.

Map No: 8

208

Tiroran House

Isle of Mull
Argyll and Bute
PA69 6ES

Tel: 01681 705232
Fax: 01681 705240
E-mail: colin@tiroran.freeserve.co.uk
Web: www.tiroran.com

Colin and Jane Tindal

The drive to Tiroran takes you through some of the wildest and most spectacular scenery in Scotland. There's a magical sense of time almost ticking backwards on the Isle of Mull - perhaps it's the single track roads that connect most of the island, or maybe it's the rolling mists that stroke the heathland landscape in shrouds of pink, orange, and purple - the alchemy of light here can be astounding. Tiroran lies on the north shore of Loch Scridain, an arm of sea that separates the Ross of Mull from nearby Ben More, the only Munro on the island. A stirring burn tumbles past the house through an enchanting garden and down to the sea; it's the dreamiest of walks. Colin and Jane used to run a bigger hotel on the mainland but they wanted something smaller, more intimate. Sit under the shade of a grape vine in the conservatory, or relax in one of two lounges, with log fires and nautical prints. Jane is an excellent cook, so meals are a special occasion, and Colin, ever helpful, is full of suggestions. Bedrooms are all different and most have garden views; binoculars are provided to spot grazing deer. *Children 12 and over welcome.*

Rooms: 3 twins, 3 doubles.
Price: £82-£104; singles £56-£67.
Meals: Breakfast until 9am. Dinner, 3 courses, from £25. Packed lunch by arrangement.
Closed: November-March, open by arrangement.

From Craignure or Fishnish car ferries, A849 towards Bunessan & Iona car ferry, then right on B8035 towards Gruline for 4 miles. Left at converted church. House 1 mile further.

Calgary Hotel and Dovecote Restaurant

Calgary
Nr. Tobermory
Isle of Mull
Argyll and Bute PA75 6QW

Tel: 01688 400256
Fax: 01688 400256
E-mail: calgary.farmhouse@virgin.net
Web: www.calgary.co.uk

Julia and Matthew Reade

On a good day, you could be in Italy or France, such is the Mediterranean feel of the place. Matthew and Julia have let their world evolve naturally and they do their own thing brilliantly: tea shop, restaurant, art gallery, the occasional free-range child, a very relaxed atmosphere and lots of commitment. The fabulous restaurant has brick arches, whitewashed walls, polished wood floors and a simple, crisp, country elegance. Matthew, who renovated the entire place himself, makes huge wooden chairs in his work shop - they could pass for Balinese thrones, and those in the restaurant get booked in advance by returning guests. In the courtyard, wrought-iron tables and terracotta pots are scattered around a fountain, and the gallery has fine local art and ceramics, all of which you can buy; a woodland sculpture walk is on the way. Bedrooms fit the mood perfectly: pretty fabrics, whitewashed walls, comfy beds - nothing disappoints. Walk down to Calgary beach for wonderful sunsets. A truly inspiring place not to be missed.

Rooms: 4 doubles, 2 twins, 2 family, 1 single.
Price: £66-£72; singles from £33.
Meals: Breakfast 8.15-9am weekdays, 8.30-9.30am weekends. Light lunch from £5. Dinner, 3 courses, about £18.
Closed: December-February. Open weekends only November and March.

From Dervaig, B8073 for 5.5 miles. House signed right before Calgary Bay.

Highland Cottage

Breadalbane Street
Tobermory
Isle of Mull
Argyll and Bute PA75 6PD

Tel: 01688 302030
Fax: 01688 302727
E-mail: davidandjo@highlandcottage.co.uk
Web: www.highlandcottage.co.uk

David and Jo Currie

Highland Cottage would be a wonderful place to arrive on a dark, stormy night; welcoming, informal and fully insulated against the elements. This award-winning hotel set in a quiet conservation area looks down over the harbour, with its many yachts and fishing boats. Tobermory is the largest settlement on the Isle of Mull, famous for its brightly-coloured buildings along Fishermen's Pier - Dulux painted them free to promote a new range of paints. You're just a few minutes from the hustle and bustle of quayside life where there's always something going on - Highland games, art festivals, yachting regattas, or just the daily to and fro of islanders stocking up on supplies. David and Jo are a friendly couple, who will point you in the right direction. Bedrooms are in a traditional cottage-style, with pristine bathrooms and thoughtful luxuries; the four-posters are especially attractive. There's a cosy upstairs lounge with hundreds of books to browse through and an honesty bar. Downstairs, enjoy a drink in the sunny conservatory before a candlelit dinner, before rounding off the evening with a glass of Tobermory malt.

Rooms: 2 four-posters, 3 doubles, 1 twin.
Price: £90-£110; singles from £72.50.
Meals: Breakfast until 9.30am. Dinner, 4 courses, £26.50.
Closed: Mid-October-mid-November & Christmas. Restricted opening in January & February.

From Oban ferry, A848 to Tobermory. Across stone bridge at mini-r'bout, then immediate right into Breadalbane St. Highland Cottage on right opposite fire station.

Kilcamb Lodge

Strontian
Highland
PH36 4HY

Tel: 01967 402257
Fax: 01967 402041
E-mail: kilcamblodge@aol.com
Web: www.kilcamblodge.com

Anne and Peter Blakeway

Peter, once a racing skipper in the America's Cup, comes from 10 generations of fishermen; water is in the blood; it's also at the end of the garden. Loch Sunart leads to Mull, Coll, Tiree, America. The position is breathtaking with Glas Bheinn in the distance, rising from the loch shore. Walk down to the water's edge along grass paths flanked by bluebells, a wonderful spot to be shipwrecked. In good weather, they'll take you out in the boat to catch langoustine, lobster and crab for your supper. The house is exquisite; small, relaxed and welcoming. Smart red carpets in the bar, cut-glass crystal in the rich green dining room, a crackling fire and comfy sofas in the drawing room. Bedrooms are excellent, with fresh flowers, lovely fabrics and big, spoiling bath towels. After a fabulous dinner, head for bed to find curtains drawn and the bed turned down. A drive west to the end of the road brings you to Ardnamurchan, the most westerly point in Scotland - they say it's even further west than Land's End. *Cots and highchairs available.*

Rooms: 4 doubles, 7 twins/doubles.
Price: £60-£130.
Meals: Breakfast 8.30-10am; Continental £8.50, Full Scottish £12.50. Lunch from £6. Dinner, 2 courses, £20.50; 4 courses, £29.50.
Closed: December-February.

From Fort William, A82 south for 10 miles to Corran ferry, then A861 to Strontian. Hotel just west of village, signed left. Driving round from Fort William, via A830, then A861 south, takes an hour longer.

Map No: 8

212

Stein Inn

Stein
Waternish
Isle of Skye
Highland IV55 8GA

Tel: 01470 592362
Fax: 01470 592362
E-mail:
angus.teresa@steininn.co.uk
Web: www.steininn.co.uk

Angus and Teresa McGhie

White cottages bob by the quay in this remote, tiny fishing village sparkling in the salty breeze, the setting for Skye's oldest inn. At the beer-seasoned bar of this rough hewn, fire-warmed hostelry, Angus stocks 80 single malts and thirst-quenching real ale under blackened joists. If the weather is good, sit out by the sea loch's shore. Across the water, the headland rises up dramatically, while to the north a few low-slung islands lie scattered about. It is a perfect place to lose yourself and I sat out with my pint watching the locals potter around in their boats. The food is really good against a beautiful sunset and if cosiness comes from contrast and setting then the clean, closely-eaved, blue-carpeted and pine-panelled rooms above are perfect. From your window watch the catch landed, hauled from the sea to your plate, impossibly fresh. There are moorings for yachts - sailors can ring ahead and Angus will have your provisions waiting – but why not spoil yourselves with a couple of nights on land...

Rooms: 4 doubles, 1 single.
Price: £47-£57; singles £23.50-£28.50.
Meals: Breakfast until 9.30am. Bar lunch from £4.50. Dinner, 3 courses, about £13.
Closed: 24 December-1 January.

From Isle of Skye Bridge, A850 to Portree. Follow sign to Uig for 4 miles, then left on A850 towards Dunvegan for 14 miles. Hard right turn to Waternish on B886. Stein is 3.5 miles along loch side.

Map No: 11

Viewfield House

Portree
Isle of Skye
Highland
IV51 9EU

Tel: 01478 612217
Fax: 01478 613517
E-mail: info@viewfieldhouse.com
Web: www.viewfieldhouse.com

Hugh and Linda Macdonald

Viewfield may look a touch imposing but it's actually gracious, relaxing and unstuffy with liberal helpings of laid-back grandeur. The big, bright, elegant sitting room has huge windows and shutters, polished wooden floors and rugs, lovely furniture and lots of "stuff", according to Linda; "stuff" being sculpture, crystal, and silver. It's still a home, albeit quite a grand one, but Linda and Hugh remain delightfully unfazed by the magnificent surroundings; no hushed voices, no trembling guests wondering if it's alright to borrow a book, instead everyone dives in to enjoy it all. The dining room is superb with 1887 wallpaper, Hugh's ancestors on the walls and stained-glass windows. Eat dinner-party, Aga-cooked food either communally around the huge mahogany table, or separately at small tables. Bedrooms are just as good, just as warm, just as fun. Climb through woods to Fingal's Seat for 360° views and a loch to swim in. A great place run by great people and hard to beat for that house-party warmth. *Washing machine and tumble dryer available to guests.*

Rooms: 5 twins, 4 doubles, 1 single; 1 double, 1 single sharing bath and shower.
Price: £80-£90; singles £35-£60. Dinner, B&B £55-£67.50 p.p.
Meals: Breakfast 8.30-9am. Packed lunch £4. Dinner, 4 courses, £20.
Closed: Mid-October-mid-April.

On A87, coming from south, drive entrance is on the outskirts of Portree, opposite BP garage.

Map No: 11

Glenelg Inn

Glenelg
By Kyle of Lochalsh
Highland
IV40 8JR

Christopher Main

Tel: 01599 522273
Fax: 01599 522283
E-mail: christophermain@glenelg-inn.com
Web: www.glenelg-inn.com

Why drive to the shops when you can skim across the water in your motor boat? Catch Christopher going your way and he may give you a lift. As for his inn - just perfect. Bedrooms are extremely good - Colefax and Fowler fabrics, bowls of fruit, great views; splash out on the suite and get an *enormous* room, beautifully decorated, where you can have breakfast in bed while gazing over the sea to Skye – wonderful. There's also a restaurant, bar and sitting room. The latter is more 'country house drawing room', with leather sofas, an open fire and oil paintings, but the epicentre of this lively place is the panelled bar: fishermen, farmers and sailors all come for the unpretentious atmosphere. Low beams and fires, and in one corner a pile of old fish boxes to sit on (which might sound awful, but they're perfect). Come here for excellent bar meals - steamed mussels, wild salmon, venison - and music pipers, fiddlers and folk musicians all pass by. In summer, sit in the garden with its awesome views. Close by, the tiny Kylerhea ferry will take you across to Skye.

Rooms: 2 doubles, 2 twins (with extra bed), 1 suite, 1 family.
Price: Dinner, B&B £72 p.p.; suite £92 p.p.
Meals: Breakfast 8.30-9.30am. Bar meals from £7. Dinner, 4 courses, £25.
Closed: Occasionally in winter.

West off A87 at Sheil Bridge. Keep left into village and inn on right. The Kylerhea ferry from Skye is a beautiful alternative.

Map No: 11

Applecross Inn

Shore Street
Applecross
Wester Ross
Highland IV54 8LR

Tel: 01520 744262
Fax: 01520 744400

Judith Fish

No Highland fling would be complete without a pint at the Applecross, firmly fixed on the west coast trail in an awesome position - the inn sits on the bay with views off to Rassay and Skye. There are two ways in: the spectacular coastal road and *Bealach-Na-Ba*, Britain's highest mountain pass; the latter is not for the light-hearted, cut off by snow for much of the winter, but the view from the top across mountain peaks and Hebridean seas is stupendous. Down in the tiny village of Applecross, at low tide, acre upon acre of golden sand appears - a great place to walk. Judith has given the place a makeover; extending and refurbishing, exposing a stone wall and putting Caithness slate and a woodburning stove in the bar. The hallmark of the Applecross is its simplicity: the peat fires, the half pints of fresh prawns, the piper who plays early mornings in summer to get guests up, and the tiny single with its gigantic view. Lots of fish on the excellent menu, a family feel and one of the best views in Scotland.

Rooms: 1 double, 1 twin, 1 family, 1 double, 1 twin, 2 singles, sharing 2 bathrooms.
Price: £50-£60; singles £25.
Meals: Breakfast 7.30-9.30am weekdays, 8-10am weekends. Bar meals from £5. Dinner, 3 courses, approx. £20.
Closed: New Year's Day.

From Loch Carron, A896 north for 5 miles, then left over Bealach-Na-Ba pass for 11 miles to village, inn on left. When snow closes pass, use road via Kenmore.

Map No: 11

Scarista House

Isle of Harris
Western Isles
HS3 3HX

Tel: 01859 550238
Fax: 01859 550277
E-mail: timandpatricia@scaristahouse.com
Web: www.scaristahouse.com

Patricia and Tim Martin

In a book where views count, Scarista takes the oatcake. The landscape here is nothing short of magnificent. The beach? Two or three miles of pure white sand, hidden from the rest of the world and you'll probably be the only person on it. Then there's the gentle curve of the crescent bay, ridges running down to a turquoise sea and sunsets to astound you. One of the most beautiful places I have ever visited - anywhere in the world. When Patricia and Tim took over it was the fulfilment of a dream. They have been coming to the island for many years - they can guide you to its secrets - and are absolutely committed to their life here. Their house - an old manse - is a perfect island retreat: shuttered windows, peat fires, rugs on bare oak floors, whitewashed walls. Bedrooms are just right, with old oak beds, mahogany dressers, maybe a writing desk facing out to sea. Food is delicious; Tim and Patricia cook brilliantly. Kind island staff may speak in Gaelic, books wait to be read. There's golf - the view from the first tee is surely the best in the game. Worth every moment it takes to get here.

Rooms: 3 doubles, 2 twins.
Price: £130; singles from £75.
Meals: Breakfast 8.30-9.30am. Packed lunch £5.50. Dinner, 4 courses, £35.
Closed: Occasionally in winter.

From Tarbert, A859, signed Rodel. Scarista is 15 miles on left, after golf course.

Pool House Hotel

Poolewe
Wester Ross
Highland
IV22 2LD

Tel: 01445 781272
Fax: 01445 781403
E-mail: enquiries@poolhousehotel.com
Web: www.poolhousehotel.com

Peter, Margaret, Mhairi and Elizabeth Harrison

Fabulous ostentation is not a quality usually associated with Scotland but in a small corner of the Highlands, one hotel has taken luxury to a sublime level. We liked what we saw the first time we visited the Pool House on the shores of Loch Ewe. Since then, the Harrisons have courageously converted 14 rooms into four sumptuous suites with sea views and a sumptuous single. The result is awe-inspiring. The *Diadem* suite is based on a Titanic theme - Margaret is related to the ship's captain. The room's brass light fittings were made with the same moulds used on the Titanic and the Edwardian bath, with its original shower column, was made in 1912, the year the fated liner set sail. Elsewhere, beautiful French furniture, a Regency clock, Art Deco beds – truly impressive stuff. It's also the greenest hotel in Scotland, with worm farms making liquid compost and waterless toilets, as used by Nasa, scooping the coveted Loo of the Year award. Everyone here is lovely and the food's top notch - some things never change. You may see a sea eagle, or the *Aurora Borealis. Children over 14 welcome.*

Rooms: 4 suites, 1 single.
Price: £250-£350; single room £90. Dinner, B&B £125 p.p.
Meals: Breakfast 8-9.45am. Set lunch from £14. Dinner, 4 courses, £25-£35.
Closed: January & February.

Poolewe is on A832 south of Laide and north of Gairloch. Hotel on Loch Ewe.

Summer Isles

Achiltibuie
By Ullapool, Ross-shire
Highland
IV26 2YG

Tel: 01854 622282
Fax: 01854 622251
E-mail: summerisleshotel@aol.com
Web: www.summerisleshotel.co.uk

Mark and Geraldine Irvine

Geraldine's description of the Summer Isles as a "roof in a lovely location" is a wonderful understatement. This old fishing inn may be unremarkable from the outside, but the laid-back house-party feel inside is irresistible. It's been in Mark's family since 1969; he and Geraldine took it over a few years back having opted out of London life - friends have been beating a path to their door ever since. Both are natural hosts, with a deep affection for this beautifully remote part of the west coast of Scotland. Geraldine paints and her artistic leaning infuses the hotel with distinction: dried grass shoots out of terracotta pots, pebbles collected on the beach spill onto windowsills and blobs of colourful art hang on the walls. From the wonderful suites with sea views to the quirky log cabin rooms, all feels at ease; just as the simple unstuffy elegance of the dining room is an ideal setting to be wooed by Michelin-rated food from Chris Firth Bernard. Easily one of the best places to stay in Scotland. *Children six and over welcome. Sea trout fishing on Loch Oscaig June-September.*

Rooms: 4 suites, 9 doubles.
Price: £104-£220. Singles £95-£150.
Meals: Breakfast until 9.30am. Light lunch from £4. Dinner, 5 courses, £40.
Closed: Mid-October-Easter.

From Ullapool, A835 north towards Unapool for about 9 miles, then left on single track road, signed Achiltibuie. Follow signs to village. Hotel on left, sea on right.

Map No: 12

The Albannach
Baddidarrach
Lochinver
Highland
IV27 4LP

Tel: 01571 844407
Fax: 01571 844285
E-mail: the.albannach@virgin.net

Colin Craig and Lesley Crosfield

Colin and Lesley would be anarchists if they took life seriously, which luckily they don't. Instead, they prefer to chew the cud, drink good wine, cook fine food and live with just a little irreverence and a lot of laughter. Colin thinks Lochinver a touch metropolitan but manages to cope by sailing Lesley off to holidays on deserted islands to get away from it all. They spend their days on dry land hatching new plans for the table. Gillian, a friend, crofts the veg - you may get an impromptu herb tasting - the waitress's father catches the crayfish and Colin dives for scallops. Seriously good food is fabulously fresh - expect your supper to be divine... rather like their home. They've done it all themselves, brilliantly of course - renovated, extended, panelled the downstairs, built the terrace, designed the conservatory. Sink into wicker chairs amid rugs and erupting greenery and gaze out across water to Suilven rising majestically in the distance; climb it as well. Bedrooms are just right, fit the mood perfectly and have heaps of comfort; but it's the indefatigable spirit here that makes it so special.

Rooms: 3 doubles, 2 twins.
Price: Dinner, B&B £82.50-£115 p.p;
Meals: Breakfast 8.30-9.45am. Dinner, 5 courses, included; non-residents £36.
Closed: 1 December-15 March and most Mondays.

A837 for Lochinver. Approaching town, right over bridge for Baddidarrach. 1st left and house signed right after 100m.

2 Quail Restaurant
Castle Street
Dornoch
Sutherland
Highland IV25 3SN

Tel: 01862 811811
E-mail: stay@2quail.com
Web: www.2quail.com

Michael and Kerensa Carr

One of the best restaurants in Scotland; small, stylish and set in the genteel surroundings of the Royal Burgh of Dornoch, one of the few places in the Highlands that can be truly described as 'pretty' - the stone used in the buildings has a hint of the Cotswolds. Officially a county 'town', it's really a small village and 2 Quail is right in the middle. Michael and Kerensa look after you impeccably, with a combination of good humour and contrasting styles; he does calm chef in control of superb ingredients; she does dynamite front of house, sizzling with energy and enthusiasm. You eat in one of two dining rooms either side of the hallway; beautiful wool carpets of Buchanan tartan, russet tablecloths and shelves of books worth reading suggest the warmth of autumn, of leaves just turning. Upstairs, two pleasant rooms have a mixture of authentic Victorian and Edwardian furniture; all is welcoming and comfortable. Settle in the small sitting room and dream about the meal to come as the smell of the stockpot wafts invitingly up the stairs. *Children eight and over welcome.*

Rooms: 1 double; 1 twin/double, with private bath/shower.
Price: £70-£90.
Meals: Breakfast 8.30am weekdays, 9am weekends; other times by request. Dinner, 4 courses, £30; booking essential. Packed lunch by prior arrangement.
Closed: Christmas & 2 weeks in February/March.

From Inverness, A9 north for 44 miles,
then right on A949, signed Dornoch.
Restaurant on left before Cathedral.

The Dower House

Highfield
Muir of Ord
Highland
IV6 7XN

Tel: 01463 870090
Fax: 01463 870090
E-mail: stay@thedowerhouse.co.uk
Web: www.thedowerhouse.co.uk

Robyn and Mena Aitchison

Neither a restaurant nor a hotel, this historic house in the Cottage *orné* style happily defies attempts to apply a convenient label. To say it's a must for those who enjoy good food in intimate country house surroundings doesn't truly do it justice. It's more like the Mini that Robyn somehow coaxed into transporting several of the larger artefacts here: small and adorable. Mena describes Robyn's eclectic brand of no frills cooking as "gutsy and colourful". That could just as well describe the chef himself, a broad presence dressed in bold colours, whose enthusiasm and eye for the extraordinary infuse the house. Impeccable rooms hold some beautiful discoveries; tinkle a tune on the pianola, marvel at the magnificent Victorian half-tester or enjoy a lazy soak under a trompe l'œil of climbing wisteria. Dinner is served in a graceful dining room - with a piano at one end - and finishes with home-made truffles and coffee in front of an open fire in the cosy sitting room. In case you're wondering what you've done to deserve all this - it's because you do. A gem of a place. *Self-catering in lodge house, sleeps 2-5.*

Rooms: 1 suite, 2 doubles,
2 twin/doubles.
Price: £110-£130; suite £150;
singles £65-£85.
Meals: Breakfast 8-9.30am. Dinner,
3 courses, £35.

*A9 north of Inverness to Tore r'bout,
then left on A832, signed Muir of Ord.
In village, A862, signed Dingwall.
Entrance 1 mile on left.*

Clifton House

Nairn
Highland
IV12 4HW

Tel: 01667 453119
Fax: 01667 452836
E-mail: macintyre@clifton-hotel.co.uk
Web: www.clifton-hotel.co.uk

J Gordon Macintyre

Inverness may be a touch far-flung, but Clifton House is worth a detour from just about anywhere. Unique, powerful, magnetic - this is easily one of our favourite hotels: an artistic cauldron yet remarkably, without the slightest hint of pretension. Gordon has fashioned his world over the years, keeping it beyond the designer's grasp. Everywhere something exceptional draws the eye: Pugin wallpaper, of Lord Chancellor fame, in a drawing room stuffed with beautiful things; red silk on the walls of the long corridor; a handmade marbled table in the dining room; sprays of fresh flowers and wall-hugging art in the yellow sitting room. Gordon is gently passionate about opera, art and life; in winter, plays, concerts and recitals grace the beautiful rooms. He cooks sublime food, a symphony he orchestrates in tandem with his son Charles. The bedrooms, some with views of the Moray Firth, are all different, all delightful, with Zoffany fabrics, Vogue prints, busts ... if this all sounds a bit over-the-top, blame it on our exuberance. A very special place.

Rooms: 4 singles, 4 doubles, 4 twins.
Price: £85-£117; singles £60.
Meals: Breakfast until 11.30am.
Dinner, à la carte, about £25.
Closed: Christmas & New Year.

From Inverness, A96 west. In Nairn, left at only r'bout, signed to beach. Continue along seafront with sea on right. Hotel signed on left.

Map No: 12

Boath House

Auldearn
Nairn
Highland
IV12 5TE

Don and Wendy Matheson

Tel: 01667 454896
Fax: 01667 455469
E-mail: wendy@boath-house.demon.co.uk
Web: www.boath-house.com

"A bin of wine, a spice of wit, a house with lawns enclosing it, a living river by the door, a nightingale in the sycamore." Robert Louis Stevenson could have been writing about Boath. This wonderful late Georgian mansion, set in 20 acres of lake, stream and mature woodland, lies in a warm micro-climate known as Scotland's 'banana belt'. Don and Wendy spent four years restoring it from a derelict state and intuitively know what works, the result, perhaps, of many years travelling; plaudits are raving and awards are rolling in - not bad for a first attempt. "We're just doing what we like as well as we can," says Don, with a broad Highland grin. He does front of house with aplomb; a fastidious foodie, the story of what you're eating is as important as the taste. It helps that Wendy and chef Charlie Lockley prepare amazing food. This is fine dining, *par excellence*, the sense of well-being afterwards is immaculate. Climb graceful stairs to stylish bedrooms, with plush carpets, big beds, nice antiques and lots of light, and pamper yourself in a basement spa with an Aveda treatment, or a sauna. Bliss. *Uses mostly organic produce.*

Rooms: Main house: 2 twin/doubles, 4 doubles; Cottage: 1 double.
Price: £135-£200; singles £95; cottage £175.
Meals: Breakfast 8.30-10am. Lunch, 4 courses, £24.95. Dinner, 5 courses, £35. Packed lunch by arrangement.
Closed: Last 3 weeks in January.

From Inverness, A96 for 16 miles to Auldearn. House on left off village bypass.

The Cross
Tweed Mill Brae
Kingussie
Highland
PH21 1TC

Tel: 01540 661166
Fax: 01540 661080
E-mail: relax@thecross.co.uk
Web: www.thecross.co.uk

Tony and Ruth Hadley

It may not be deep country, but this is a special destination in its own right. Unwind on a beautiful terrace, surrounded by copper beech, hazel, willow, alder, and sycamore; the trees enfold you in peace and quiet. They bring wildlife, too: dippers, heron, otters, red squirrel - even a roe deer. Inside, whitewashed stone walls meet cool, contemporary design, with plush red carpets, old wooden beams, an open-plan feel and modern art scattered pleasingly about the place. Upstairs, clean lines and light rooms have a Scandinavian feel, with skylights in eaved walls. Bedrooms have the same smart, minimalist feel with halogen lights and excellent beds. Rooms on one side have the river right below them; one has a small balcony. Above all, the heart of The Cross is the restaurant - one of the best in Scotland. Ruth's exceptional food has won stacks of awards, so climb that mountain in the afternoon and have no guilt at supper. Not a place to be hurried. *Children over eight welcome.*

Rooms: 7 doubles, 2 twins.
Price: Dinner, B&B £95-£115 p.p.
Meals: Breakfast 8-10am; healthy/Continental only. Dinner, 5 courses. Restaurant closed Tuesdays.
Closed: 1 December-28 February.

At the only traffic lights in Kingussie, right up hill if coming from north, signed left.

Old Pines Restaurant with Rooms
Spean Bridge
By Fort William
Highland
PH34 4EG

Tel: 01397 712324
Fax: 01397 712433
E-mail:
specialplaces@oldpines.co.uk
Web: www.oldpines.co.uk

Bill and Sukie Barber

Old Pines is a must for anyone in search of that appealing combination of relaxed informality and seriously good food. Sukie and Bill do things effortlessly, be it marshalling one of their children off to bed while greeting a guest, or sitting down in the garden for a chat while chopping herbs from their organic garden. In between, Sukie somehow finds time to prove her fast-growing reputation as one of Scotland's top chefs, cooking up truly ambrosial food that's eaten communally in the stone-flagged, chalet-style dining room. Bill readily shares his enthusiasm for local scenery, wildlife, history and culture; nothing at Old Pines is too much trouble. Pretty rooms, comfortable sofas, log fires and loads of books await inside, while plants and flowers frame Ben Nevis in the conservatory. Kids can eat and play with the Barbers' brood; a fenced garden and a playroom with pool and table tennis provide ample distraction. Bedrooms are chalet-style with stripped pine walls and duvets, all perfect, but it's the Barbers who really make this place so special; kind, generous, fun and thoroughly down-to-earth. Don't miss it.

Rooms: 2 family, 2 twins, 2 doubles, 2 singles; 1 single with private bathroom.
Price: Dinner, B&B £60-£80 p.p.; children £10 sharing with parents; B&B (Mondays) from £45.
Meals: Breakfast times flexible. Dinner, 5 courses & afternoon tea included; non-residents £30. Supper on Sundays £20.
Closed: Rarely. Dinner and lunch not available Mondays.

On A82, 1 mile north of Spean Bridge left just after Commando Memorial onto B8004 to Gairlochy. Old Pines 300 yards on right.

Map No: 12

Balfour Castle

Shapinsay
Orkney
KW17 2DY

Tel: 01856 711282
Fax: 01856 711283
E-mail: balfourcastle@btinternet.com
Web: www.balfourcastle.co.uk

Patricia and Andrew Lidderdale

"There is doubt as to whether one should reveal this lovely place to a living soul," wrote a Norwegian journalist of this magical place, the most northerly castle hotel in the world and a perfectly preserved example of the Victorian laird's estate. Balfour was completed in 1848 in the 'calendar house' style, with seven turrets, 12 exterior doors, 52 rooms and 365 panes of glass. It stands in magnificent scenery on the tiny island of Shapinsay, surrounded by an ancient sycamore wood whose boughs gnarl and twist like skeletal armour. Its authenticity is also protected by a strange twist of fate; the last Balfour left no heir, so he bequeathed it all to Captain Tadeusz Zawadski, a Polish cavalry officer who settled after being posted to Orkney during the Second World War. Balfour believed the Pole could undertake the huge task and how right he was, for his descendants run the place with the same warmth and affection today. Each room is a wonderful discovery; the library is a favourite, with carved busts of Greek thinkers denoting the subject matter below. Take long walks, explore the island and leave the world behind for a while; lucky folk may even see a rainbow lit by the northern lights. *Pets by arrangement.*

Rooms: 2 doubles, 1 twin; 1 triple, with private bathroom, 2 doubles, sharing private bathroom.
Price: Dinner, B&B £100 p.p.
Meals: Breakfast times flexible. Dinner, 3 courses, included.
Closed: February-March.

Shapinsay car ferry from Kirkwall (25 mins). Regular sailings. Castle minibus will collect foot passengers.

Woodwick House

Evie
Orkney
KW17 2PQ

Tel: 01856 751330
Fax: 01856 751383
E-mail: woodwickhouse@appleonline.net
Web: www.orknet.co.uk/woodwick

Ann Herdman

"Drink here voyager, you about to embark on the salt sound towards Eynhallow and the Kirk of Magnus"; so reads poet George MacKay Brown's inscription in the garden of this quiet haven. Trees are in short supply on Orkney but Woodwick sits in a wild sycamore wood fed by a burn that tumbles down to a small bay overlooking the island of Gairsay; walk through wildflowers and hanging lichen to the sound of rushing water and babbling crows - magical. Woodwick promotes "care, creativity and conservation", so come here to think, free of distraction. The house is nothing fancy, just clean and homely, friendly and peaceful. Built in 1912, it stands on the site of a larger building destroyed during the Jacobite rebellion; all that remains is a remarkable "doocot", a perfect space for quiet contemplation. There's a wisteria-filled conservatory, a candlelit dining room - food is organic where possible - two sitting rooms, an open fire, a piano, books and lots of old films you've been meaning to see for ages. A nearby ferry takes you to some of the smaller islands, while the Italian Chapel and numerous ancient sites are an absolute must. *Cots available. Pets £7 for duration of stay.*

Rooms: 2 doubles, 2 twins; 3 doubles, 1 twin, with basins, sharing 1 bathroom.
Price: £56-£78; singles £32-£48.
Meals: Breakfast 8.30-10am. Dinner, 3 courses, £22. Lunch & packed lunch by arrangement.
Closed: Never.

From Kirkwall or Stromness, A965 to Finstown, then A966, signed Evie. After 7 miles, right, just past Tingwall ferry turning, then left down track to house.

Map No: 13

228

Quick reference indices

WHEELCHAIR FRIENDLY
These owners have told us that they have facilities for people in wheelchairs.

Birmingham
9

Devon
59

Dorset
63 • 64

Gloucestershire
69 • 76

Herefordshire
86

Northamptonshire
107

Oxfordshire
114 • 119

Sussex
140

Yorkshire
159

Scotland
197 • 198 • 200 • 211 • 214 • 222 • 224 • 226

LIMITED MOBILITY
These places have bedrooms and bathrooms that are accessible for people of limited mobility. Please check details.

Bath and N. E. Somerset
1 • 2 • 4 • 5

Berkshire
8

Birmingham
9

Bristol
10

Channel Islands
11

Cornwall
15 • 16 • 17 • 24

Cumbria
27 • 28 • 34 • 35 • 36

Derbyshire
40

Devon
41 • 45 • 48 • 53

Dorset
64

Durham
65

Essex
66

Gloucestershire
72 • 73 • 79

Hampshire
81 • 83

Herefordshire
85 • 86

Isle of Wight
88

Kent
91

Lancashire
95 • 96 • 98 • 100

Northumberland
104 • 105 • 108 • 109

Nottinghamshire
111

Oxfordshire
112 • 113 • 115 • 117 • 118 • 120

Shropshire
121

Somerset
126 • 128

Suffolk
136

Quick reference indices

ROOMS UNDER £80
These places offer a double or twin room based on two people sharing for under £80 per night. Check when booking.

RESTAURANTS-WITH-ROOMS
These places are licensed restaurants that also have accommodation.

Quick reference indices

ORGANIC & GROWN
These owners use mostly organic
ingredients, chemical-free, home-
grown or locally-grown produce.
Entry numbers 52, 67, 85 & 177
have been certified as totally
organic by the Soil Association.

Quick reference indices

SWIMMING POOL
A swimming pool is available on
the premises for guests to use.

TENNIS
A tennis court is available on the
premises for guests to use.

Hotel Soap Opera

The following letters are taken from an actual incident between a hotel and one of its guests.

Dear Maid - Please do not leave any more of those little bars of soap in my bathroom since I have brought my own bath-sized Imperial Leather. Please remove the 6 unopened little bars from the shelf under the medicine chest and another 3 in the shower soap dish. They are in my way.
Thank you, S. Berman

Dear Room 635 - I am not your regular maid. She will be back tomorrow, Thursday, from her day off. I took the 3 hotel soaps out of the shower soap dish as you requested. The 6 bars on your shelf I took out of your way and put on top of your Kleenex dispenser in case you should change your mind. This leaves only the 3 bars I left today which my instructions from the management is to leave 3 soaps daily. I hope this is satisfactory.
Kathy, Relief Maid

Dear Maid - I hope you are my regular maid. Apparently Kathy did not tell you about my note to her concerning the little bars of soap. When I got back to my room this evening I found you had added 3 little Camays to the shelf under my medicine cabinet. I am going to be here in the hotel for two weeks and have brought my own bath-size Imperial Leather so I won't need those 6 little Camays which are on the shelf. They are in my way. Please remove them.
S. Berman

Dear Mr. Berman - My day off was last Wed. so the relief maid left 3 hotel soaps which we are instructed by the management. I took the 6 soaps which were in your way on the shelf and put them in the soap dish where your Imperial Leather was. I put the Imperial Leather in the medicine cabinet for your convenience. I didn't remove the 3 complimentary soaps which are always placed inside the medicine cabinet for all new check-ins and which you did not object to when you checked in last Monday.
Please let me know if I can of further assistance.
Your regular maid, Dotty

Dear Mr. Berman - The assistant manager, Mr. Kensedder, informed me. that you called him and said you were unhappy with your maid service. I have assigned a new girl to your room. I hope you will accept my apologies for any inconvenience. If you have any future complaints please contact me between 8AM and 5PM so I can give it my personal attention. Thank you.
Elaine Carmen, Housekeeper

Dear Miss Carmen - It is impossible to contact you by phone since I leave the hotel for business at 7.45 AM and don't get back before 5.30 or 6PM. That's the reason I called Mr. Kensedder last night. You were already off duty. I only asked Mr. Kensedder if he could do anything about those little bars of soap. The new maid you assigned me must have thought I was a new check-in today, since she left another 3 bars of hotel soap in my medicine cabinet along with her regular delivery of 3 bars on the bath-room shelf. In just 5 days here I have accumulated 24 little bars of soap. Why are you doing this to me?
S. Berman

Hotel Soap Opera

Dear Mr. Berman - Your maid, Kathy, has been instructed to stop delivering soap to your room and remove the extra soaps. If I can be of further assistance, please call extension 1108 between 8AM and 5PM. Thank you.
Elaine Carmen, Housekeeper

Dear Mr. Kensedder - My bath-size Imperial Leather is missing. Every bar of soap was taken from my room including my own bath-size one. I came in late last night and had to call the bellhop to bring me 4 little Cashmere Bouquets.
S. Berman

Dear Mr. Berman - I have informed our housekeeper, Elaine Carmen, of your soap problem. I cannot understand why there was no soap in your room since our maids are instructed to leave 3 bars of soap each time they service a room. The situation will be rectified immediately. Please accept my apologies for the inconvenience.
Martin L. Kensedder, Assistant Manager

Dear Mrs. Carmen - Who the hell left 54 little bars of Camay in my room? I came in last night and found 54 little bars of soap. I don't want 54 little bars of Camay. I want my one damn bar of bath-size soap. Do you realize I have 54 bars of soap in here. All I want is my bath size Imperial Leather. Please give me back my bath-size soap.
S. Berman

Dear Mr. Berman - You complained of too much soap in your room so I had them removed. Then you complained to Mr. Kensedder that all your soap was missing so I personally returned them. The 24 Camays which had been taken and the 3 Camays you are supposed to receive daily (sic). I don't know anything about the 4 Cashmere Bouquets. Obviously your maid, Kathy, did not know I had returned your soaps so she also brought 24 Camays plus the 3 daily Camays. I don't know where you got the idea this hotel issues bath-size Imperial Leather. I was able to locate some bath-size Ivory which I left in your room.
Elaine Carmen, Housekeeper

Dear Mrs. Carmen - Just a short note to bring you up-to-date on my latest soap inventory. As of today I possess:

- *On shelf under medicine cabinet - 18 Camay in 4 stacks of 4 & 1 stack of 2.*
- *On Kleenex dispenser - 11 Camay in 2 stacks of 4 & 1 stack of 3.*
- *On bedroom dresser - 1 stack of 3 Cashmere Bouquet, 1 stack of 4 hotel-size Ivory, & 8 Camay in 2 stacks of 4.*
- *Inside medicine cabinet - 14 Camay in 3 stacks of 4 &1 stack of 2.*
- *In shower soap dish - 6 Camay, very moist.*
- *On northeast corner of tub - 1 Cashmere Bouquet, slightly used.*
- *On northwest corner of tub - 6 Camays in 2 stacks of 3.*

Please ask Kathy when she services my room to make sure the stacks are neatly piled and dusted. Also, please advise her that stacks of more than 4 have a tendency to tip. May I suggest that my bedroom window sill is not in use and will make an excellent spot for future soap deliveries. One more item, I have purchased another bar of bath-sized Imperial Leather which I am keeping in the hotel vault in order to avoid further misunderstandings.
S. Berman

Annual Events 2002

January 1: London Parade
floats & marching bands leave
Parliament Square at noon
020 8566 8586

January 11-13: Saturnalia Beer
Festival, Llanwrtyd Wells, Powys
01591 610666

January 12-27: London
International Mime Festival,
The South Bank
020 7637 5661
www.mimefest.co.uk

January 25: Burns Night;
celebration of Scottish poet

February 8-10: Cheltenham Folk
Festival 01242 227979

February 12, Shrove Tuesday:
Chinese New Year

Purbeck Marblers & Stonecutters
Day, Corfe Castle, Dorset; football
game through village
lesh@corfe-castle.demon.co.uk

March 2-10: Bath Literature
Festival 01225 463362
www.bathlitfest.org.uk

March 8-10: Folk 'n' Ale Weekend,
Llanwrtyd Wells, Powys
01591 610666

March 12-14: Cheltenham Gold
Cup; national-hunt horseracing
festival 01242 226226
www.cheltenham.co.uk

March 29-April 1: British Juggling
Convention, Cardiff
www.bjc2002.co.uk

March 29, Good Friday: Marbles
Championship, Tinsley Green,
nr. Crawley, Sussex
www.marblemuseum.org

March 30, Easter Saturday: Oxford
and Cambridge University Boat Race
www.theboatrace.org

Nutters Dance, Bacup, Lancashire
01706 870119

April 1, Easter Monday: Hare Pie
Scramble and Bottle Kicking,
Hallaton, Leicestershire
0116 265 7310

April 4-6: Grand National, Aintree,
Liverpool; national-hunt horseracing
www.aintree.co.uk

April 5-7: Cheltenham Festival
of Literature 01242 227979

April 19-20: Scottish Grand
National, Ayr; horseracing
01292 264179
www.ayr-racecourse.co.uk

April 21: London Marathon
020 7620 4117
www.london-marathon.co.uk

April 26-28: Mull Music Festival,
Isle of Mull
01688 302009

April 30-May 3: Minehead Hobby
Horse, Somerset; pagan festival
01643 702624

May-July: Glyndebourne Opera
Festival, East Sussex
01273 813813
www.glyndebourne.com

May 1, May Day: Padstow Obby
Oss, Cornwall; pagan festival
01872 322900

May Morning Celebrations,
Magdalen College, Oxford; choir
sings at dawn 01865 726871

May 1-6: Cheltenham Jazz Festival
01242 227979

May 8: Helston Furry Dance,
Cornwall; pagan festival
01872 322900

May 12: May Fayre and Puppet
Festival, St Paul's church,
Covent Garden, London
020 7375 0441

May 17-June 2: Bath International
Music Festival - 01225 463362
www.bathmusicfest.org.uk

Annual Events 2002

May 21-24: Chelsea Flower Show, Royal Hospital, London
020 7834 4333
www.rhs.org.uk

May 23-27: Orkney Folk Festival, Stromness
01856 850773

May 26-29: Llanelli Festival of Walks, Carmarthenshire
01554 770077

May 27, Spring Bank Holiday Monday: Cheese Rolling, Brockworth, Gloucestershire
01452 421188

May 31-June 9: Hay-on-Wye Literature Festival, Herefordshire
www.hayfestival.co.uk

Early June: Fleadh, Finsbury Park, North London; Irish music festival
020 8963 0940;
www.meanfiddler.com

June 1: Man Versus Horse, Llanwrtyd Wells, Powys; runners compete vs horse riders over 23 miles
01591 610666

June 1-2: Seafood Festival, Eyemouth, Borders, Scotland; food, dancing, street theatre
018907 50678

June 7: Cotswold Olimpicks, Chipping Campden, Gloucestershire; rustic sports festival & torchlight procession
www.chippingcampden.co.uk

June 7-23: Aldeburgh Festival, Suffolk; classical music
01728 687110
www.aldeburgh.co.uk

June 8: The Derby, Epsom, Surrey; flat horseracing - 01372 470047
www.epsomderby.co.uk

June 20-23: Royal Highland Show, Edinburgh; agricultural display
0131 335 6200
www.rhass.org.uk

June-Mid-August: Royal Academy Summer Exhibition, London; everyman art
020 7300 8000
www.royalacademy.org.uk

June 6-12: Appleby Horse Fair, Appleby-in-Westmorland, Cumbria
01452 421188

June 18-21: Royal Ascot, Berkshire; flat racing
01344 622211
www.ascot-authority.co.uk

June 21: Kithill Midsummer's Night Bonfire, Bodmin Moor, Cornwall - 01872 322900

June 21-23: Round Mull Yacht Race, Isle of Mull
01631 569100

June 21-26: St. Magnus Festival, Orkney; classical music
01856 871445
www.orkneyislands.com

June 22: World Worm-Charming Championships, Willaston, Cheshire
01270 663957

June 24-July 7: Wimbledon Lawn Tennis Championships
www.wimbledon.org

June 28-30: Glastonbury Festival, Somerset
www.glastonburyfestivals.co.uk

June 29-30: Scottish Traditional Boat Festival, Portsoy; old boats, ceilidhs
01261 842951
www.sixvillages.org.uk/boatfest

July-early September: The Proms, Royal Albert Hall, London
020 75898212
www.royalalberthall.com

July 3-7: Henley Royal Regatta, Oxfordshire - www.hrr.co.uk

July 5-14: Frome Festival; arts, theatre, music
01373 455690

Annual Events 2002

July 6-7: Game Fair,
Scone Palace, Perth
01620 850577
www.scottishfair.com

July 6-21: Cheltenham
International Festival of Music
01242 227979

July 8-14: Llangollen International
Musical Eisteddfod, North Wales
01978 861501
www.international-eisteddfod.co.uk

July 12-14: Swanage Jazz Festival,
Dorset - 01929 422885

July 18: Tobermory Highland
Games, Isle of Mull
01688 302001

July 25-28: Cambridge Folk Festival
www.cam-folkfest.co.uk.

July 26-28: Womad Rivermead,
Reading; world and dance music
01225 744494
www.womad.org

August 2-9: Sidmouth International
Festival, Devon; folk music, arts
www.mrscasey.co.uk/sidmouth

August 8-12: Bristol Balloon Fiesta,
Ashton Park
www.bristolfiesta.co.uk

August 9-11: Brecon Jazz Festival
Powys - www.breconjazz.co.uk

August 11-31: Edinburgh Festival;
comedy, theatre, film
www.eif.co.uk

August 17-25: Victorian Week,
Llandrindod Wells, Powys;
period costume
01597 822600

August 24-26, Bank Holiday
weekend: Notting Hill Carnival,
London; Caribbean festival
www.nottinghillcarnival.org.uk

Cartmel Races, Cumbria; horseracing
0151 5232600

August 26, Bank Holiday Monday:
World Bog Snorkelling
Championships,
Llanwrtyd Wells, Powys
01591 610666

September 9: Abbots Bromley
Horn Dance, Staffs; Pagan dance
www.abbotsbromley.com

September 14: Leuchars Air Show,
nr. St Andrews
01334 839000
www.airshow.co.uk

September 19-21: Ayr Gold Cup;
horseracing
01292 264179
www.ayr-racecourse.co.uk

September 21: World Gurning
Championships,
Egremont, Cumbria
01946 821554

October 11-13: Tour of Mull Rally,
Isle of Mull; rally driving
01254 826564

November 3: London to Brighton
Veteran Car Run
01753 681736

November 5: Guy Fawkes Night

November 16: Biggest Liar in the
World, Bridge Inn, Wasdale,
Cumbria
019467 26221

December 31, New Year's Eve:
Scotland Hogmanay

Picadilly Circus, London

Tar Barrels Parade, Allendale,
Northumberland

Mari Llwyd Torch Lit Walk,
Llanwrtyd Wells, Powys
01591 610236

What is Alastair Sawday Publishing?

A dozen or more of us work in two converted barns on a farm near Bristol, close enough to the city for a bicycle ride and far enough for a silence broken only by horses and the occasional passage of a tractor. Some editors work in the countries they write about, e.g. France and Spain, others work from the UK but are based outside the office. We enjoy each other's company, celebrate every event possible, and work in an easy-going but committed environment.

These books owe their style and mood to Alastair's miscellaneous career and interest in the community and the environment. He has taught overseas, worked with refugees, run development projects abroad, founded a travel company and several environmental organisations - many of which have flourished. There has been a slightly mad streak evident throughout, not least in his driving of a waste-paper-collection lorry for a year, the manning of stalls at impoverished jumble sales and the pursuit of causes long before they were considered sane.

Back to the travel company: trying to take his clients to eat and sleep in places that were not owned by corporations and assorted bandits he found dozens of very special places in France - farms, châteaux etc - a list that grew into the first book, French Bed and Breakfast. It was a celebration of 'real' places to stay and the remarkable people who run them.

The publishing company is based on the unexpected success of that first and rather whimsical French book. It started as a mild crusade, and there it stays - full of 'attitude', and the more appealing for it. For we still celebrate the unusual, the beautiful, the individual. We are passionate about rejecting the banal, the ugly, the pompous and the indifferent and we are passionate too about promoting the use of 'real' food. Alastair is a trustee of the Soil Association and keen to promote organic growing and consuming by owners and visitors.

It is a source of deep pleasure to us to have learned that there are many thousands of people who share our views. We are by no means alone in trumpeting the virtues of standing up to the destructive uniformity of so much of our culture.

We are building a company in which people and values matter. We love to hear of new friendships between those in the book and those using it and to know that there are many people - among them farmers - who have been enabled to pursue their lives thanks to the extra income the book brings them.

www.specialplacestostay.com

Adrift on the unfathomable and often unnavigable sea of accommodation pages on the Internet, those who have discovered www.specialplacestostay.com have found it to be an island of reliability. Not only will you find a database full of honest, trustworthy, up-to-date information about over a thousand *Special Places to Stay* across Europe, but also:

- Direct links to the web sites of hundreds of places from the series.
- Colourful, clickable, interactive maps.
- The facility to make most bookings by email - even if you don't have email yourself!
- Online purchasing of our books, securely and cheaply.
- Regular, exclusive special offers on books from the whole series.
- The latest news about future editions, new titles and new places.
- The chance to participate in the evolution of both the guides and the site.

The site is constantly evolving and is frequently updated. By the time you read this we will have introduced an online notice board for owners to use, where they can display special offers or forthcoming local events that might tempt you. We're expanding our European maps, adding more useful and interesting links, providing news, updates and special features that won't appear anywhere else but in our window on the world wide web.

Just as with our printed guides, your feedback counts, so when you've surfed all this and you still want more, let us know - this site has been planted with room to grow!

Russell Wilkinson, Web Editor
editor@specialplacestostay.com

Alastair Sawday's
Special Places to Stay series

ALASTAIR SAWDAY'S

Special
places to stay

ITALY

A stunning selection of places, all special in some

ALASTAIR SAWDAY'S

Special
places to stay

BRITISH BED & BREAKFAST

A mouthwatering selection of more than 900 very special B&Bs in England, Scotland and Wales.

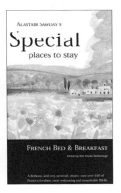

ALASTAIR SAWDAY'S

Special
places to stay

FRENCH BED & BREAKFAST

A brilliant, and very personal, choice: now over 650 of France's loveliest, most welcoming and remarkable B&Bs

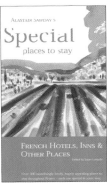

ALASTAIR SAWDAY'S

Special
places to stay

FRENCH HOTELS, INNS &
OTHER PLACES

Over 300 irresistibly lovely, hugely appealing places to stay throughout France - each one special in some way.

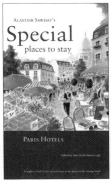

ALASTAIR SAWDAY'S

Special
places to stay

PARIS HOTELS

A night in Paris for not precious to the slept in the wrong hotel.

ALASTAIR SAWDAY'S

Special
places to stay

IRELAND

From the sublime to the eccentric, the sophisticated to the simple! Here is the best of Ireland's best.

ALASTAIR SAWDAY'S

Special
places to stay

SPAIN

A feast of over 300 wonderful places all over mainland Spain and its islands

ALASTAIR SAWDAY'S

Special
places to stay

PORTUGAL

From the sublime to the eccentric, the sophisticated to the simple! Here is the best of Ireland's best.

ALASTAIR SAWDAY'S

Special
places to stay

GARDEN BED & BREAKFAST

Gardens with buds? Well - sort of. Ninety-nine very special houses with gardens to match. Sleep and stroll in peace.

www.specialplacestostay.com

The Little Earth Book - 2nd Edition

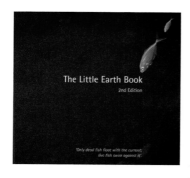

The Little Earth Book
2nd Edition

'Only dead fish float with the current; live fish swim against it.'

A fascinating read. The earth is now desperately vulnerable; so are we. Original, stimulating mini-essays about what is going wrong with our planet, and about the greatest challenge of our century: how to save the Earth for us all. It is pithy, yet intellectually credible, well-referenced, wry yet deadly serious.

Alastair Sawday, the publisher is also an environmentalist. For over 25 years he has campaigned, not only against the worst excesses of modern tourism and its hotels, but against environmental 'looniness' of other kinds. He has fought for systems and policies that might enable our beautiful planet - simply - to survive. He founded and ran Avon Friends of the Earth, has run for Parliament, and has led numerous local campaigns. He is now a trustee of the Soil Association, experience upon which he draws in this remarkable book.

Researched and written by an eminent Bristol architect, James Bruges, *The Little Earth Book* is a clarion call to action, a mind-boggling collection of mini-essays on today's most important environmental concerns, from global warming and poisoned food to economic growth, Third World debt, genes and 'superbugs'. Undogmatic but sure-footed, the style is light, explaining complex issues with easy language, illustrations and cartoons. Ideas are developed chapter by chapter, yet each one stands alone. It is an easy browse.

The Little Earth Book provides hope, with new ideas and examples of people swimming against the current, of bold ideas that work in practice. It is a book as important as it is original. Learn about the issues and join the most important debate of this century.

Did you know.....

- If everyone adopted the Western lifestyle we would need five earths to support us.

- In 50 years the US has - with intensive pesticide use - doubled the amount of crops lost to pests.

- Environmental disasters have created more than 80 MILLION refugees.

www.thelittleearth.co.uk

Order Form UK

All these books are available in major bookshops or you may order them direct. Post and packaging are FREE.

	Price	No. copies
Special Places to Stay: **Portugal**		
Edition 1	£8.95	
Special Places to Stay: **Spain**		
Edition 4	£11.95	
Special Places to Stay: **Ireland**		
Edition 3	£10.95	
Special Places to Stay: **Paris Hotels**		
Edition 3	£8.95	
Special Places to Stay: **Garden Bed & Breakfast**		
Edition 1	£10.95	
Special Places to Stay: **French Bed & Breakfast**		
Edition 7	£14.95	
Special Places to Stay: **British Hotels, Inns** and other places		
Edition 3	£11.95	
Special Places to Stay: **British Bed & Breakfast**		
Edition 6	£13.95	
Special Places to Stay: **French Hotels, Inns** and other places		
Edition 2	£11.95	
Special Places to Stay: **Italy**		
Edition 2	£11.95	
Special Places to Stay: **French Holiday Homes**		
Edition 1 (available January '02)	£11.95	
The Little Earth Book	£5.99	

Please make cheques payable to: **Alastair Sawday Publishing**   **Total** [   ]

Please send cheques to: Alastair Sawday Publishing, The Home Farm Stables, Barrow Gurney, Bristol BS48 3RW. **For credit card orders call 01275 464891 or order directly from our website www.specialplacestostay.com**

Name:

Address:

Postcode:

Tel: Fax: BH3

If you do not wish to receive mail from other companies, please tick the box ❑

Order Form USA

All these books are available at your local bookstore, or you may order
direct. Allow two to three weeks for delivery.

	Price	No. copies
***Special Places to Stay:* Portugal**		
Edition 1	$14.95	
***Special Places to Stay:* Ireland**		
Edition 3	$17.95	
***Special Places to Stay:* Spain**		
Edition 4	$19.95	
***Special Places to Stay:* Paris Hotels**		
Edition 3	$14.95	
***Special Places to Stay:* French Hotels, Inns and other places**		
Edition 2	$19.95	
***Special Places to Stay:* French Bed & Breakfast**		
Edition 7	$19.95	
***Special Places to Stay:* Garden Bed & Breakfast**		
Edition 1	$17.95	
***Special Places to Stay:* Italy**		
Edition 2	$17.95	
***Special Places to Stay:* British Bed & Breakfast**		
Edition 6	$19.95	

Shipping in the continental USA: $3.95 for one book,
$4.95 for two books, $5.95 for three or more books.
Outside continental USA, call (800) 243-0495 for prices.
For delivery to AK, CA, CO, CT, FL, GA, IL, IN, KS, MI, MN, MO, NE,
NM, NC, OK, SC, TN, TX, VA, and WA, please add appropriate sales tax

Please make checks payable to: The Globe Pequot Press   **Total**

To order by phone with MasterCard or Visa: (800) 243-0495. 9a.m. to 5p.m.
EST; by fax: (800) 820-2329, 24 hours; through our web site:
www.globe-pequot.com; or by mail: The Globe Pequot Press, P.O. Box 480,
Guilford, CT 06437.

Name: Date:

Address:

Town:

State: Zip code:

Tel: Fax:

Report Form

Comments on existing entries and new discoveries.

If you have any comments on entries in this guide, please let us know.
If you have a favourite house, hotel, inn or other new discovery, in Britain
or elsewhere, please fill out the form below.

Book title: _____ Entry no: _____ Edition: _____

New recommendation ☐ Country: _____

Name of property: _____

Address: _____

_____

Postcode: _____

Tel: _____

Date of stay: _____

Comments: _____

_____

_____

_____

_____

_____

From: _____

Address: _____

_____

Postcode: _____

Tel: _____

Please send the completed form to: **Alastair Sawday Publishing,
The Home Farm Stables, Barrow Gurney, Bristol BS48 3RW** or go to
www.specialplacestostay.com and click on contact.

Thank you.

Celebrate 75 years of Garden Visiting with the
NATIONAL GARDENS SCHEME
in 2002

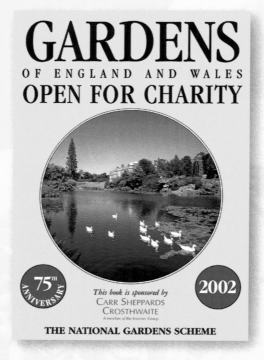

The **Gardens of England and Wales Open for Charity** Guide 2002 lists around 3500 gardens of quality and interest open to the public during the 75th Anniversary year of the National Gardens Scheme. Gardens listed in this renowned publication, known as the 'Yellow Book' range from small suburban plots packed with plants, through cottage gardens, spilling over with summer colour, to large country mansions set in picturesque parkland. Some of the gardens listed have been opening for over 50 years. All of the gardens listed are waiting to welcome visitors in 2002.

Garden Finder, a search and mapping facility on the NGS website gives detailed information, often with accompanying photographs, about the gardens. Plan your visiting using the latest opening information announced on the NGS website **www.ngs.org.uk**

Published in February 2002, the **Gardens of England and Wales Open for Charity** is for sale in all major bookstores, price £5, It is also available through the NGS website.

The National Gardens Scheme Charitable Trust, Hatchlands Park, East Clandon, Guildford, Surrey GU4 7RT
T 01483 211535   **F** 01483 211537   **E** ngs@ngs.org.uk

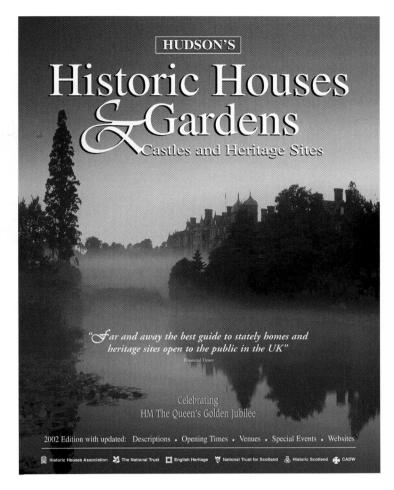

HUDSON'S

Historic Houses & Gardens
Castles and Heritage Sites

"Far and away the best guide to stately homes and heritage sites open to the public in the UK"
Financial Times

Celebrating
HM The Queen's Golden Jubilee

2002 Edition with updated: Descriptions • Opening Times • Venues • Special Events • Websites

Historic Houses Association   The National Trust   English Heritage   National Trust for Scotland   Historic Scotland   CADW

Discover the best-selling, definitive annual heritage guide to Britain's castles, stately homes and gardens open to the public.

600 pages featuring 2000 properties with
more than 1500 colour photographs.
The essential heritage companion that is also a delight to dip into.

**Available from good bookshops
or from the publisher:**
Hudson's, PO Box 16, Banbury OX17 1TF
Tel: 01295 750750

ISBN: 0 9531426 7 1   £9.95 (plus £3 p&p)

Find out what happens to the food we eat and why organic is the more natural choice.

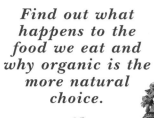

the truth about food

Soil Association

'The truth about food' - yours FREE when you join the Soil Association

PLUS £6 OFF your first year's membership when you join using this coupon

If you care about the food you eat **join the Soil Association today** and add your voice to one of the fastest growing movements of our time. As a charity we urgently need your support to fund our campaigning work to help build a sustainable future for the British countryside.

Join today and you will receive

The truth about food, a fascinating 40 page full colour booklet which addresses many of the most pressing issues concerning the food we eat in the 21st century. ***Plus*** quarterly editions of our award winning magazine *Living Earth*. ***Plus*** £6 off your first year's membership

---

YES. I want to discover 'the truth about food' and save £6 off my first year's membership of the Soil Association

I enclose a cheque for a total of £18.00

OR/ Please debit my VISA/Mastercard/Access a total of £18.00

Card No. _____

Expiry Date _____ Issue Number (Switch only) _____

NAME _____

ADDRESS _____

_____

_____ POSTCODE _____

Tick here if you do not want further appeal information ☐

Return this coupon to: the Soil Association. FREEPOST (BS4456) Bristol BS1 6ZY

Registered Charity No. 206862

Index by Property name

Index by property name

Index by property name

Index by place name

Index by place name

Index by place name

Exchange rate table

£ Sterling	US $	Euro €
1	1.47	1.61
5	7.37	8.07
7	10.31	11.30
10	14.73	16.14
15	22.10	24.21
17	25.05	27.44
20	29.47	32.28
25	36.83	40.35
30	44.20	48.42
35	51.57	56.50
40	58.93	64.57
45	66.30	72.64
50	73.55	80.71
75	110.33	121.06
100	147.11	161.41

Rates correct at time of going to press September 2001

COMPETITION

All our books have the odd spoof hidden away within their pages. Sunken boats, telephone boxes and ruined castles have all featured. Some of you have written in with your own ideas. So, we have decided to hold a competition for spoof writing every year.

The rules are simple: send us your own spoofs, include the photos, and let us know for which book it is intended. We will publish the winning entries in the following edition of each book. We will also send a complete set of our guides to each winner.

Please send your entries to:

Alastair Sawday Publishing, Spoofs competition,
The Home Farm Stables, Barrow Gurney,
Bristol BS48 3RW.

Explanation of symbols

Treat each one as a guide rather than a statement of fact and check important points when booking:

 Working farm.

 Children are positively welcomed, with no age restrictions, but cots, high chairs etc are not necessarily available.

 Pets are welcome but may have to sleep in an outbuilding or your car. Check when booking.

 Vegetarians catered for with advance warning. All hosts can cater for vegetarians at breakfast.

 Owners use only certified organic produce.

 Most, but not necessarily all, ingredients are organic, organically grown, home-grown or locally grown.

 Full and approved wheelchair facilities for at least one bedroom and bathroom and access to all ground-floor common areas.

 Basic ground-floor access for people of limited mobility and at least one bedroom and bathroom accessible without steps, but not full facilities for wheelchair-users.

 No smoking anywhere in the house.

 This house has pets of its own that live in the house: dog, cat, duck, parrot...